BLACK BEAR

BLACK
BEAR

A STORY OF SIBLINGHOOD AND SURVIVAL

Trina Moyles

ALFRED A. KNOPF CANADA

PUBLISHED BY ALFRED A. KNOPF CANADA

Knopf Canada, an imprint of Penguin Random House Canada
320 Front Street West, Suite 1400
Toronto, Ontario, M5V 3B6, Canada
penguinrandomhouse.ca

Knopf Canada and colophon are registered trademarks
of Penguin Random House LLC.

The authorized representative in the EU for product safety and compliance is Penguin Random House Ireland, Morrison Chambers, 32 Nassau Street, Dublin D02 YH68, Ireland. https://eu-contact.penguin.ie

"Lead" by Mary Oliver
Reprinted by the permission of
The Charlotte Sheedy Literary Agency as agent for the author.
Copyright © 2005, 2017 by Mary Oliver with permission of Bill Reichblum

Library and Archives Canada Cataloguing in Publication

Title: Black bear : a story of siblinghood and survival / Trina Moyles.
Names: Moyles, Trina, author
Identifiers: Canadiana (print) 2025011321X | Canadiana (ebook) 20250113228 |
ISBN 9781039010161 (hardcover) | ISBN 9781039010178 (EPUB)
Subjects: LCSH: Moyles, Trina. | LCSH: Moyles, Trina—Family. | LCSH: Black bear—
Alberta, Northern. | LCSH: Human-animal relationships—Alberta, Northern.
| LCSH: Petroleum industry and trade—Environmental aspects—Alberta,
Northern. | LCSH: Fire lookouts—Alberta, Northern—Biography. | LCSH: Siblings
of suicide victims—Alberta, Northern—Biography. | LCSH: Siblings—Death—
Psychological aspects. | LCGFT: Autobiographies.
Classification: LCC QL737.C27 M69 2026 | DDC 599.78/5092—dc23

Cover design and illustration: Lisa Jager
Text design: Lisa Jager
Typeset by: Daniella Zanchetta

Printed in Canada

10 9 8 7 6 5 4 3 2 1

Penguin
Random House
KNOPF CANADA

For Brendan

Author's Note

This is a true story of my lived experience, although I recognize that memory is subjective. The way I recall how the story went may differ from the one that my loved ones remember. I am grateful to my family for trusting me to tell my story. Some names and identifying details have been changed.

Contents

I tell you this
to break your heart,
by which I mean only
that it break open and never close again
to the rest of the world.

—MARY OLIVER, "LEAD"

NORTHERN ALBERTA

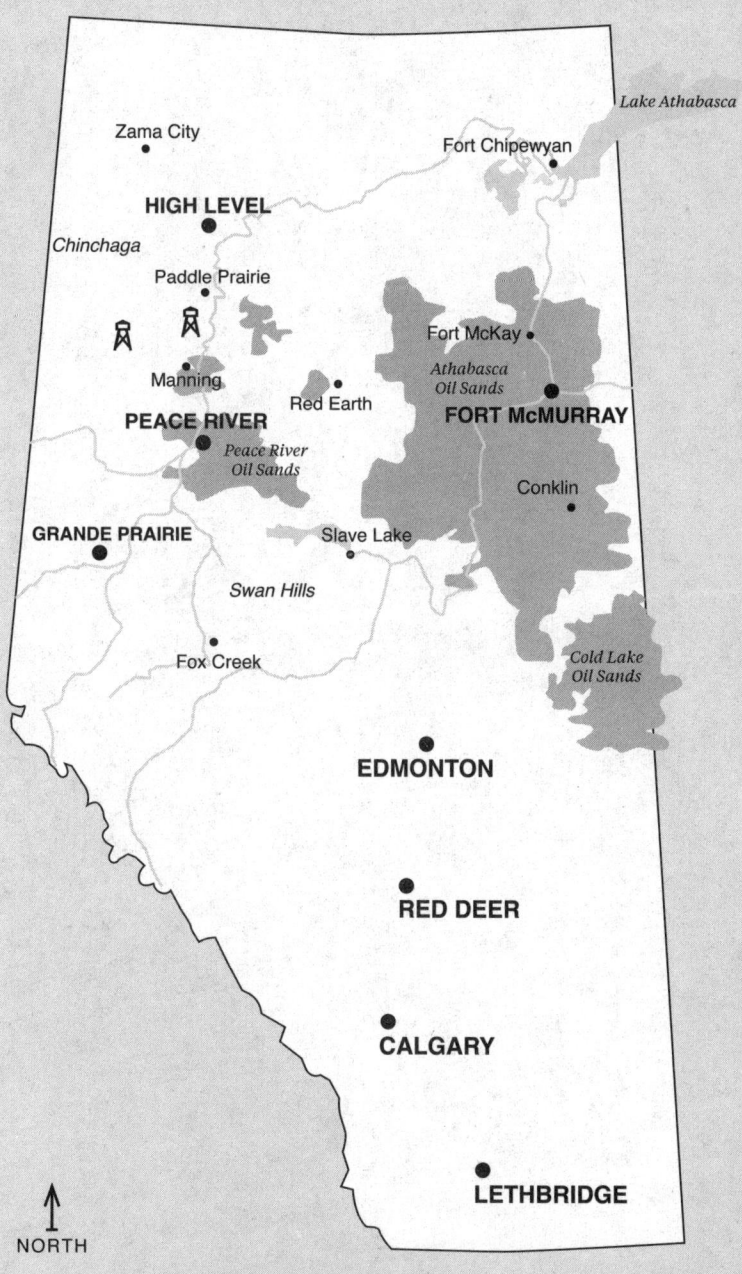

Introduction

I was five years old when I had my first encounter with a black bear. In the spring of 1990, my father, a wildlife biologist, brought home an orphaned three-month-old cub in a cardboard box. The cub's mother, having burrowed beneath the roots of an old tree, had been killed in the den by a logging excavator, but the cub, weighing barely more than a bag of apples, survived. Forestry workers caught the young bear and dropped it off at the Fish and Wildlife office in Peace River, Alberta, where my dad worked, and he called my mom with the news.

"The cub is going to stay in the basement for the night," she told us.

My brother, Brendan, older by three years, raced out the front door, jumped on his bike, and pedalled down the street to tell his friends. Between the two of us, Brendan was the extroverted child, collecting friends the same way I sought the company of books. Our basement was a den to my brother's rambunctious sleepovers. The boys wrestled on an old futon and played mini-hockey using a pair of rolled-up socks as a puck, the basement reverberating with their banter and peals of laughter.

The kids who lived on our street often joked that we "lived in a zoo." Previously, my dad had brought home three orphaned coyote pups that tumbled in play on the concrete floor. On another occasion, there was a barred owl with an injured wing. The summer before, my dad had helped to rescue a moose calf that had been stranded on the riverbank after its mother swam across the kilometre-wide Peace River. The tenderness with which he took off his blue sports jacket and gently wrapped it around the calf's eyes so that it wouldn't be frightened by the crowd of people that gathered on the riverbank to watch has always stayed with me. My dad's work as a biologist felt heroic, even godly, to my five-year-old mind. He seemed to be able to communicate with animals in their wordless languages. He wasn't afraid to get close, handling them with the same affection he showed when tucking us in at night.

My dad spent hours on the phone that day, trying to find a zoo willing to take the orphaned cub, as was commonly practised by biologists in the 1980s. Today, orphaned black bear cubs are typically taken to wildlife rehabilitation centres, or euthanized—it's considered a more humane option than living in captivity. "We'll take her," a zookeeper from the Calgary Zoo told him. "But you know, what we really want is a grizzly."

The zoos were already brimming with black bear cubs, a species of bear so abundant in North America that they could be found from as far north as the Arctic treeline down to the border of Mexico. Black bears, the oldest evolved species of bear on the continent, reproduce faster than grizzly bears and polar bears. They're smaller, often perceived to be less threatening, and so commonplace they are often referred to by negation, that is, everything they are not. Not a grizzly bear. Not a polar bear. As the expression goes, "It's just a black bear." In other words, they wouldn't create the same excitement as a grizzly bear or a polar bear cub's arrival at a zoo.

Brendan and I paced at the bottom of the driveway as if waiting for the arrival of a third sibling into our family. My dad pulled up in our family's burgundy Dodge van and emerged with a cardboard box in his hands. I could hear mewing and tussling coming from inside it. My heart pattered in anticipation.

Once in the basement, my dad set the box on the cool concrete floor, donned a pair of leather work gloves, and opened the flaps. Brendan and I and a small gang of his friends hovered nearby while my mother snapped photos on a Canon 35-millimetre film camera. The cub's head sprouted up out of the box and sniffed the air with its bright-pink nose.

"Awwwww!" I cooed, extending a hand to touch the cub's glossy black fur.

"Careful," my dad cautioned, intercepting my hand and pointing out the cub's sharp, curled claws, an evolutionary trait that's allowed black bears to become adept tree climbers. It's one of the first things black bear cubs learn to do when they come out of the den, he explained—climb to safety. But without its mother, who would teach this cub how to climb? I wondered.

The cub was female, he said.

Did she have a brother or sister? I asked, but he couldn't say. She was the only one who'd survived.

Even at five years old, I felt the cruelty of the events.

My dad held the cub in his gloved hands and invited me and my brother to gently stroke her fur. The feeling of the bear was paradoxical: Her long guard hairs were coarse to the touch, but underneath, her coat was soft as a goose down pillow. To feel the warmth of a live bear, a creature that embodied the word *wild*, provoked an upwelling of wonder in me. The cub looked at me and I was surprised to see that her eyes were a shade of blue not unlike my own.

She frolicked about in the basement, entertaining us, batting around the cardboard box and peeing on the floor. We oohed and aahed and shrieked with delight. She didn't seem afraid. What must she have sensed?

My dad explained that her ability to "scent us" was even more powerful than her ability to see us. Bears, like dogs, experience the world through scent, although bears can smell up to seven times better than a bloodhound. In the wild, they leave scent deposits rich with information about their desires and motivations—to breed, mark territory, secure habitat—on the trunks of trees, thin sapling boughs, rocks, and the very ground on which they step. Bears have scent glands between their toes, so even their footsteps tell stories about who they are and where they're going. My brain weighed three times more than hers, yet the percentage of the cub's brain devoted to scent was at least five times greater. My olfactory bulb was the size of a pencil eraser; hers was the size of a Dubble Bubble gum stick. Our family's home, laden with human smells—the lasagna in the oven, the sweat beneath our armpits, the shot of bleach that my mother sprayed onto the basement floor, cleaning up where the cub peed—must've been an overwhelming shock to her. The scent equiv-alent of peering into a toy kaleidoscope and witnessing a dizzying explosion of colours and shapes.

After an hour or so, my brother and the other boys grew bored of the small bear, who seemed to grow bored of us. They left, clamber-ing up the stairs, catapulting their bodies back outside, scouting for another adventure.

I watched Brendan depart, tempted to race behind in his foot-steps. I'd been following my rowdy, affectionate brother around since the day I learned to crawl. Brendan was my magnetic north, but on that day I was fascinated by the tiny cub who brayed and bounced around the basement like a bright-eyed kitten. I stayed and studied her behaviours, as though she were my own baby sister.

The cub fell asleep on the cold floor as I kept vigil next to her. My mother took a photograph of us: a pigtailed girl crouching next to the bear, who is coiled into a tight black ball. There is a strange sense of symmetry to it. Two cubs of different kinds—*Ursus ameri-canus*, a solitary species, and *Homo sapiens*, a species that's evolved through socialization—curling into the protection of their soft, gummy bodies. My small fingers are interwoven, hands clasped. My eyes, wide as planets, express wonder and empathy for the creature who'd lost her family.

Children aren't afraid to cross over into the world of plants and animals. Psychologists refer to this as "naive biology": a child's natural ability to see themselves as part of, rather than separate from, the biological phenomena around them. Naive biology enables children to innately trust and form relationships without question; to extend care beyond friends and family to the natural world. I loved the bear the same way I loved my family—without boundaries. I couldn't imagine facing the world without the protection of my parents, or my brother.

Growing up in bear country in northern Alberta during one of the province's greatest oil booms, Brendan and I would inevitably learn to draw boundaries and brace ourselves for different forms of loss. Like most children, we faced dangers—wild and human—and discovered our own strategies for belonging and protecting ourselves from harm. Somehow, over the years, we lost track of each other and the primal pull to love without question. This is a story of reorientation, of fear and survival, of bears and oil, and of finding our way back to family—and the wilderness that inspired us.

PART I

BEAR COUNTRY

One

I grew up in northern Alberta along the muddy banks of the Peace River, a wide brown waterway that surges north through the boreal forest, nourishing the land and braiding itself into the Peace–Athabasca Delta. From a bird's-eye view, the river appears like a long, sinewy muscle. At close range, the tracks of black bears, coyotes, and moose are visible on its shores. That is where you'd find us: my brother, with a Swiss Army knife in hand, stripping poplar boughs to build a fort, and me, wandering without a direction, humming a made-up song, scavenging for bits of twisted driftwood that resembled bodies and stones so smooth they felt as though they could merge into the palm of my hand.

In the early days, there was no separation between Brendan and me, in the way it can be with close-in-age siblings. There was only us. People always said we looked alike. His hair was dirty blond and curly whereas mine was the colour and texture of cornsilk. But we had the same impish smile and chipmunk cheeks and the same colour of eyes, somewhere between blue and grey, the colour of a swollen thunderhead on a hot day in July. As the older brother, Brendan was the one I always turned to to ask: Where do we go from here? He was naturally brave and athletic and fond of me, doting on me from an early age.

Brendan was always toeing the edge of risk, whereas I was more fearful about the ways in which we might get hurt. He was patient with my uncertainty and lovingly coaxed me into his adventures. "C'mon, Treen," he'd croon, trying to pump me up with confidence. "It will be *fun*!" We catapulted our bodies off huge boulders and swam in the river. We swallowed the river water and got bellyaches from beaver fever. We paddled north with the current in a canoe, anchored between our parents. Once, Brendan fell off the dock and almost got swept away by the river's current. My dad reached for him and hauled my brother out by the collar of his shirt. Twice, in early spring, the river rose and surged, heaving continents of ice and water over the banks, and we had to evacuate our home in the flats for higher ground. Our family took refuge with my brother's best friend's family, and Brendan and I laughed and played with the other kids, indifferent to the high waters threatening to flood our home.

When I was seven, he plunked me down on the back of his black GT snow racer and tied it with a long rope behind his friend's snowmobile. They gunned the engine and I screamed and gripped the steering wheel and hung on for my life. We whipped along a snowy trail through a tightly knit stand of poplars and I worried I might smash into a tree. Brendan kept looking back over his shoulder, making sure I hadn't fallen off. I clutched the wheel until I started to enjoy myself, my body leaning into the turns and the thrill of acceleration. When they braked the snowmobile in the middle of a snowy alfalfa field, Brendan jumped off and raced towards me, his boots punching through the snow. He high-fived me.

"How was it, Treen?" he asked with a wild grin.

"Awesome!" I answered in a shot, breathless, my cheeks two red apples against the cold.

It was as though he was always writing me into his own version of Choose Your Own Adventure, the younger playmate he was trying to toughen and wisen up.

Together, we were survivors of our childhood in northern Alberta, bound by blood and our shared social environment, playing witness to the same elemental world and at ease in each other's constant company.

In 1989, when I was four, we moved five hundred kilometres north from Edmonton to Peace River, where my dad took a job as a provincial biologist. Business was booming in those days—oil and gas, logging, coal mining, and cash-crop agriculture—but you could count the number of northern biologists on one hand. My dad was responsible for a wildlife management region the size of a small country. His colleagues in the city, or those who worked coveted jobs in the Rocky Mountains, teased him: Who did you piss off to get sent north? Many of his peers didn't want to live and work in a blue-collar resource town with a population of six thousand, but my dad didn't want to work as what he called an "armchair biologist." He longed to study the wild, up close and hands-on: flying over the forest in a Cessna four-seater, listening for the telemetry pulse of radio collars worn by woodland caribou, searching out their ghostly forms for aerial counts, and drawing blood samples from tranquilized grizzly bears caught in culvert traps.

Being a biologist in northern Alberta meant he had the opportunity to work with a wide range of megafauna, including black bears, grizzly bears, woodland caribou, moose, white-tailed and mule deer, wolverines, elk, and woodland bison. It would also mean he'd be a voice for the wild in a political arena that favoured industry over biodiversity.

There was a devastating side to my dad's work. He'd witness rapid deforestation of the boreal forest for canola fields and pine plantations and pipelines, and the steady decline of habitat for woodland caribou and grizzly bears. The bureaucracy and politics of trying to protect habitat that was continually sold off to the highest bidder, of trying to slow down the pace of industry, often got him down. He didn't talk much about it, but his frustrations were etched on his face.

My parents built a small house down by the river, in a neighbourhood called Lower West Peace, or "Moccasin Flats." Many of our neighbours were Cree, Dene, and Métis. The expression "Moccasin Flats" carried a derogatory slant, but as a child, I didn't yet understand these colonial divisions. Together, we cruised the streets of the neighbourhood on our five-speed bikes, slept over at one another's homes, and rendezvoused at the boat launch down by the river.

Towering poplars, carved with scars from black bears, were visible from our living room window. Mule deer wandered the streets and fed on the highbush cranberry tree in our front yard. Standing in front of the large window, you could see across the river to the other side of the valley. In late April, my dad and I scanned the south slope, spying for that particular shade of newborn green that exists only in the first days of spring, a green so soft and muted that it's easy to miss. That's how my dad taught me to look for the signs of changing seasons and for our wild neighbours who lived close by: patiently and with perseverance. Day after day, don't stop looking, or listening for the hopeful song of the black-capped chickadees (chick-a-DEE-DEE-DEE-DEE), for the flock of pine grosbeaks feeding on the rotted, shrunken crabapples, for the leafy deciduous trees unfurling their unassuming shade that reminded us: You've survived another winter.

We lived in what my dad called Bear Country, by which he meant we lived in the bears' habitat—their homeland, so to speak—and not the other way around. We followed the laws of living with bears with the fundamental knowing that, as soon as we laced up our shoes to go outside, we could meet a bear, anywhere, along the riverbank, on the playground, or ambling down the middle of the street. Though, for the most part, we did not. The orphaned bear cub was a rare encounter. Our early first-hand experiences with bears were fleeting, harmless sightings mostly witnessed from the safety of our parents' van. Black bears loitering at the edges of grain fields, scampering across the road, or grazing in the ditches. As kids, we mostly experienced bears as an invisible entity, always present but hidden out of sight.

"Just because you don't see them doesn't mean they aren't around," my dad cautioned us.

He pointed out the clues they left behind: piles of berry-laden scat, the aspen trees they dug into with their short, curled claws, a tuft of hair snagged on rough tree bark. He pointed out the sticky balsam poplar buds in spring—"the first thing they eat when they come out of the den"—and beaver dams—"bears love nothing more than feasting on a fat beaver." Bears will eat pretty much anything, my dad taught us, and for that reason we grew up aware that unsecured garbage bins, or the foods we grew or carried with us, could draw them closer.

The playground at my elementary school bordered on bear country, backing onto the southern-facing, rolling slopes dotted with stands of aspen and birch and willows. Once, a teacher spotted a black bear in the hills and the school went into lockdown. "Everyone is to stay inside," boomed the principal's voice over the school intercom. My classmates and I pressed our faces up against the glass windows and spotted a black blob in the distance. Conservation officers arrived and drove their truck onto the far edge of the playground and honked their horn, which was enough to frighten the bear farther up into the hills.

The following day, recess resumed and we all forgot about the bear that we were supposed to be afraid of. Years later, I'd realize that bears likely denned behind the schoolyard, not far from where we made snow angels and built snow forts and chased one another around in games of tag.

"Bears are more herbivore than carnivore," my dad pointed out. "They're a fierce predator of dandelions," he declared with a chuckle. Why were we meant to be afraid of an animal that mostly ate grass and flowers? I wondered.

My grade school drawing of a food chain: The worm, at the bottom, eats the organic matter in the soil. The robin bobs for the worm. The grass grows from the fertilized soil. The deer eats the grass. The girl, at the top of the chain, eats the deer. This felt familiar to me. Every fall, my dad filled our family's freezer with moose roasts and deer sausages and elk burger. He took me and my brother to the gun range and taught us how to fire the old Remington .22 long rifle that once belonged to my Nana, my dad's mother. He'd remind me that he wanted me to someday inherit it. "It should belong to the women in our family," he said. Brendan and I would line up empty tin cans and pop cans, lie flat on our bellies, and take turns aiming.

My brother was an excellent shot. Although he was always small for his age—often the smallest guy in his class—he was naturally athletic and excelled at physical tasks. In school, he didn't seem to care about achieving perfect grades, but socially, he thrived, playing hockey and team sports. I was the opposite. I strove for straight A's but lacked confidence on the volleyball or basketball court. I preferred lacing up my ice skates and gliding alone in wide loops. Brendan was patient with my daydreaming ways and physical hesitancy.

When we were shooting, he would instruct me to aim the bead through the rear sights—"just a hair below"—and squeeze the trigger. It always frightened me to pull my finger on the trigger and feel the gun bucking against the soft spot between my shoulder and collarbone. But the satisfying *PING!* as a can went flying and my brother's congratulatory excitement made it worthwhile. His big grin validated my shot.

We used the same .22 rifle to go grouse hunting every September. On one hunting trip, Brendan dropped a ruffed grouse from a low tree branch. Dad opened the bird up and showed us inside the stomach gizzard, a handful of green clover, perfectly intact, not yet digested. "The grouse swallows pebbles to help grind up the clover," he explained. Amazed, I palmed the pebbles and shook them in my cupped hands like dice. Grouse eats the clover and pebbles. Girl eats the grouse. I could understand myself in this cycle.

But where did the bear belong in the food chain? We didn't hunt bear, not for meat, certainly not for trophy—the paws, hide, and head. I knew that some of my First Nations classmates' families hunted black bears for meat, using bear grease for cooking and making medicines. But they had a different relationship with the bear. Some referred to them as they would people, "Grandfather" or "Brother." I wasn't sure where to place the bear. We were both omnivorous. We both slept in dens. We played and wrestled with our siblings. When I drew the bear beside the stick figure of the girl, my teacher told me to erase it.

"Humans are at the top," she explained, directing me to place the bear beneath the girl.

I nodded but wasn't convinced, and when she walked away, I drew the bear off to the side like a satellite entity, an unlike object I wasn't sure what to do with.

Two

I didn't play with Barbie dolls, with their too-long legs the colour of orange peels, whittled waists, pointed toes, manicured hands, and lipstick smiles. My own skin was fish-belly white, rivers of pale-blue veins and arteries visible beneath the surface. It was easier to turn myself into an animal. I wanted to grow fur and walk on all fours. I played with small bear figurines with a thin sheen of velvet covering their bodies, that could walk upright on two flat feet—just like us. I dressed the bears up in human clothes and played with them in my doll house, where they slept in beds and bathed in a claw-footed bathtub. I sculpted from kids' clay miniature meals of spaghetti and meatballs, hamburgers, sirloin steaks, scrambled eggs, and ice cream. The bears feasted at a dining room table made of shiny oak.

In the summer, I brought the bears camping in the bush. Made homes for them in the bowels of mossy logs. We denned together in my tent. The bears slept next to me like talismans, like worry dolls tucked under my pillow.

During these trips, Brendan was never idle. He wasn't inter-ested in my bears or imaginary games. He could swing a hatchet and split spruce logs into kindling. He could harvest old man's beard, lichen hanging off the boughs of old spruce, and make a nest

of dried materials for lighting a fire. He could carve a stick for roast-
ing sausages and tie a silver lure onto a fishing rod and reel in a
northern pike.

Together, we once constructed a fort made of spruce limbs and
twine. Brendan expertly carved off the branches with a handsaw,
lashed a limb between two trees, and made an A-frame by leaning
sticks up against the beam. I gathered up spruce boughs to pile on
top and layer on the ground to make a carpet. My parents took a
photograph of us, curled up next to one another, beaming, safe in
the den we'd built together.

On a camping trip in Jasper National Park, I was helping my
mother make pancakes while my brother sat at the picnic table,
playing his Gameboy, when my father looked up and in a low voice
uttered, "Brendan, don't move." A female elk stood only a few centimetres behind Brendan, who was ten years old at the time. We were all
surprised how she'd entered the clearing so silently, so unheard. My
brother, not knowing what was behind him, heeded my dad's advice.
He made himself into a statue. The elk sniffed the back of his baseball
hat, so close that he later told us, "I could feel its breath on the back
of my neck." She stayed for less than a minute before ambling off into
the forest. Bren's quiet bravery helped to avoid injury from the elk,
who could've easily trampled him with her powerful hooves.

On these trips, my brother and I would sleep inside a green nylon
tent. The walls were thin enough to hear everything beyond: wind
through the creaky pine limbs, mosquitoes whining their desperation. We lay on our bellies and devoured Choose Your Own Adventure
novels and R.L. Stine's Goosebumps series by flashlight. When I woke
in the middle of the night, too afraid to leave the tent to go pee, I'd
comfort myself by listening to my brother next to me, snoring faintly.
I anchored my breath to his breath and eventually fall back asleep.

Whenever we slept in tents, my mother made my dad sleep with
a rifle.

She was fearful of bears, although she loved watching them from afar. While driving through the Rockies, if we encountered a bear feeding on clover in the ditch, she'd make my dad pull over on the side of the road so she could take photographs. But sleeping in tents worried my mother. She'd stir every few hours, nudging my dad awake. "Dave, what was that?" On more than one trip, she abandoned the tent to sleep in the vehicle, taking us kids with her. She'd been a city girl all her life, growing up in her family's stucco bungalow in Burnaby, BC. When she was seventeen, she left the city for the mountain town of Jasper, Alberta, with her friends, and got a job waiting tables. She later moved to Edmonton to study early childhood development at college and met my dad, freshly back from a canoe trip on the Yukon River. My mom felt attracted to my dad's adventures in the wilderness. He proposed to her while on a hiking trip in Jasper, winding a paper clip around a throat lozenge to make his own engagement ring, and she joyfully accepted.

Shortly after my parents were married in 1980, my father's colleague gave them a "wedding gift," an invitation to tag along on his grizzly bear research project in the eastern slopes of southern Alberta, which involved capturing bears with leg snares, sedating them, and taking physiological measurements and samples.

"It was completely insane," my mother said, shaking her head. "I wasn't convinced those drugs were strong enough. It was a cowboy operation."

"Your mother isn't wrong," my dad admitted, noting that research protocols and the tranquilizers used had changed substantially over the past decades.

Though I hadn't felt instinctive fear of wildlife as a little girl, eventually I came to be afraid of the sound of footsteps, the crunching of gravel at night, knowing that only a thin membrane separated us from wild things that lurked in the bushes.

"No food in the tent," instructed my father, who meticulously packed everything in a cooler and stored it in the back of our van. "No chocolate or snacks." Even, "No toothpaste."

The spring I turned six years old, a male black bear ambushed a boy named James in his tent in the Marten River campground, just north of the town of Slave Lake, Alberta. The boy was only a few years older than Brendan. He'd pitched his tent next to his parents' trailer, but in the morning, when they woke, the tent was completely gone. Everything—tent, sleeping bag, mattress, boy—dragged off into the bush. No, he hadn't brought food into the tent, the boy's father told media, adding that his son had wanted to be a park ranger or naturalist. Fish and Wildlife officers later destroyed a black bear found in the vicinity of the campsite.

These kinds of attacks were extremely rare. My dad knew this. We had a significantly higher chance of being killed in a head-on collision with a logging truck, or a bull moose running out in front of our van. However, fear began to take root in our small bodies and minds, creating distance from the wilderness that had once seemed like an extension of ourselves. We were learning to anticipate worst-case scenarios—to imagine dangerous behaviour from beings unlike us—to keep ourselves safe.

Three

My dad was known as "the bear guy" in Peace River. He often got the call to advise on what to do with "problem bears" reported by the public. Now and then they'd get a call from a farmer about a grizzly bear, but for the most part the culprit was a black bear that had wandered into town or was nosing through somebody's trash bins. "Problem bear" or "nuisance bear" were the terms commonly used by wildlife managers to describe bears that showed no fear of people, fed on anthropogenic food sources, and edged close enough to threaten a person's perception of safety. *Perception* being the key word there, my dad would later grumble. It was a tricky thing to assess and manage, because everyone's perception of risk was different. Some people tolerated a bear wandering through their backyard. Others viewed the bear as a threat to their children's safety. For everyone, the distance or threshold between the bear and their circle of comfort, the perception of a situation going from harmless to dangerous, could be markedly different. There was no clear line, no border drawn in the sand, that signalled to bears: *You shall not pass.*

Reports of problem bears were most frequent from late April, when bears crawled out of hibernation, through the spring and summer months, and into October, when they entered hyperphagia, a state of extreme hunger. Most of the calls to conservation officers about "problem bears" were regarding black bears, hands-down, owing to the fact that the grizzly population in northwestern Alberta was significantly less and, for the most part, tended to avoid people. The expression "problem bear" almost always refers to a black bear, even today.

"There's a goddamned bear breaking into my shed!"

"There's a bear prowling the riverbank. I'm scared for the safety of my kids."

"There's a bear up in a tree behind my house. I threw rocks at it, but it won't budge."

"Human safety is always our number one concern," my dad would say. "But it's about keeping the bear safe too."

When a call came, my dad would don his government uniform, a sand-coloured button-up shirt with the Fish and Wildlife badge of a bighorn sheep stitched on the shoulder. Over the years, the name on the badge would change from *Fish and Wildlife* to *Sustainable Resources*, symbolic of the Government of Alberta's expanding agenda of prioritizing resource extraction over environmental conservation. Sometimes I'd beg to go along with him, eager to witness some of the action, but he never allowed it. As my brother and I got older, however, the public reports of nuisance bears came frequently enough that the novelty of it wore off.

"Where's Dad?" I'd ask my mom.

"Oh, he's responding to a call about a bear down in the Southend," she'd say, and I'd nod nonchalantly.

One evening, our community made the national news when a black bear waltzed right through the automatic doors of the IGA grocery story and beelined for the bakery. Brendan and I laughed when we watched the footage captured by the store's security camera: the bear strolling through those doors as if he'd done it a thousand times before, eventually chased out by the store manager with an industrial broom. The story made for a comedic segment on the six o'clock news, as no one was harmed, the bear included. My brother and I were excited, even proud, that the news of the bear had put our small town on the map. Maybe it was a problem bear, but it was *our* problem bear. For my dad, it was just business as usual.

Another day, another nuisance bear.

In the 1990s, wildlife managers relied on a bear management concept called "mutual avoidance," a term that was coined and popularized by Stephen Herrero, a behavioural ecologist and author of *Bear Attacks: Their Causes and Avoidance*, a book published in 1985 that became, and remains today, widely influential. "Mutual avoidance is a desirable end state," wrote Herrero in *Bear Attacks*. He called for a "standoff between bears and people rather than the petting, feeding, and garbage eating that have characterized the past." Herrero argued that a century of tolerating, and in some cases even encouraging, bears feeding on anthropogenic food sources had created a legacy of food-conditioned and habituated bears. *Bear Attacks* was one of the first books to draw a connection between food habituation and fatal maulings, arguing that a food-habituated bear is a dangerous bear. His logic was sound: Close the garbage dumps, clean up unmanaged food sources, and scare away food-habituated bears through persistent negative, or adverse, conditioning. My dad agreed.

He and his colleagues used negative conditioning to send problem bears a message, loud and clear: You aren't welcome here. Mostly, they'd rely on non-lethal methods, driving bears off by vehicle, honking the horn, or turning on a loud siren. They'd fire off a round of cracker shells at the bear, or shoot them with rubber bullets.

"We aim for the fat on the bear's rump," my dad told me. "The rubber slug will certainly sting and send them a message, but it won't cause any harm to the bear."

Some of the problem bears would be captured in culvert traps, a live-bear trap designed like an open culvert: long enough for a bear to worm in, pull on bait at the back of the trap—typically a beaver

carcass or roadkill—and trigger the door to slam behind them. Biologists would tranquilize the bear and take its physiological measurements: body weight, length, sex, and general health. They'd age the
bear by examining its teeth, the wear on its canines and incisors,
looking for the presence of yellow dentine, which would indicate an
older bear. Sometimes my dad would extract a tooth with pliers and
send it for analysis in Edmonton. Under a microscope, a lab tech-
nician would count the number of rings on a tooth root, like the
growth rings on a tree stump, to determine the bear's age. The problem bear would receive a bright-yellow or -orange ID ear tag. Some
would get a radio collar, so biologists could follow its whereabouts
like a prisoner released on parole. The problem bears entered the
system as numbers, so repeat offenders could be identified.

Most wildlife managers had a three-strikes-you're-out policy.
For bears that didn't get the memo on mutual avoidance, their story
ended with a lead bullet. "Put down" was the common expression,
or "cull," like *kill* made soft, or "euthanized," as though the bear was
akin to our family's dog, Sage, whom we said goodbye to on the operating table at the veterinary clinic. "Destroyed" was another word
used by wildlife managers, and as a child I imagined them blowing
up the bear into ten thousand tiny pieces the same way they detonated the Death Star in *Star Wars*.

Bears that remained afraid of people and avoided areas used by
humans would have the best chance at survival, my dad reminded us.

The calls from the public about problem bears wore on him,
however.

"Who's really the problem here—bears or people?" he'd complain.

Bears were just being bears, he'd say, drawn by their noses to
unmanaged food sources, including unsecured garbage bins, or
cooking oil dumped behind a restaurant in town, or an apple tree,
or raspberry bushes in somebody's backyard. Or maybe someone
left their barbecue wide open, or forgot a bag of dog food out on

the front steps of their house. Or perhaps it was a bear just passing through town, using the paved walking trail as a corridor to travel. In cases where bears would refuse to budge from people's backyards, sometimes they'd discover small cubs clinging to the upper branches of nearby trees, which the mothers guarded from below.

At the root of every problem bear, my dad would say, is a human problem. The idea of a "bad bear" was solely a human construct. The bear was just trying to pack on enough pounds to survive the winter. If it discovered a human-made food source, that was our fault, not the bear's.

But for all the resources that went into dealing with these so-called problem bears in town, the bears that actually killed people seemingly appeared out of thin air, like a sleight of hand. Their victims never saw it coming. These black bear attacks, although incredibly rare, mostly happened in remote areas where human activity encroached on their habitat.

In 1980, several people were attacked by a large male black bear at an isolated oil and gas camp near Zama City, a hamlet northwest of Peace River. The first victim, a geologist, had been fatally attacked from behind while walking alone along a stream bed, surveying rocks. When the geologist didn't return to camp, two of his colleagues began to search the forest for him, and the same bear attacked them. One worker fled up a tree—a deadly mistake with a species that's evolved to climb—and the bear dragged her down by the ankle. The other ran back to camp to get help, but it would be too late.

Biologists determined it was a clear case of predation. The bear hadn't attacked in defence of its own safety, or because it was protecting cubs or a food source. It had treated the people as potential prey. Biologists called it a "surplus kill," no different from a fox in a chicken coop, killing more hens than it can possibly eat.

These rare encounters lodged themselves in my imagination. I knew that fatal bear attacks were exceedingly uncommon, only one, maybe two, occurring in Canada every year, but nor were they impossible. Perhaps some fear, particularly in such remote country, was warranted.

When I was in tenth grade, my forestry class was preparing for a two-week field course outside Swan Hills, Alberta, an area located to the south of Peace River where there's a high density of grizzly bears and black bears. My dad came to my high school to give a presentation on bear safety, specifically, how to protect ourselves from or avoid bear attacks. I'd grown up listening to these cautionary stories and instructions, but somehow the repeated telling felt as visceral as the first. He told us a story about sixty-three-year-old Cree trapper Bella Twin, who, in 1953, encountered and defended herself against one of the world's largest recorded grizzly bears in this same region and astonishingly put down the bear with a .22 rifle, a firearm meant for hunting small game like grouse and rabbits. I shivered in awe of Bella's bravery, and my classmates' eyes were wide with admiration. Even the boys nodded with respect. I was proud of my father, standing in front of our class like a bear guru of sorts.

We were instructed to respond differently in a close encounter with a grizzly bear versus a black bear. The two species had, behaviourally speaking, evolved differently. Whereas black bears evolved in trees, often fleeing and climbing to safety in frightening encounters, grizzly bears evolved on treeless plains where they had to stand their ground and fight back in defense situations. If it was a defensive grizzly bear attack, a mother protecting her cubs, for example, he advised us to play dead, which would potentially defuse the attack. "You've got to convince her that you're not a threat," he said. Often, in defensive grizzly attacks, bears would eventually leave after initially wounding or impairing a person.

"Cover the back of your neck with your hands," he told us. "Try to stay on your stomach. The bear will likely try to flip you over, but if you can, stay on your stomach and protect your vital organs."

If it was a black bear attack, he said, "you've gotta fight with everything you've got."

We learned of a ten-year-old girl from Williams Lake, BC, who fought off a black bear with an axe and a pot of boiling water, which she flung in the bear's face.

Black bear attacks in North America occur more frequently than grizzly bear attacks, he explained, but when grizzlies do attack, it often results in serious injury or death. There were other key differences between grizzly bears and black bears.

He pointed to research from Herrero's *Bear Attacks* that found the majority of fatal grizzly bear attacks occurred in national parks, where bears had become food habituated and accustomed to people. On the flip side, nearly all the fatal black bear attacks took place in rural, remote areas—not so different from Peace River or the Swan Hills. Although these incidents were extremely rare, Herrero found that black bears would stalk and attack their victims in broad daylight, whereas the majority of grizzly bear attacks occurred at night. Perhaps that's due to the fact that grizzly bears, as their habitat has shrunk in size and fragmented, have adapted to become more nocturnal. In over half the accounts, black bears preyed on people of smaller stature, their victims often women or children. There was an assumption that grizzlies were more dangerous than black bears, but just because black bears tended to be smaller didn't mean they were any less deadly. "[Black bears] can bite through live trees thicker than a man's arm," Herrero wrote in *Bear Attacks*. "They can kill a full-grown steer with a bite to the neck."

"If a black bear is stalking you, you're probably not going to see it coming," my dad told us. "When they get into predatory mode, it's like the flick of a switch. They're *on*. They're focused."

A collective hush fell over the room, all eyes glued to my father.

No doubt he was thinking of the tragic bear attacks that had occurred only a few years earlier at Liard River Hot Springs, a remote campground in northern British Columbia. On August 14, 1997, an adult black bear stalked a woman named Patti McConnell and her thirteen-year-old son, Kelly, near the upper hot springs pool. The bear attacked McConnell and then turned on her son, who had attempted to beat the bear off his mother with a stick. When Ray Kitchen, a fifty-six-year-old trucker, heard their screams, he went running to intervene, but the bear charged and knocked him over. As people heard the attacks, they fled from the hot springs for the parking lot, and in the ensuing panic the bear mauled a fourth victim, a twenty-eight-year-old man. Eventually, two bystanders came running with rifles. They shot the bear, but both Patti McConnell and Kitchen died from their wounds.

My classmates and I had learned about the gruesome attacks, right down to the goriest details, on the television news. It made the front page of the newspapers with headlines that read: DEADLIEST ATTACK IN NORTH AMERICAN HISTORY. *Reader's Digest* published a story called "Rogue Bear on the Rampage" that depicted the thirteen-year-old boy watching the bear "engulf his mother's almost naked body." The story read like a thriller novel; it was impossible to tear your eyes away from the sensational account. "[Kelly's mother] lay beside him, her skin ashen, her eyes open and unblinking," the article read. "The animal's foul, rancid breath made Kelly want to vomit. He closed his eyes. He knew he was about to die."

There was something unsettling about the way people leaned in to the bear attack story, some kind of twisted desire to consume every last gruesome detail. We were drawn to the blood lust of bear attacks with a magnetic intensity. It was hard to look away from the onslaught of headlines, but then again, we were kids growing up in a culture obsessed with violence inflicted by predators of all kinds—from wrestlers bashing one another over the head with folding chairs to movies about serial killers and rapists. Bears were just another bad guy.

But when it comes to bears, a fatal, predatory attack is never personal. It's not evil or malicious, or premeditated. It's about the animal's attempt to survive and evolve. The media's obsession with bear attacks generates sales and dollars, but more often than not, it fails to bring us any closer to understanding them as a species.

The detail about the woman's "almost naked body" reminded me of the opening scene in Spielberg's cult classic *Jaws*, a movie we worshipped as kids, that opens with a young woman with long blond hair running along a beach, giggling and taking off her clothes. A drunken suitor follows behind, slurring, "What's your name again?" "Chrissie!" she says. "Where are we going?" "Swimming!" she responds. As she pulls off her sweater, revealing her breasts, the man says with a laugh, "I'm definitely coming!" Chrissie swims elegantly out into the calm ocean waters as the guy drunkenly struggles out of his clothes and passes out on the beach.

The point of view changes to that of the great white shark, lurking beneath Chrissie, rising up towards her. The camera zooms in on her naked body, a perfect Barbie replica, and the theme music, the two single notes produced by a tuba that *Jaws* would become world-famous for—*duh duh, duh duh, duh duh*—warns us that she's about to get attacked. The *Reader's Digest* story about the Liard River Hot Springs bear attack used similar stylistic tactics, only the rogue predator on a killing spree was a black bear instead of a shark. And the "almost naked" woman was an actual human victim.

At the root of my discomfort about the sensationalized story was not only the conscious fear of being attacked by a wild predator, but an unconscious one too, which began to take up space in my body. The fear of what it meant to be a girl on the brink of adolescence in the North.

Four

The summer I was ten years old, one of Brendan's friends from the city rode the Greyhound north to visit. The boys were thirteen. We pedalled our bikes across the Peace River bridge to the Reddi-Mart and sat outside on a picnic table in the hot sun, sucking on jumbo cups of blue slush. My brother's friend, Daniel, a boy several inches taller and much bulkier than my brother, looked over at me and sneered.

"You see that road over there? Trina's breasts are flatter than that road."

I froze. Daniel laughed and my cheeks flushed pink with embarrassment. I turned to Brendan for help, but I saw that he was laughing.

I didn't know how to react. I sensed the cruelty behind his friend's words, as though what he was really saying to me was: *Your body doesn't belong to you.* Shame rose up from my belly button, between my tiny girl breasts, to my lips. The boy's words hurt me, but what hurt more was my brother's laughter. It felt like a betrayal.

I didn't know what else to do, so I laughed.

Psychologists have a word for this behaviour. They call it "fawning," an unconscious response to try to maintain connection in an unsafe environment or relationship. It's considered the fourth trauma response: fight, flight, freeze—and fawn. One becomes more appealing to the threat, pacifying conflict in order to establish safety.

It was the first time I could remember my body being sexualized. Made into a *thing* that someone else could talk about, and in that sense take ownership of. It was also the first time I realized that my brother couldn't protect me from harm. Although he laughed as if in on the joke, Brendan must've been uncomfortable. He didn't often show it, but my brother was a sensitive boy. I know he'd felt the hurt the same way I did—I was his kid sister, I was a part of him. But we were transitioning into adolescence, which would send us on divergent paths according to what society expected of our genders.

Growing up, I wore Brendan's hand-me-down clothes—grunge jeans that hung off my sapling frame and baggy Nirvana T-shirts—with pride. I cut my long blond hair into a mushroom cut, a popular hairstyle in the early 1990s, just like he did. We rocked out to the same music: the Offspring, Pennywise, NOFX. I remember sitting with my brother in the back seat of our parents' Dodge van, drumming on the back of the driver's and passenger's seats, Green Day full blast on the stereo, gleefully bellowing the lyrics: *WELCOME TO PAR-A-DISE!*

On the weekends, he played in hockey tournaments and I religiously attended, even travelling with the team to away games. The ice was my brother's preferred habitat, the place where he seemed the happiest, where he came alive. My mom said she used to take him to the arena where they lived at the time, in Brooks, Alberta, when he was a baby and his eyes would follow the game, watching the players zip back and forth. By the time Brendan could walk, he could skate.

For me, the hockey arena was a different kind of wilderness. The other players' younger siblings and I would scurry up and down the side ramps, chasing rogue pucks that flew over the glass, and search beneath the bleachers for sticky quarters to buy scorching hot Styrofoam cups of hot chocolate and bags of hickory sticks from the vending machines. They called us "rink rats." We were scavengers of sorts, allowed to freely roam the arena. But when my brother set foot on the ice, I would rush back to the bleachers where my parents sat and watch him like a hawk. I'd perch behind his team in the players' box, cheering until my lungs were hoarse. As they played, the scent of the boys' damp, sweat-saturated hockey gear—gloves, pads, socks, uniforms—filtered up towards us. I secretly loved that smell, even when, after games, my brother grabbed me and playfully threatened to zip me up in his equipment bag.

Brendan's dream—like many other boys' dreams in Canadian towns and cities—was to play on a team for the National Hockey League. Somehow, when we were kids, it didn't seem so far out of reach. We were of a generation force-fed those inspirational slogans printed on laminated posters tacked up on the walls: *IF YOU CAN BELIEVE IT, YOU CAN ACHIEVE IT*. Brendan was always one of the strongest players, and our family organized our lives around his great love and his dream of playing in the NHL. During the summer months, we travelled as a unit, towing a tent trailer behind the Dodge van, to Penticton, BC, where he could attend hockey skills camps. At home, he would position me as the goalie in front of a miniature net and fire away, perfecting his shot. I never complained, content to be the loyal hockey sister, the rink rat, the accomplice to his dreams.

While I had begun to struggle with a growing sense of my body as an object of appraisal, never quite measuring up, my brother had to contend with his own perceived shortcomings: He was always one of the smallest guys in his class and on his hockey team. Over the years of playing minor hockey in Peace River, coaches often told him, "Too bad you aren't bigger." That he wasn't an "alpha male"— a term that seemed to imply being physically big and dominant-spirited—weighed on him. Later, I'd reflect back on that day outside the Reddi-Mart when Brendan didn't stand up to his friend Daniel. Perhaps he'd been afraid of him. Like me, he fawned in the face of the boy's cruelty.

Our coming of age in a resource town in northern Alberta would require different survival strategies. I would learn how to avoid getting unwanted attention from boys or men. I would learn how to fawn and please, but also how to physically fend off an attack and defuse threats—not only from bears, but from boys and men. Defensive tactics of a different kind. Even then I sensed that the cultural onus seemed to be on us, as girls, to protect ourselves from harm.

And so, at thirteen, I signed up for a self-defence course with my best friend that was taught by my dad's colleague, Allen, a conservation officer with a black belt in karate. In the late 1970s, Allen had been hired by the government to set leg snares for bears. Catch a bear, kill a bear—that was the policy back then. But in the 1990s, it was more a game of catch and release, unless a bear broke the three-strikes policy, or killed someone. Allen knew what it meant to have an angry bear come charging at him like a racehorse. *Steady the breath, aim for the lungs, and shoot.* Maybe that's why he taught self-defence to youth: He wanted others to be prepared, to develop the same inner calm he'd learned to cultivate in the face of danger.

Most of the participants in the self-defence class were girls. Allen taught us escape moves, how to break free if someone grabbed our wrists by rotating the arm and applying pressure against their thumb and forefingers. How to hit an attacker in the "vital areas," jabbing the eyes, striking the nose, jaw, or temple. How to carry car keys between our knuckles when walking to our vehicles at night. I didn't even have my learner's permit yet, but that was a trick I'd carry with me long into adulthood.

My brother didn't take a self-defence class, but early on he would learn how to try not to get shoved in a locker, or hung up on a coat hook by his underwear—both of which happened—or socially persecuted for being a small male. He compensated with his talent at hockey and his boisterous, extroverted personality. He was quick-witted and funny and likeable. No one could tease or hurt Brendan if he became the life of the party. "B-Mo," his peers called him fondly. They adored him, and by extension they loved me, calling me "Moyles's little sister." The boys homed in on a shared behaviour of ours, an unconscious habit of tugging on our earlobes while deep in thought. They teased us both about it. When I walked down the hallways at school, they'd gently flick my ear, and my cheeks burned red with embarrassment. But the boys' teasing seemed playful and non-threatening. It was attention, even a kind of social validation. People saw me because they saw my brother, and that offered a protective buffer. No one would ever mess with me because of Brendan's talent on the ice and his popularity at school.

When he was fifteen, Brendan started getting "fucking smashed," as he liked to say, with his hockey teammates on the weekends. He tried to hide it from my parents; alcoholism ran on both sides of our family, our mother always warned us. She spoke often of her childhood, growing up with an alcoholic father whose own father, a Ukrainian immigrant, had struggled with substance abuse. But booze flowed like the river in the North. The only way to drink was to drink hard. Get blackout drunk. "If you can't remember what happened, you know it was a good night," the saying went.

Brendan gifted me with a mickey of lemon gin, hidden in a small wooden chest he'd made in his grade eleven industrial arts class, the summer I was fourteen years old. My first sip of alcohol triggered cringe and disgust, followed by a warmth that rocked my body like ocean swell. I tasted relief in alcohol. I swam in the sea of disembodiment. The fear and anxiety that was gradually accumulating in my girl body found release.

We drank religiously every weekend in the bleachers at Friday night hockey games, at bush parties, in gravel pits, and next to the gravesite of Twelve Foot Davis, a legendary trapper who'd improbably struck it rich on a twelve-foot-wide gold mining claim during the Klondike gold rush. We got high, standing atop a large cement pad where Twelve Foot's remains were entombed, overlooking the Peace River valley, the lights of town glittering down below. We gathered around stacks of burning pallets, Metallica's "Enter Sandman" blasting out of one of the hockey gods' vehicles. Boys on shrooms and cocaine dared one another to jump over the dancing flames. Someone emptied a jerry can of fuel on the fire and it exploded. We waterfall-chugged and drank until we couldn't walk. We drank until the red-and-blue lights flickered through the bush and the RCMP extinguished the flames and shut down the party and everyone drove home drunk.

More than once, my friends carried me, rag doll, out of a party. My brother was mortified.

"Get her home," he'd snap at them.

Often, he'd come search me out at a party and scold me.

"You've had enough for one night," he'd grumble.

But that weightless, out-of-body experience of inebriation had a powerful pull on me. I craved the momentary release and suspected my brother felt it too, because neither of us stopped drinking or partying, in spite of our parents' disapproval, and no matter that we woke up the next morning feeling as though our bodies had been run over by a gravel truck. We just got better at hiding it.

While we'd been trained to deter problem bears, and to protect ourselves against predatory wildlife attacks, there were quiet, embedded risks to growing up in northern Alberta. There were other predatory forces we wouldn't see coming—and no soundtrack to indicate an incoming threat.

It was my intoxicated classmate at the bush party, stumbling into the back seat of one of the hockey gods' trucks. The next week at school, they wouldn't call her a victim, they'd call her a slut.

Don't be a Chrissie—she had it coming.

"Bear spray is more effective than a gun," my dad had informed my classmates and me in his presentation before our field trip to Swan Hills. "It's faster and safer."

How many of my female classmates were also thinking what I was thinking?

Maybe it could work on guys too.

As teenagers, we had a significantly greater chance of dying from alcohol poisoning and drug overdose, or operating vehicles or ATVs while drunk, than of being mauled by a bear. Yet, in some ways, we were better equipped to fend off predatory wildlife than we were to cope with social pressures and substance abuse. As my brother and I began to prioritize partying on the weekends, we inherently spent less time with our family on the land, camping, canoeing, and hunting. We were just teens in a small northern town, doing what teens do. Experimenting beyond the boundaries of our family culture, moving towards independent social behaviour. But there were consequences to our actions; too many of our peers died—far too young.

In 1999, when I was fourteen years old, my friend, a shy boy with pale skin and eyes as blue as a glacier, was racing on his snowmobile at high speed when he lost control and the machine skidded off a steep embankment, fatally crushing him. The following year, a sixteen-year-old girl whom I played basketball with was riding on the back of a snowmobile on a gravel road when a truck hit them, killing her. The snowmobile driver had gunned the engine, trying to beat the truck across the road. The year after that, a friend of Brendan's took a punch to the back of the head while trying to break up a fight outside the Moon Saloon, a local bar in town. The coroner's report found that he died on impact. He was twenty-one years old.

These events didn't stop us from drinking and climbing into cars with drunk drivers, racing at breakneck speed down gravel roads.

We toasted our lost friends like fallen comrades, pressed the bottle of Jack Daniel's to our lips, and taunted one another on, *drink, drink, drink, drink.*

On that grade ten field trip to Swan Hills, we didn't encounter a single bear.

There was one instinct that continued to differentiate Brendan and me. I savoured being alone. I could spend long hours by myself, wandering the riverbank or getting lost in the pages of a novel. I sculpted animals from clay and carved feathers from soft, buttery wood. I wrote short stories and essays, which my mother saved and collected in a scrapbook.

Brendan relied on a brotherhood of teammates and friends. On the weekends, he invited them over to our family's house for sleepovers. There was always an extra plate or two set at the dinner table. The more the merrier, in Brendan's mind.

His mood would turn sour, bordering on angry, when vacations with family friends came to an end. He never wanted to say goodbye to the people he loved. Once, while on a trip to Hawaii with close family friends, Brendan defiantly took off on Waikiki Beach, a hot spot for professional surfers, boogie board tucked under his arm, after the adults told us to pack up our belongings. Horrified, we all watched my seventeen-year-old brother, who weighed barely more than a hundred pounds, launch himself into the face of a six-metre-high swell. He paddled and kicked furiously as the wave descended upon him, the water threatening to swallow him up.

"Brendan!" my mother screamed.

But he caught the swell and surged forward in the ocean's spray. It would have been beautiful, watching him, balanced atop his board, porpoising through the water, had it not been so terrifying knowing how the ocean could have barrel-rolled him under to hit rock bottom. But Brendan rode the wave triumphantly to the shore.

"Did you *see* that?" he cried, his eyes bright and wild, water dripping off his skinny frame, his frustration now satiated by this daredevil pursuit, and perhaps by the fact that he'd frightened us all. Our family would come to laugh about this story for years, but I privately wondered what triggered Brendan's passionate response, why he'd so willingly chucked himself into danger.

Brendan felt beckoned by the raging waves, whereas I was repelled by the risk. I began to sense that there were limits to where I would, or could, follow my brother.

When I was fourteen, I saved up my paycheques from working at the town's recreational centre, wiping down gym equipment and selling memberships, and bought a horse. Doctor Pepper, or Pepper as I called him, was a silver giant with a charcoal mane, so tall I had to step up on a milk crate to swing my leg over the saddle. I boarded him at my dad's colleague's acreage, located on rolling alfalfa pastures at the edge of a birch forest overlooking the Peace River valley. Every day after school, I rode the bus out of town and got dropped off at the end of the long driveway. I'd run to Pepper's paddock, calling his name, and he'd hang his large, ghostly head over the wooden fence, ears perked up at the sound of my voice.

I'd saddle him up and use the fence to climb onto his wide back, and away we'd go. My friend Jessica lived down the road at her family's farm and she'd meet us on the trail halfway, astride her own horse, Doc Boy, a spunky Arabian the colour of caramel. We spent nearly every afternoon on horseback, hiking up our stirrups and crouching over their necks, pretending to be jockeys. We raced the silica mine semi-trucks that went screaming down the gravel road, the horses' hooves pounding, kicking up the scent of alfalfa.

We wove through the forested trails of the river valley and climbed up and down the hills, scouting for new vantage points of the snaking river below. I never felt afraid atop Pepper's back, whether I was riding alone or with company. I trusted him as I trusted my own instincts. Being on the land was like a salve. When I rode through the forest, my fear and anxiety fell away.

One afternoon in early autumn, Jessica and I rode our horses along a steep ridge. The birch bore brilliantly coloured tangerine leaves that glimmered against a blue sky scrubbed clean of clouds. Pepper's hooves shuffled through leaf fall. The scent of decay stung my nostrils.

Ahead on the trail, Doc Boy skidded to a halt.

"Look!"

I glanced down a ridge to see a furry two-legged creature standing as tall as a grown man, staring back up at us. It took us a few seconds to whisper the word out loud.

"Bear!"

It was the first time I'd ever come face to face with a bear in the wild. Everything my dad had taught me couldn't prepare me for the shock of it. My mind and body flooding with fear and awe. Only it wasn't *fear* that I felt—not the same paralysis and disconnect I experienced when I overheard guys make a violent joke about a girl. It was precisely the opposite feeling. I felt wholly *in* my body, as though every single hair on my skin was alert, as if I'd grown fur. I couldn't take my eyes off the bear. We were two animals wondering: *What's the other going to do?* But the bear didn't flinch. It was huge and beautiful, the same swirling colour as cream poured into black coffee. Jessica and I were stunned into silence.

My first thought was, *Grizzly bear?*

I examined the angle of the bear's Roman nose, a telltale sign that it was a black bear, not a grizzly, as my dad had taught me. The sunlight caught its golden fur. Biologists called it a cinnamon-phase black bear, which is caused by a mutation in a gene involved in melanin pigment production. The same mutation causes a form of albinism in people. Cinnamon bears were much rarer than black bears, but I knew they existed in northern Alberta.

Pepper broke the trance. His muscles shivered beneath me. The horse trembled, shifting his hooves. We danced nervously on the spot.

There was no talk of what to do next. I gently touched the rein to Pepper's neck and leaned back in the saddle. Instinctively, he sank down on his haunches, spinning around like a top. I clicked my tongue and he launched forward into a flat-out gallop, the orange leaves swarming his hooves like honeybees. Jessica, atop Doc Boy, followed. We never once looked back.

Five

Brendan moved south to Edmonton to study systems used in the oil and gas industry when he was nineteen years old, in 2001. My parents and I stood outside our family's small, grey house and watched him drive away in his maroon-coloured sports car. After he left, our house felt vacant. It wasn't a surprise he'd decided to go. Many young people we grew up with would eventually leave the North, head south to bigger cities like Grande Prairie, or Edmonton, or Calgary to study and look for work. Some of Brendan's peers went straight from high school to Fort McMurray to work in the oil patch, where they were raking in six figures a year. A high school diploma wasn't necessary for the job; if you could hack it living in an isolated camp, you could strike it rich in Fort Mac. But my parents convinced Brendan to pursue higher education before seeking employment.

Alberta was on the cusp of one of the biggest economic booms in the province's history. Since the late 1980s, when we were kids playing along the muddy riverbank, the government had been investing in the infrastructure and technology required to extract and separate oil from vast deposits of bitumen, a heavy and viscous form of petroleum, buried under the beaver ponds and muskeg swamps and black spruce we grew up with. They called it "unconventional oil." Politicians boasted, "It's going to be bigger than the gold rush." The government would come to call it "the Alberta advantage." There were three known bitumen deposits in Alberta, including smaller reserves in Peace River and Cold Lake, along with the Athabasca oil sands north of Fort McMurray, the largest deposit, which would prompt a mass influx of workers from across Canada. The population of Fort Mac would more than double between 2000 and 2007, reaching nearly eighty thousand people, prompting a rental and real estate crisis. People said Peace River was next, that change was coming to our hometown of six thousand people, and we braced ourselves for the boom, but—by some stroke of luck—it never happened.

A year before Brendan's departure, his dreams of moving up the ranks into professional hockey had come to an end. He'd tried out for several Junior A teams, which is a step below the farm league for the NHL. At a tryout in Vernon, BC, my brother played with every inch of his heart, but he was barely five foot eight and nearly a hundred pounds lighter than the other guys. Afterwards, a scout told him that he was "talented, but too small to make it." He was despondent for days, locking himself in his room in my parents' basement and refusing to come up for meals. I'd never witnessed him so low before. I ventured down one evening with a plate of food, in an attempt to coax him out.

"Hey, you okay?" I rapped my knuckles against the glass pane of the door.

"Yeah, I'm fine," he said, his voice lacklustre, unconvincing. I stood there, holding my breath, not sure what to say to my brother who was usually so confident.

"Leave me alone, Treen," he mumbled.

A week after the call from the scout, Brendan emerged from the basement and we resumed partying on the weekends. I was relieved to have him back, but I could tell that something had changed in him. That naive, boyish enthusiasm Brendan was known for had dulled, or hardened. I wasn't sure if his friends recognized it, but I saw it—felt it. When he left for Edmonton, I sensed that he was burdened by his perceived failure, though he wouldn't talk about it.

Like many other young men his age, Brendan saw an opportunity in oil, which surprised me, given that we'd both grown up listening to our father speak openly about the negative impacts of resource extraction on the environment. My dad wasn't fundamentally opposed to oil. He saw the important role that extractive industries played in the economy, and admitted that some companies were "better than others," but it infuriated him how the Alberta government green-lit every project with hardly any long-term planning or environmental oversight. The way I remembered my dad telling it, it was that the oil and gas industry was causing irreparable damage to the landscape we'd grown up on. Had my brother even been listening?

The promise of financial gain and the social impetus to join his friends were big factors in his decision. The oil industry was heavily dominated by a male labour force in the early 2000s. Even twenty years later, women account for fewer than a quarter of workers employed by mining and oil and gas industries in Alberta.

When Brendan called me after settling in the city, he sounded like himself again; there was a familiar spark in his voice. He told me he was enjoying his new-found independence, and I was full of excitement for him.

"You're gonna love it here, Trina," he gushed to me over the phone.

I'd graduate from high school in less than a couple of years and I knew that I'd follow him south to Edmonton.

But over those two years, the phone calls from Brendan became less frequent. While I missed him, I was too distracted by what was going on in my own life—volunteering in my high school's student union, riding my horse, and waitressing at a Mexican restaurant—to realize that he might have been struggling to adapt to life in the city.

There were signs that he was spiralling. One year after Brendan moved away, he was gunning it back north to Peace River on the highway, rushing the five-hundred-kilometre trip to catch the last set of Wide Mouth Mason, the mainstage act at PeaceFest, an annual music festival. My girlfriends and I poured cherry-flavoured vodka into plastic bottles of Pepsi and snuck them in past security. I checked my flip phone for an update from my brother. He should be here by now, I thought. *0 new messages.*

At midnight, I got the call from my mother.

"Brendan's been in a car accident," she told me. "But he's okay."

Some 250 kilometres north of Edmonton, around the town of Fox Creek, Brendan drifted off to sleep at the wheel. No doubt he'd been up late partying the night before. He'd been driving over the speed limit when his car veered off onto the shoulder of the highway, caught a bit of loose gravel, and flipped into the air. It rolled into the ditch, crushing the front end and smashing the windshield. Somehow Brendan stumbled out from the wreckage. An ambulance took him to the hospital in Fox Creek, where a nurse tweezed out dozens of shards of glass embedded in his shoulders and back. He bore the scars from that accident—a network of large purple welts that covered his back—like unwanted tattoos. He hated them, a reminder, perhaps, of his close brush with death, and refused to talk with me about it.

Instead of slowing down, he only seemed to hit the gas harder. He partied more frequently during the week and began failing classes. I overheard my parents arguing with him over the phone, threatening to cut him off financially if he didn't get his act together. When we spoke over the phone, Brendan seemed preoccupied with a social world I didn't belong to.

———

After graduating from high school, I moved south to Edmonton to go to university, but I found that I no longer recognized my brother. His appearance had changed. His neck had grown wide as a tree trunk and his skin had turned the colour of tomato paste from baking in a tanning bed. He flexed his biceps and joked, "Who wants a ticket to the gun show?"

He had been struggling to pass his exams and was forced to redo the second year of his program.

It was hard to pin Brendan down for a visit, but I knew he'd begun working as a bartender in a country bar called Cowboys. Throughout the city, Cowboys plastered up billboards of blond-haired women sucking on highballs, their breasts thrust towards the camera, and guys with their shirts off, flexing six-pack abs and ripped biceps. When I went to see him there, he couldn't sit down with me and catch up. I wanted him to ask about my life. I wanted to tell him about my first year of college. I wanted to gush to him about the creative writing course I was taking and how, sometimes, on the walk back to my apartment, I'd get so excited about an idea for a poem or story that I found myself sprinting the last kilometre home.

I sucked back gin and sodas, but the buzz did nothing to change my mood with the cheesy country songs pumping. I'd begun to feel embarrassed about my own drinking habits, and hid the stories of getting blackout drunk from the friends whom I met at college, where I was majoring in anthropology and minoring in English lit. There, I was encountering new perspectives and starting to reframe what we'd all normalized as "harmless fun" in Peace River. Cowboys was basically an upscale version of the Moon Saloon, where the young man had died from the punch to the back of the head, and it brought back bad memories. I was trying to distance myself from a culture of hard drinking, but Brendan seemed to be forging a new sense of belonging at Cowboys. He'd always loved being on a team. Only now, his teammates seemed more interested in scoring coke and ecstasy.

That night at the bar, women swarmed my brother. He went to the bathroom and came back with wide, bright pupils.

One of his friends, a guy from back home, looked me up and down as though inspecting a cow at an auction.

"Hey Moyles, your sister is getting hot," he said.

It was as if I were ten years old again and back sitting on that picnic table outside the Reddi-Mart. Maybe my brother's friend thought he was giving me a compliment. But it was just a reminder that geography hadn't changed a thing. Brendan laughed. I laughed.

I went home with his friend that night. I suppose that I was lonely, too, unsure of who I wanted to be, and longing for a connection to Peace River. But I woke up the next morning in his crumpled sheets, hungover and full of regret. He tossed a ten dollar bill at me and I took a taxi home.

There were early signs of what would become my growing discomfort with and eventual estrangement from Brendan. He was becoming increasingly irritable and moody and difficult to contact. Now and then he'd call and sound like his old self and make promises to spend time together, grab a coffee, or go for a walk in the river valley, but then he'd cancel last minute. Once, after he promised to drive me to the airport, I nearly missed my flight because he'd slept in after a late night out. He'd become less available, less reliable, and as a result I began to distance myself from him. I ignored his calls and texts. *I'll call him back later*, I'd think, but then I'd forget. It was a kind of mutual avoidance. If we didn't see each other, we couldn't disappoint each other.

In my second semester at university, I enrolled in an American literature class and was surprised to sit next to a boy named Devon from a neighbouring town in the North who'd played hockey with my brother. He was a popular, handsome Cree kid who partied hard like the rest of us. He told me that he was taking his bachelor of arts degree, like me, and wanted to become a lawyer. I didn't say as much, but I would've pegged him for the type who'd be working a camp job in Fort Mac.

But I was wrong about the hockey boy. Devon raised his hand often in class to comment on one of the books we'd been assigned to read. He was kind and sensitive in a way that wasn't commonly expressed by many of the boys we grew up with. That semester, he became my friend.

"Do you ever wonder about the culture up north?" I asked him one day before class started. I hesitated. "Like, the heavy drinking and all . . . ?"

"Yeah, it's pretty fucked up," he said, running a hand through his hair. "My cousin went to work in Fort Mac and it's even worse there. He went completely off the rails. It got so bad that my uncle paid for him to go to some rehabilitation centre in the woods. They fish and hunt there and my cousin said it was all right. He came back clean. For now, anyway."

"Yeah, I worry about my brother sometimes," I said. "But I'm not sure."

Devon looked at me for a few seconds, as if making up his mind to tell me something.

"Yeah, Trina, I'm just gonna say it. Your brother is an addict. Straight up."

The word *addict* struck like a stone. When I thought of an addict, I thought of one of the homeless people who pushed a shopping cart up Main Street in Peace River and hung outside the Mac, a rough bar across from the pharmacy where no one I knew went. Once, when I entered the pharmacy, a homeless guy asked me to buy him a bottle of mouthwash. I'd looked at him, confused.

"You can get pretty messed up if you drink enough of it," a friend later told me.

I associated the word *addict* with individual failure, believing that addiction was something that happened to other people in other families—not my own.

My brother was not that kind of guy. In my mind, he was still the brave boy who remained calm during the encounter with the elk. He was the star hockey player. The popular kid whom everyone loved. The boy riding the six-metre wave. My ally and protector. At that time, I couldn't imagine how he could be all those things *and* someone who struggled with addiction.

Devon's words followed me home like a stray dog. They began to gnaw at me as I tried to reconcile what I thought I knew about Brendan and what my friend had told me. He had no reason to lie.

I told my parents what I'd learned, over the phone, and they didn't question it. I suppose they already knew more than I did. Maybe we all knew but didn't want to admit it. They decided to organize an intervention for my brother in Edmonton. We would all be there, including a close family friend, Allen, a conservation officer, the same man who'd taught the self-defence course. Allen had been trained to remain calm in high pressure, even dangerous scenarios with problem bears in the Peace Country. He knew how to keep his cool in the face of hostile, unpredictable energy, with bears and people too. I was relieved that he would be there.

I didn't say a word when we gathered at Brendan's apartment. I could barely look at my brother when my parents confronted him. When they used the word *addiction*.

"Brendan, we're all here today as an intervention," my mother told him. "We love you and want to help you get better."

He jumped up and paced the room, stomping his feet. "You guys are fucking overreacting," he said. "It's just partying. It's what we do on weekends. I'm not an addict. What a fucking joke."

"If you don't get help, we're going to cut you off," my mom said, her voice breaking.

Brendan's face turned an ugly, mottled red. The muscles in his neck bulged. He became enraged like a bear who had taken the bait and was caught in a culvert trap.

It was as if he could scent my involvement in the intervention. "You told them, didn't you?" he said, thrusting his fist in my face. "You think you're so perfect, golden child? Why can't you mind your own fucking business?"

I cowered on the couch, saying nothing. It was the first time I remember feeling afraid of Brendan. His eyes were full of accusation. How could I have betrayed him?

He stormed out of the living room and slammed his bedroom door.

Six

After the intervention, Brendan's addiction worsened. He'd binge on booze and drugs and then disappear during the comedown, going silent for days. Only a month after the intervention, a childhood friend of his informed my parents that Brendan hadn't been attending his classes at college. Scenes of worst-case scenarios played out in my mind. What if he borrowed money from the wrong person? I saw him crumpled in the parking lot outside Cowboys. I imagined some guy kicking his head into a street curb. I texted him.

Hey. Where are you? We are all worried about you.

Nothing. I tried again, five minutes later.

Bren, I know we haven't been close lately, but you know I'm always here for you.

I woke up the next morning and reached for my phone. *0 new messages.*

Later that morning, my mother called to let me know that she'd finally heard from him. Brendan was okay, she said. Staying with a friend whom she didn't know.

When my brother disappeared on a bender, I felt a kind of grief that reminded me of something my father had taught us: When hunting deer, or elk, or moose, take the lung shot—aim one palm width behind the front leg—to ensure a quick, clean death. Wounding the animal would prolong its pain and suffering. In my mind, Brendan was a badly wounded animal, running deeper into the woods while we searched for a blood trail, desperate to locate him but terrified of what we might find.

I didn't know you could grieve someone who hadn't died.

I immersed myself in my writing as a way of coping with the immense fear that had taken up occupancy in my body. I clung to the words on the page as if they symbolized a trail out of the woods, away from the pain and uncertainty, a map that allowed me to move forward in my own life.

A year later, my parents finally convinced Brendan to sign up for a rehabilitation program in Edmonton. My father travelled down to the city to stay with my brother for six weeks. Brendan made it through the program and began attending Alcoholics Anonymous meetings. He asked a former hockey teammate from Peace River to be his sponsor.

Hey, I'd really like it if you could come with me to an AA meeting, he texted me.

Hesitantly, I agreed.

We drove to a location on 118th Avenue where an AA meeting was being held in a basement beneath an Ethiopian grocery store. We sat down at the back of the room on plastic chairs. Brendan, wearing his bright white sneakers, two-hundred-dollar designer jeans and a flashy sports jacket, stuck out from the crowd of mostly older folks. The leader of the AA meeting, an Indigenous man in his sixties, led the opening prayer. I looked over at my brother, who was reciting it word for word. *God, grant me the serenity . . .*

The roomful of people appeared friendly, though weathered. A few people smiled and nodded at me when my brother stood up to say, "My name is Brendan and I'm an addict. I'm seventy days clean now. I wanted to bring my sister here with me for support today."

"Welcome to you both," said the facilitator. "Did you want to share more with the group about why you're here today?"

"I'm tired of letting my family down," my brother said, gesturing a hand towards me. "I want to do better by them. I want to have a relationship with my sister again."

I shifted uncomfortably in the plastic chair. The others looked at me and I avoided eye contact, staring instead at the floor with tears pooling at the edge of my eyes. I wanted to believe that Brendan's words were in earnest, that he'd brought me there to show me that he was really trying to get better for his sake and our family's sake too. But I knew, deep down, I didn't really trust the words coming out of his mouth. They felt too rehearsed. Too clean, like his bright white sneakers. He'd said these things to my parents and me before. I wondered if he'd really brought me there so I'd go back to them and convincingly say, "It's true, he really is making an effort to change. He's staying clean," and they'd give him more money. Rather than being moved by his words, I felt angry and distrustful.

He dropped me off at my apartment in his jacked-up truck. How could he afford such a truck, anyway? I couldn't wait to get out of the vehicle. "Thanks, Treen," he said as I reached for the door handle. "We should go for coffee soon."

I softened at the sound of my childhood nickname. Only the people closest to me called me that. I looked over at him and felt a pang of regret. Maybe I shouldn't have doubted him. He needed me.

"Okay," I said. "I'd like that."

But the call to hang out never came, and shortly after, he began using again.

———

I wasn't sure how to reach and help my brother, and eventually I stopped trying. The naive biology that had allowed us to exist as one when we were children had been replaced by its opposite: a seemingly irreparable divide, an inability to understand each other.

What does it mean to become estranged? The Merriam-Webster dictionary defines it as "mutual indifference where there had formerly been love," or "a state of alienation from a familial relationship." Estranged, from Old French *estranger*, "to treat as a stranger."

Slowly, we were becoming strangers to one another. We saw one another now and then, linked by our parents' efforts to stay together as a family, but we lacked any warmth and desire for connection in our communication. Indifference divided us like fog in a river valley, obscuring the view of the other side, and gradually we forgot the other was even there.

My life was growing in new directions in Edmonton. I began to volunteer with a human rights group at my university and we organized documentary screenings and social justice workshops. I shaved my head for a fundraiser for cancer research and liked the way I looked in the mirror: strong, confident, an antithesis to the sexualized women plastered on the Cowboys billboards. I wore T-shirts with slogans like BE THE CHANGE YOU WANT TO SEE IN THE WORLD. When ethnic violence broke out in Darfur, Sudan, we organized a student protest march from Calgary to Edmonton, walking three hundred kilometres along the highway, calling for the University of Alberta to divest from arms companies supplying weapons of genocide and war. I made good friends through my volunteer work and found a sense of belonging—even family.

Although I hadn't graduated from university yet, I began working for a human rights organization in the city that had been founded in the 1970s by the diaspora community from Latin America, people who'd fled from brutal US-backed dictatorships in Chile, Argentina, Guatemala, and El Salvador. My work allowed me the opportunity to travel with my colleagues to rural communities in Guatemala and Nicaragua to participate in building schools and health care facilities. My eyes were cracked wide open in Latin America, hearing stories of people who'd survived the US-funded Contra War in Nicaragua, or Guatemalan farmers fighting against Canadian-owned gold mining companies who were operating without legal consent. I devoured the pages of Eduardo Galeano's *Open Veins of Latin America*, a book that laments the legacy of colonial resource extraction—of gold, silver, nickel, salt, and even guano—and the slavery and abuse of workers in the Americas. I'd come back to Edmonton, after my travels, feeling politically charged and incensed and poured that energy into my writing and activism work. I was starting to make connections between human rights abuses occurring in Indigenous communities in Latin America and abuses that were occurring right in my own backyard: Alberta's oil sands.

In 2007, when I was twenty-two years old, I organized a social justice conference for Alberta high school and college students, where an activist from Edmonton's Greenpeace chapter delivered a passionate speech about the environmental impacts of the oil sands in northern Alberta, including the issue of toxic runoff from tailings ponds into the Athabasca River.

Organized opposition to the oil sands was just taking off in Alberta. The speaker, a charismatic guy in his mid-twenties, spoke convincingly about the industry's massive carbon emissions that were fuelling climate change. A month earlier, he and other activists had rappelled off the High Level Bridge in Edmonton, dropping an enormous banner that read STOP THE TAR SANDS. Those sympathetic to—reliant upon—the oil industry, including my twenty-five-year-old brother, were incensed.

"Fucking tree huggers," he huffed when I saw him at a family dinner.

I tried to interject, to point out that, given the far-reaching effects of the climate crisis, the protesters might actually have everyone's best interests in mind, but my brother shook his head and wouldn't meet my eye. It was as if an invisible, soundproof wall had been erected between us, barring any kind of productive conversation.

While organizations like Greenpeace were accusing the oil sands industry of "ecocide," the Alberta government began referring to protesters as "environmental terrorists." The year before, Dr. John O'Connor, a physician working in First Nations communities located north of Fort Mac, raised the alarm on the disproportionately high rates of cancers in Fort Chipewyan and Fort McKay, suggesting that the oil sands could have played a role. In 2007, members of Health Canada and the Alberta Cancer Board, assisted by Alberta Health, charged O'Connor with causing "undue alarm" about environmental pollution.

My activist friends circulated emails with attachments of photographs of deformed, lesion-covered whitefish from Lake Athabasca with golf ball–sized tumours protruding from their spines.

Meanwhile, Alberta's oil sands were making international headlines. "There's an oil boom going on right now. Not in Saudi Arabia, or Kuwait, or any of those places, but 600 miles north of Montana," crooned a *60 Minutes* news anchor in an episode on Alberta's oil sands that aired in late January 2006. "The oilmen up there aren't digging holes in the sand and hoping for a spout. They're digging up dirt—dirt that is saturated with oil. They're called oil sands, and if you've never heard of them then you're in for a big surprise because the reserves are so vast in the province of Alberta that they will help solve America's energy needs for the next century."

That same year, Brendan dropped out of his college program and got a job working for an oil and gas company in Nisku, a suburb of Edmonton. Despite attending AA meetings, he continued to struggle with addiction, staying clean for weeks before bingeing on booze and coke. We found ourselves fiercely divided over oil.

"Well, you benefit from petroleum every day," he'd argue with me. "What do you think your running shoes are made of? How do you think the bus you catch every day gets around the city?"

"That shouldn't give government or companies the pass on community health and environmental monitoring," I'd retort. "Have you even seen those images of the deformed fish?"

"Pfft, those communities are benefiting—believe me," he scoffed. "Anyways, we can't all *save the world* for a living," he said mockingly. "Just don't go and chain yourself to a truck, or something stupid, okay?"

Over the Thanksgiving weekend in 2007, my mother found anabolic steroids in my brother's gym bag and she confronted him about the risks. Steroids could cause extreme mood swings, depression, and other long-term psychiatric problems. My brother detonated with a rage that shook and dominated every corner of the house. I heard him berating my parents from behind my closed bedroom door. I hated that I no longer felt safe in my childhood home.

Often, my friends and colleagues were surprised when they learned I even had a brother.

"Oh, you never mentioned a brother. You never talk about him."

"We're not close," I'd say with a shrug, avoiding the complexity of it all.

"I'm putting him at arm's length," I threatened to my mom. "I've got to do it." The distance between us felt more essential than ever, but my mother begged me to keep in touch with Brendan.

"Don't, Trina," she pleaded with me. "You don't know how these things can go on for years. You need each other."

I burned with an anger that surprised me. Since Brendan's addiction had grown to take up so much space in our lives, I found myself resentful of him. I looked back on our childhood and reframed the way I'd perceived things. Maybe it had always been *his needs* before my own. My brother had been the sun we all orbited around: the hockey star, the extroverted boy, the child whose voice dominated conversation at the dinner table. Nothing had changed, only now he was gleaning all the parental attention and energy for the mistakes he couldn't stop making.

Two months later, I reluctantly drove back north to Peace River for the Christmas holidays. A part of me wanted to stay and celebrate with my activist friends in the city. I worried that everything was about to implode. Brendan and I made the five-hundred-kilometre drive along Highway 43 in separate vehicles. When I heard the sound of his truck door slam shut, my jaw tensed. Even my parents seemed to walk on eggshells around my brother, careful not to set him off.

He partied with friends on Christmas Eve at the Moon Saloon, came home in the early hours of the morning, and crashed hard. On Christmas morning, he didn't come upstairs. My mom knocked on the door of his bedroom in the basement. No answer. He was out cold.

We didn't hear the sound of his footsteps until my parents and I had set the table for Christmas dinner. Brendan stomped upstairs and sat down at the table in front of the empty plate, wearing a pair of grubby sweatpants and a gym T-shirt. He didn't speak or look up at us.

"Merry Christmas," I said sarcastically, and he glared at me.

I resented him deeply at that point. The way his problems had taken over our lives, the way my mother embodied sadness and anxiety, the way my dad had a permanent scowl on his face.

I can't remember what I said to make him snap; I only remember his reaction. How he lunged across the dinner table as though he was going to wrap his hands around my neck and choke me, his eyes expressing something like hate. My dad had to hold him back. I fled downstairs to my room and packed my bags. My mom begged me not to leave, but I was done with the charade of pretending it was all going to be okay. That night, I wrote Brendan a letter. In the morning, I slipped it under the door, hugged my parents goodbye, and drove back to the city.

Brendan and I didn't see one another or speak for over a year. I let go of imagining our future together as adult siblings. I learned to become an only child. To harden and brace myself to expect the worst from my brother.

I never brought the incident up with my parents, avoiding the memory of violence between me and Brendan, along with the words I'd written—*I don't want you in my life anymore.*

PART II

PROBLEM BEAR

Seven

In the 1990s, my father and his colleagues relocated a four-year-old male grizzly bear originally from southwest of Grande Prairie four hundred kilometres north to the Chinchaga, an area of boreal forest north of the town of Peace River, and a favoured location in the 1990s and early 2000s for relocating problem bears from elsewhere in the province. Relocation was considered a more humane option than the bear being destroyed, although this approach was practised more frequently with grizzly bears than with more abundant—and hence dispensable—black bears.

They put a VHF radio collar on the problem bear and dropped it off at the end of a logging road. Only a month later, a fixed-wing aircraft pilot picked up the bear's radio signal at the edge of an airstrip in Fairview. The bear had wandered more than three hundred kilometres back south. A few days later, the pilot picked up his signal again, this time farther to the southwest, in Saddle Hills County, "only a stone's throw away from houses," as my dad remembers. He called the local Fish and Wildlife officers to advise them that a problem bear was on the move.

"What impressed me about that bear is that no one ever saw him," said my dad. "He was bedding down during the day and moving at night to avoid people."

Adult male bears, both grizzlies and black bears, are long-distance travellers. Although it may seem like the more humane option, often relocation doesn't work. Relocated bears are forced to try to make a living in an unfamiliar habitat and face many risks, including being preyed upon by larger, more dominant bears who already live and den in the area.

Even if it took them months, some bears would travel over a thousand kilometres to get back home.

"What is it that guides them?" my dad would often wonder. "The stars? Some kind of magnetic or navigational pull home? It's just incredible."

When I asked him why the bear was relocated in the first place, he couldn't remember that part of the story. It was far less memorable than the animal's desire to find its way back home.

After graduating from university in Edmonton, I'd spent seven years working with human rights organizations in Latin America and East Africa, but I couldn't ignore the magnetic draw to return to my roots in the Canadian north. In 2016, when I was thirty-one years old, I moved back to Peace River to finish writing my first book, *Women Who Dig*, and prepared for my rookie season working at a fire tower.

For the past decade, Brendan and I had lived estranged from each other. Our mother tried desperately to keep the emotional connection between us alive, sending us updates about the other and urging us to repair our relationship. But the thought of reconciling with my brother—when there were so many things unsaid—completely overwhelmed me. I felt a range of emotions: sadness, anger, and guilt for keeping him at arm's length for so many years, even knowing there had been no denying how difficult or abusive he could become under the influence of drugs and alcohol. I wanted to try to heal our relationship, but I wasn't sure how, or where to begin.

"Your brother's doing a lot better now," my mom insisted. "You should really reconnect."

While I'd been living in Nicaragua, Cuba, and Uganda, my brother had spent the last decade working in the oil and gas industry, taking contracts across northern Alberta in Fort Mac, Red Earth, and Fox Lake, and often working week-long shifts at workers' camps. During that time, he'd been briefly married and then divorced, and had struggled on and off with addiction.

Shortly after I arrived back in the North, Brendan got hired on as a well-site operator in the Peace River oil sands, working shifts of fourteen days on, seven days off, and making the five-hundred-kilometre commute between Peace River and Edmonton every two weeks. He'd asked my parents if he could stay in their guest room while working in Peace River—and they obliged.

I was surprised by how healthy he looked. I noticed how Brendan had aged, his dark-brown hair threaded with silver, which made his eyes appear bluer. He was handsome. Thirty-four looked good on him. Though Brendan lifted weights at the gym every day, he'd given up the anabolic steroids and his body appeared muscled but in proportion. His arms were saturated with tattoos that he'd had done shortly after his divorce. He rolled up his shirt sleeve to show me his artwork. A Bengal tiger leapt back at me, jaws open, snarling. I didn't ask him, but I wondered if Brendan identified as the tiger, considered to be the most powerful of wild cat species, with the capacity to lift twice its body weight and take down its prey with the single swipe of the paw. Indeed, the tiger represented strength, ferocity, and unpredictability. Maybe it was a symbol for battling the tiger within himself, the desire to drink and binge on cocaine.

"I've been clean for over a year now," he told me.

I felt a shot of hope when my brother embraced me exuberantly, as if nothing had happened between us, sensing a return of his boyish vitality.

"It's like the old Bren is back again," my mother said.

But instinctively, I kept my guard up. My brother's sobriety felt as tenuous as the oil and gas industry he worked in: boom-and-bust.

"Children change everything," people sometimes said to me about my brother. "It will get easier when you're older and you guys have kids. Wait and see."

I'd always responded to this with cynicism, but the same year we moved back to Peace River, my brother brought home his new girlfriend, Amanda, and her three-year-old child, a boy named Max, to celebrate Halloween. From across the basement room, I watched Amanda paint Brendan's face like a vampire and tie a cape around his shoulders. We carved the giant pumpkins that my parents sowed from seed in the backyard. Max zipped around the basement and played with Brendan's old pirate ship Lego set. He was small for his age and whip-smart. Something in the boy reminded me of my brother when he was young.

Brendan was firm but gentle and loving with Max. He confessed to me that he'd never felt such a love before, for his partner and her child.

"Come visit us in Edmonton," Brendan urged me before they left. "I want you to be an Auntie. I want you to be in my son's life."

I didn't know what it meant to be an Auntie, and a part of me remained deeply skeptical and fearful that my brother, with his addiction struggles, could hold everything together. I was afraid to get too close. What if he relapsed and disappeared on us again?

A month later, Brendan and his partner shared the news: They were expecting a baby. My parents were ecstatic, but I wasn't sure how to feel. Everything seemed to be happening so fast. My brother's foot, heavy on the gas.

On July 9, 2017, at 7 a.m., I woke to a text from Brendan.

A photograph of my brother dressed in a yellow hospital gown, cradling a newborn child, his arms covered in tattoos right up to his knuckles. He was grinning with a familiar boyish intensity. His eyes were wet with tears.

You had to be the first to know, Treen, he wrote. He hadn't even texted our parents yet.

It was a moment of witnessing not only the birth of my niece, but Brendan passing into a new stage in his life. As usual, he was a few steps ahead. I kept returning to the message over the next several weeks, examining the photograph as proof of life, the sight of my newborn niece, Brianna, cradled in my brother's arms, his tattoo of the Bengal tiger visible. My brother's words: *You had to be the first to know.*

I knew that reconciliation with Brendan wouldn't happen overnight. Despite our close bond as children, the distance between us had eroded any sense of trust or familiarity. We didn't know one another as adults—not really. But I could see that he was genuinely trying to reach across that which had divided us and I wondered if maybe it was true what people had told me.

Children soften the spaces between us. They cannot heal the wounds of the past, but they require our mutual love and ask that we show up for them, and in that sense we had a new reason to show up for one another.

Eight

A mother black bear and two cubs sauntered north of the fire tower through the cutblock, a clearing where the forest had been logged several years before. The aspen and birch saplings hadn't yet grown tall enough to obscure the view. The bears stuck out against the landscape, their black fur shining like polished stones against the dead grass and leafless brush. Banks of snow sheltered against the willows. The fire moss, a carpet of coral-stemmed lichen, glowed in the afternoon sun. From up in the fire tower, I watched the bears. It appeared as though they were walking across a bed of hot coals.

It was May 2019 and I was in my fourth season as a fire tower lookout in northwestern Alberta, where I was tasked with spotting smoke from a hundred-foot-high tower and alerting firefighting crews to potential burns. However, while surveying the land, my eyes were often drawn to an abundance of wildlife: migratory birds, moose and their gangly-legged calves, mysterious lynx, and groundhogs that emerged from their dens, standing on guard like foot soldiers. The cabin beneath the tower, my base camp, gave me an on-the-ground perspective. If I wasn't watching for fire from the tower, I was watching for wildlife from my cabin windows.

From afar, the bears were beautiful. Fixed in time and space like a landscape painting, or a photograph in a gallery that I could pause in front of and appreciate without feeling threatened. I knew that bears were mostly afraid of people. These bears didn't want anything to do with me.

The animals looked huge, as bears do to the average person who rarely sees them. The human mind, when seeing a bear, often reacts with shock and awe, as though the animal's astonishing bulk of fur, muscle, tooth, and claw has appeared out of thin air, like a sleight of hand, a magic trick, as though bears belong only in our imaginations and not along the peripheries of our daily lives. *Now you see me, now you don't.* An appearance that might be accompanied by the click of a camera shutter or the sound of a rifle firing. Sounds that translate to: We love bears and we hate them.

The bears grazed on fireweed and coltsfoot emerging from the bare earth. They appeared calm and at home on the land. Unbothered by the tower, the cabin, the scent of a woman and her dog, and even the forestry radio that chirped alive with human voices.

I hoped they wouldn't edge any closer.

Every April for the previous four years, the melting snow and the geese returning to the northern skies signalled it was time to pack my boxes of food rations, books, clay and pottery tools, and climbing gear, and prepare for another season alone watching for wildfires. In a world gone digital, many people are surprised to learn that such a job even exists, but there are a hundred active fire towers remaining in Alberta. Lookouts are the first line of defence in wildfire detection in the province, responsible for keeping vigil over the forests and grasslands and reporting the faintest trace of smoke.

I was thirty-four years old. Seasons at the fire tower—April to September—enabled me to slow down and do what I'd always wanted to do since I was a child: write. Write articles and books about the social and environmental issues I cared about. I loved the thrill of climbing one hundred rungs up a vertical ladder to reach my office every morning, and the extraordinary views of the forest and skies. Whenever I spied a tendril of smoke rising out of the forest, my heart beat as fast as a hummingbird's wings. Blood rushed to my head. Even though the isolation could wear me down, there was a kinetic draw to life at the tower I struggled to resist. And the pay was good. I was on my way to becoming a "lifer," which is what we affectionately call the lookouts who migrate back to the job year after year.

This would be my first season at Hawk Tower, a site located in what Western scientists and land managers often refer to as the Wildland Urban Interface (WUI), which describes the transitory zone between wilderness and land developed by human activity. Fifteen kilometres to my north lay a Métis farming community. The closest human structure, a mobile home on a quarter section of farmland, was only five kilometres away. Studies show that settlements in the WUI are more likely to be affected by catastrophic wildfires and experience human–wildlife conflict.

I'd previously worked at Muskeg Tower, located fifty kilometres west as the crow flies, where I saw the tracks of my wild neighbours—moose, bear, wolf—but rarely saw the creatures themselves. I assumed that my dog, Holly, kept most of the wildlife wary and away from the cabin. An electric fence surrounded the site, as did one at Hawk Tower, but I often left the gate wide open at Muskeg. The risk of a wildlife encounter seemed low.

My only close encounter with a bear at Muskeg Tower happened on a rainy afternoon when I was down in the cabin, designated on low fire hazard, and practising yoga in my kitchen. I went outside to pee. I couldn't be bothered to walk the hundred metres to the outhouse, so I squatted down on a patch of grass beside the cabin. I looked up, startled to see a large cinnamon black bear less than twenty metres away—*inside* the fence, with no barrier between us. The bear was under my fire tower, lackadaisically propped up on its huge rear end and using a front paw to tear at the long grass and shovel it into its jaw. I noticed the bear's muddy tracks on the sidewalk, which ran parallel to the cabin. I'd probably been upside down in downward dog as the bear strolled right through the open gate.

Knees shaking, heart jackhammering in my ears, I pulled up my pants and tiptoed back into the cabin. The bear didn't seem to register my presence as I watched it gorging like a hungry cow. It was the same colour as the bear I'd encountered while riding my horse on that autumn day in the river valley. I photographed the animal through the rain-pattered window, then cracked the window open, tapped on the glass pane, and gently called out, "Oh, hey there, bear!" Terrified, the bear yanked up its head at the sound of my voice, spun on the spot, and bounced towards the fence as if riding a pogo stick. I laughed. It slipped effortlessly through the uncharged wires of the fence as though it had done it a thousand times before.

After the encounter, I texted my father a photo of the cinnamon bear.

Wait a minute, came his response. *Isn't that inside your bear fence—was the fence even on?*

Sheepishly, I turned on the electric fence and never saw that cinnamon bear again.

My lone encounter with a bear at Muskeg Tower confirmed what I thought I knew about them: Save for a few bad apples, bears are mostly afraid of people.

But Hawk Tower was at a lower altitude, surrounded by mixed forest—black poplars, birch, fir, spruce, and pine—and located much closer to human activity. There was more food for a bear to forage on here. Although the towers were what we called "next-door neighbours" on the map, the two sites were markedly different. Muskeg Tower was slightly cooler and surrounded by an ocean of scraggly black spruce and swamps. The nearest community was thirty kilometres away. There were no roads that led to the tower, other than an old ATV trail, which had become overgrown with alders. From Hawk Tower, I could see farmland plots like a patchwork quilt, houses and barns with their tin roofs that, from afar, sparkled in the sun like sugar cubes, and tractors inching across the fields like ants, kicking up huge clouds of dust. Twenty kilometres to the east, the forest plunged down into the Peace River valley. When I spun around the Fire Finder, a large compass up in the cupola that we used to locate bearings on smokes, and peered through the spotting scope, I could see the sun reflecting off the river. I suspected that the ridge on which my tower was built served as a safe route for wildlife to bypass people and reach the river valley.

Leaving the fence gate wide open wouldn't be an option here.

By my fourth season at the tower, I had the seasonal routine down pat. In early April, I'd been flown in by helicopter, accompanied by my dog, Holly, a black-and-white shepherd-husky mix. Food and water would be resupplied monthly, delivered from the fire base in Peace River by helicopter. Firefighting crews would stop in every few weeks to use the site as standby for wildfire ignitions. But until the leaves faded orange and the cranes swarmed southwards in the skies, I'd be left here alone, watching for smoke, tending a small vegetable garden, reading books, harvesting wild berries, and wandering the forest with Holly.

The cabin at Hawk Tower was a modest one-bedroom structure with a tin roof, set atop a grassy hill. While I had electricity, there was no running water. I'd have to carefully ration what was flown in until the spring rains arrived and filled up catchment barrels outside my cabin. Every day, I'd climb the ladder of the steel-frame tower and keep alert in the cupola, a small octagonal dome that measured three metres in diameter. I was responsible for reporting wildfires when they were small, less than one-tenth of a football field, and providing the fire managers with a compass bearing and an estimated distance from my tower over the two-way radio. The system worked. The most experienced lookouts knew the geography and areas of human activity around their tower like the back of their hand—every lake, ridge, cutblock, gravel road, well-site, power line, rail line. They knew when to anticipate wind shifts, cumulus cloud buildup, and lightning storms.

Don, the previous lookout who manned Hawk Tower, a lifer in his late sixties, had worked on towers for over twenty years. The last ten of them he'd spent here, until he decided to move to a tower site located closer to the town of Peace River, one with a well-maintained gravel road that allowed him to drive to town in the evenings.

He'd kept the site at Hawk Tower in immaculate shape, leaving behind hardly any material evidence of who he was beyond the job of watching for wildfires. The bookshelves were empty. The desk was tidy. He'd organized the tacks on the bulletin board according to colour and lined up the pencils on the desk from the shortest—a mere nub of lead—to the tallest.

There were a few intriguing clues about my predecessor, however.

He'd hung, high up on the kitchen wall, an enlarged print of a black bear seated in the crook of a tree, as though the bear was a president or holy guru.

Tacked up to the office bulletin board, I found a black-and-white photograph of a man standing shoulder to shoulder with a black bear. In the image, the man held a pail in one hand and extended the other towards the bear. The bear placed a paw up on the man's extended arm, as if to balance itself, and appeared to sniff or lick at something on the man's fingers. The man gazed directly at the camera, not the bear, as if to say to the photographer with his eyes, "See, I've done this a thousand times before." In Don's all-caps handwriting, the caption reads: MY FATHER WITH BLACK BEAR, JASPER NATIONAL PARK, 1941.

In the early twentieth century, Canada's national parks encouraged and even facilitated "bear feeding viewings." People fed bears out of their vehicles on roadsides, encouraging black bears to stand up on their rear feet to "dance" for a hot dog or a tuna sandwich. The legacy of feeding bears in national parks would have consequences for decades to come. The bears began to associate people with food, increasing the risk for conflict. Decades later, Herrero's concept of mutual avoidance would attempt to redraw the boundaries and make bears wary of people again.

In the office, I found stacks of Don's handwritten records that he'd kept over the decade, detailed accounts of extreme weather, notable fire years, and bear observations. HIGHEST NUMBER OF BEARS OBSERVED IN ONE DAY: 12.

I wondered about Don's relationship with the bears. Only a couple of weeks earlier, as we were packing up our belongings and supplies at the warehouse in Peace River, he'd said something that surprised me. "Don't worry about the bears, Trina—they're peaceful bears," he'd told me. "But don't get close to them and talk to them like I did."

I'd stared at him a bit wide-eyed, confused. I wasn't sure how to respond.

"It's okay, Don—I definitely won't."

Surely he didn't mean "close" in terms of physical proximity. The image of a bear eating out of his hand sprang to my mind. What kind of dynamic was I about to step into?

I shared my worries with my father, and I could tell he wasn't happy about the idea of me taking over a site where bears, by the sounds of it, had been tolerated at close range.

"Sounds like you might have to redraw the boundaries," he told me.

———

On that same day, the bears I'd spotted from the tower returned—only much closer to my cabin. I dashed outside in my socks to make sure the gate was closed on the bear fence.

The electric fence hugged the edges of my yard atop the hill, protecting my cabin, a small tool shed, garden beds, and the fire tower. The fence had five wires at different heights—the highest at one and a half metres, the lowest only fifteen centimetres off the ground. A solar array charged a twelve-thousand-volt current that ran through the wires. I'd never seen the fence work. In theory, when on, if a bear tried to slip through, it would touch its nose to the wire, which would deliver a painful shock. The lowest wire was necessary to deter a curious bear cub, or even an adult bear, from worming underneath the fence on their belly.

The lifers had mixed sentiments about the efficiency of the bear fences. Don had told me he once witnessed a black bear clear the top wire like an Olympic high jumper. "The big guy hopped right over the fence!" he'd exclaimed. Several lookouts insisted the fences didn't work. One grumbled that they were essentially akin to "lobster traps."

"Bear gets in, bear can't get out. Now you're stuck inside an electric fence with a pissed-off bear," he'd told me. "*Not* good."

I stood behind my fence with its gate securely closed, my arms crossed against my chest, gazing down at the bears. Holly lifted her snout to the air and perked her ears in their direction, but I didn't know how she'd react in a close encounter with one. I trusted Holly's calm instinct, however. On one occasion, while we walked through the bush together, she'd stopped dead in her tracks, peered into a stand of alders, the fur on her back lifted, and seconds later a black wolf with yellow eyes slipped out. Holly had mimicked the wolf: She'd done nothing. She stood by my side, engaged but non-reactive. I hoped she'd do the same in a close encounter with a bear. A lookout to my south had a dog who chased a black bear only to have the bear turn on the dog. The lookout, a hunter, rushed inside the cabin to grab her rifle, and when she came back out, the bear was hot on the dog's heels. She put down the bear with a single shot.

"What are we gonna do about these bears, eh?" I said to Holly, and she wagged her tail.

The cubs appeared to be about the same size as Holly, weighing maybe fifty pounds. They were yearlings, around seventeen months old, and would be weaned before the summer's end. The cubs looked nervous, peering up in the direction of the cabin, darting closer to their mother.

I considered the faint thrum of the electric current running through the wires of the fence. If the fence failed to deter the bears, as my colleague had warned, I had other tools to choose from: two canisters of bear spray, an air horn, and a twelve-gauge shotgun. In my first season as a lookout, my dad had sent me a box of rubber bullets, as a non-lethal deterrent, and lead slugs that would be powerful enough to take down a charging bear.

"Load three bullets in the magazine," he'd instructed, demonstrating with the lightweight defender. "First, a slug. Then two rubber bullets. You want your last shot to be a fatal one—if you need it."

I decided that if the bears set foot beyond the willows into the grassy clearing around my cabin, then I'd scare them away. I went back inside and prepared vegetable pasta with wild harvested greens for lunch for the following day, when I'd be up in the tower from 11 a.m. until 8 p.m., only climbing down for a break at midday to transmit a brief weather report. It amused me to think that the bears and I were feeding on the same dandelion greens.

While cooking, I momentarily forgot about the bears. When I remembered and looked out the window, I was relieved to see they were gone. Maybe I'd been overthinking it.

At dusk, I slipped into an old T-shirt and a pair of pyjama pants and wandered outside to use the outhouse, leaving Holly inside the cabin. The cool, damp air cast shivers on my skin, but it was early enough in the season that the mosquitoes hadn't yet taken over the night sky, and I reminded myself to enjoy it while it lasted. As I reached for the outhouse door handle, I saw the mother bear and cubs on the other side of the electric fence. Panicking, I hid behind the outhouse.

Had they seen me? I peered around the corner, trying to steal a glance. Up close, the mother bear looked enormous to me, maybe *five hundred pounds*. It was not, in fact, an especially large female, probably weighing no more than three hundred pounds, but I had no reference for comparison. All I knew was that it was *big* and *close*. Way too close.

The mother bear flopped down on its belly, furiously feeding on dandelions. I was so close that I could hear its jaw clicking, molars grinding, and lips making loud smacking noises. Some lookouts joked that black bears were really "fur cows," although it's a misnomer. Unlike ruminant species like cows, caribou, and bison, which are able to glean proteins from grass in four-chambered stomachs, bears, with only a single-chambered stomach, must feast constantly in order to compensate for their less efficient digestive system—all day, all night.

The cubs flanked their mother, chewing with vigour. One was bigger, more robust than its sibling, with blond fur around its eyes as though wearing a party mask. The smaller cub had a blond muzzle and bore unusual markings on its chest: two white crescent moons. A kind of birthmark. Instinctively, I touched the freckle in the corner of my left eye that I'd had since childhood. When I was a kid, my mom called it a "beauty mark." Secretly, I loved that freckle, a subtle feature to differentiate me from others.

The small cub with the crescent moon markings seemed the most aware of my presence. It kept scenting the air, as if trying to make sense of who I was.

A part of me wanted to stay crouched there, to continue watching the small cub and its family, but my father's words about redrawing the boundaries rang in my ears.

I crept into the tool shed to grab an air horn, a canister of compressed air that, when activated, produces an extremely loud noise. They're a smaller version of what's installed on semi-trailer trucks, trains, and large ships to send out a warning or a distress alarm.

I told myself to be brave and marched right up to the fence where the bears could see me, bear spray in one hand and the air horn in the other.

"Hey bear!" I shouted down at the mother, only a few metres away. I waved my arms like windshield wipers and widened my stance.

The mother bear's head shot up. My body trembled.

"Get out of here!" I yelled at the bears. The cubs tumbled down the slope, but the mother bear didn't even flinch. The bear stood its ground, dropping its head and locking eyes with me. Its eyes were small in comparison with the size of its skull, and they felt cold and unpredictable. I tried to read the bear's intent, but our eyes had evolved differently. Solitary species don't need white sclera, or the whites of the eyes, which allows an animal to non-verbally gaze signal, or communicate with a flick of their eyes. Gaze signalling is a trait that evolved in species that hunted together in groups or packs, like humans, allowing us to silently share information and intent. But the bear was a solitary creature that hunted and foraged alone. I couldn't read a damned thing in that bear's beady-eyed stare.

I sensed that bear was not afraid of me, however. Like me, it widened its stance. I held up a deterrent in each hand as though they were loaded pistols and we were going head-to-head in a gunfight.

"You've gotta get out of here!" I pleaded with the bear. "You guys aren't safe here."

The mother bear cracked open its jaw slightly and I swore that I could hear a slight huff of breath, as though the bear was saying to me: *The new girl doesn't know who's in charge here.*

I squeezed the air horn, which let out a deafening blast, like a semi-truck barrelling down the highway at breakneck speed.

The mother bear spun and fled downhill. When the cubs, waiting at the edge of the forest, saw their mother coming at them like a freight train, they turned and sprinted into the bush.

I felt a momentary swell of self-congratulatory pride for following the advice in Herrero's rule book on bear encounters and doing what I'd seen my dad and his colleagues do all those years: chasing them back into the forest. I was redrawing the boundary between myself and the bears. Mutual avoidance was for the bears' own good, I reminded myself.

But despite my relief that the bears were gone, I couldn't sleep that night. The dog could sense my anxiety. Holly, who normally slept curled at the foot of the bed, abandoned me for the kitchen floor. I lay restless in bed, pondering my actions, unsettled by the measures required to drive them off.

Nine

I thought of my brother often while out at the lookout. The land stirred memories of us together as kids, playing in the forest and flushing ruffed grouse out of the grassy edges of cutlines. The scent of spruce and pine transported me back to the den of our childhood. From the tower, I could even see a fragment of the wide, wandering river that had witnessed it all.

While I sat in the fire tower, watching for smoke, Brendan was somewhere out there to my south, driving along remote gravel roads in the Peace River oil sands, monitoring a number of different well-sites, where heavy oil production took place. In my mind's eye, I imagined a pump jack, a symbol ubiquitous with the oil industry in Alberta, but these northern sites relied on "downhole pumps," powered by an engine and designed to extract heavy petroleum from great depths. As a well-site operator, Brendan was responsible for visiting the sites every morning to measure production levels and coordinate with trucks, which would come to haul out the oil, ready for market.

Over the last several years, the oil and gas industry had been recovering from a major economic crash that occurred in 2015 when the price of oil dropped by 70 percent and thirty-five thousand oil workers, my brother included, lost their jobs. The industry operated with the mindset of "go hard or go home," valuing high productivity at all costs, which created elevated risks for both workers and the environment.

Workers like my brother took on long shifts, which lasted weeks and sometimes even months, often isolating people in remote camps, and compensating them generously. Manhood in northern Alberta was defined by big trucks with lift kits, Ski-Doos and jet boats, and trips to Mexican resorts. Some guys bought property and invested, but many came off lengthy stints dropping thousands of dollars on booze, coke, and strip clubs. They spent all their earnings then hightailed it back to Fort Mac, or Red Earth, or Peace River for another round. The boom-and-bust cycle of Alberta's oil sands left workers vulnerable to addiction and debt and, ultimately, job insecurity. While he was raking in ten thousand dollars a month in Peace River, my brother bought a $70,000 GMC truck. I worried that, if the price of oil dropped again, he'd simply lose it all.

Over the previous winter, my brother and I had seen one another more frequently at family dinners at my parents' house. He commuted every two weeks from his home in Edmonton, where he lived with his partner and their children. Brendan was as loud as he'd ever been. Coming off a twelve-hour shift, he'd roar up in his jacked-up truck and swing open the front door. He'd kick snow off his workboots, stomp up the stairs into the living room, and crack open an Italian soda from the refrigerator.

"What a fucking gong show of a day," he'd boom, piling heaps of food onto his plate.

Brendan was moody and rarely asked my parents and me questions about our lives, but he was physically *here*, I told myself. He was safe. Maybe that was enough.

I was relieved my brother could take refuge in our parents' basement, knowing the mental health risks that living in an isolated oil workers' camp posed for him, although emotionally, I couldn't open myself up to him. I couldn't talk about the events that had transpired between us years ago—a withholding for self-preservation, perhaps.

Since the birth of his daughter, I'd begun to spend more time with his children in Edmonton. Becoming an Auntie had been far easier than I thought. Children aren't afraid of love the way adults are. When we'd watch movies together, Max always cuddled in close with me on the couch. The blast of intimacy, the strange loveliness of my nephew curling in close to my body, seeking comfort and warmth, cracked me open. It was easy to bond with the boy. We coloured at the kitchen table and played mini-hockey in their basement and watched cartoons together.

My brother insisted on teaching me how to gently change my niece's diaper. He was constantly cooing to her, praising her, and loving her. Brendan was his most tender self with his daughter. Fatherhood gave him a sense of purpose and belonging. He stood taller because of his family's love. My brother had begun to dream about the future again, one he insisted he wanted me to be a part of, and I began to imagine what that future could look like.

The bears came back the following morning. When I woke up, I glanced out the window and saw the unmistakable black hump of the mother bear's back on the other side of the fence. The bear had parked itself on the same grassy knoll, gorging on dandelions.

"Damn," I muttered. "I guess they didn't get the memo."

I studied the bears through the cabin window. The cubs were a few steps behind their mother, voraciously tearing clumps of grass. Their faces were surprisingly doglike to me, narrow, pointed snouts, sharp canine teeth, long pink tongues flicking.

I opened the window and blew the air horn. The cubs jumped back a few steps, but the mother bear calmly grazed on. I looked down at Holly, who wagged her tail nervously.

"What am I supposed to do with these bears, eh girl?"

My dad had told me a story about when he was a kid and his parents took them camping in Riding Mountain National Park in Manitoba. A black bear wandered into their campsite while my grandfather was cooking over a propane stove. He'd grabbed the cast iron pan and conked the bear over the head. Stunned, the bear took off.

I opened the stove drawer, pulled out the cast iron pan, and grabbed a small cooking pot, then walked outside to where the mother bear could see me.

"Hey!" I yelled, and the bears looked up at me. "You're not welcome here!"

I gonged the pot and pan together madly and the bears turned and torpedoed into the forest. I waited until I was sure they'd gone, swallowed by the labyrinth of branches.

I glanced up at the cupola. In less than an hour, I'd have to climb up for duty. Due to the dry, windy conditions in the forest, lookouts were designated on extreme fire hazard, which meant I'd be scouting for smoke from nine o'clock in the morning until eight o'clock at night.

I packed up my lunch, three litres of water, a thermos of coffee, and a book, and slipped my faded red climbing harness over my shoulders. At the base of the ladder, I clipped into the fall-arrest safety system, designed to catch me if I slipped, and began to climb, monkeying up one hundred rungs. As I climbed, I scanned the forest around me, looking for any trace of smoke ribboning up out of the treetops, knowing it was probably too early in the day. Most wildfires ignite around the peak heat of day, typically after one o'clock in the afternoon, depending on the severity of wind.

At the top, I used the crown of my head to push through a hatch door into the cupola. I'd grown accustomed to spending long hours in my office in the sky. The Fire Finder, a large compass, sat in the middle of the cupola. An office chair, raised to the maximum height, was on one side of the Fire Finder and a cross-shot map, which look-outs used to triangulate bearings on smokes and pinpoint the loca-tions of wildfires, was tacked up on a bulletin board on the opposite side. I rolled down several windows, letting the cool breeze sail in.

Morning. You can mark me up, I texted the lookout to my south, a woman in her sixties, a lifer who'd worked towers for twenty years. We had a "buddy system" in place, notifying our neighbours when we were on and off the ladder, in the rare chance something hap-pened and someone got stuck dangling there like a leaf in the wind.

That's copied, she texted back. *I'm up, too. It's looking pretty dry out there.*

In other words, keep your eyes peeled for fires today. It felt like a repeat of the spring of 2016, the same year the Horse River Fire burned over two-thirds of the city of Fort McMurray. It was unusually warm for early May, windy, and the deciduous trees were just starting to "green up," or leaf out, which meant the forest was dry and flam-mable as matchsticks.

I scanned the forest around me. The landscape was blotted with that brilliant newborn shade my father and I had always looked for from our front window in Peace River. As I swivelled my gaze to the east, a foreign colour and shape, balanced in the tree, caught my eye. It wasn't unlike the way I spotted wildfires, with the eye snagging on irregularities in the pattern of the landscape; a tiny tuft of white, thirty, maybe forty kilometres away could be a fire burning out of control.

"What the—" I muttered to myself, grabbing my binoculars for a closer look.

It was the bears. Nested in the branches of an old balsam poplar at the far edge of the cutblock. The mother bear was the highest up the tree, maybe ten metres off the ground. The two cubs were bal-anced on branches beneath her. I watched the mother through the binoculars, seated on her rump, legs dangling, feasting on the sticky sap-laden buds.

Black bears originated 40 million years ago from *Hemicyon*, a tree-climbing dog. They've evolved by surviving in forest ecosystems, denning beneath tree roots, feasting on buds and leaves and insect-laden deadfall, and climbing trees for safety. In the face of threat, most black bears would choose flight, my dad always taught us, although I wasn't so sure about this mother bear. She didn't seem afraid of a fight.

I glanced down at Holly, curled beneath the ladder of the tower, waiting loyally for me, as she'd done for the past several seasons. I worried about her on the ground alone. What if she slunk under the fence and went after a bear, or the opposite, what if the electric current on the fence grounded out and a bear went after her?

I dialed up Laura, a lookout neighbour who worked a tower to my southwest, a lifer with over fifteen seasons under her belt, and the same woman who'd expertly taken down the black bear that nearly killed her dog. Laura, who spent her off-seasons living in a cabin in northern BC, hunting and fishing, once described the fire season as her "social season." She was a true hermit, but she'd always been kind to me, offering advice on how to direct aircraft to "one-tree wonders," lone trees struck by lightning, often difficult to see, or how to transplant native plants—fireweed and fiddlehead ferns—into garden beds around the cabin.

Laura, like most lifers, knew bears. Especially black bears. Every lifer had at least a good story or two about black bears and what was required to deter them from getting into the yard or cabin. Back in the day, long before the introduction of bear fences, black bears would regularly bust into cabins, crawling through the windows to raid cupboards for food. Some lookouts had to escape through the windows or take refuge in their outhouses, radioing for help. The newer cabin design took marauding black bears into consideration and built the windows another metre off the ground.

Pat, a no-nonsense lifer in his sixties whose grocery list consisted solely of pinto beans and canned sardines, once told me a story about being woken up in the middle of the night by the sound of heavy breathing. He glanced up and traced the shadowy outline of a bear paw resting on the wire mesh of the window screen above him. Terrified, Pat jumped out of bed and slammed the window shut, and the bear took off. On another occasion, he'd been climbing down his tower at the end of a long day when he felt the hairs on the back of his neck tingling. Pat got the sneaking sensation he wasn't alone. Ten metres off the ground, he looked down and saw a large black bear standing at the base of the ladder, staring right back up at him. Pat hollered down at the bear, and even threw a shoe at it, trying to scare it off. Finally, after an hour, the bear gave up, ambled back into the forest, and he was able to safely climb down.

"Chaga Tower," answered a soft voice.

"Hey Laura, it's Trina at Hawk. I've got a sow here who seems just a little too comfortable," I said. "Was wondering if you had any advice for me."

I heard myself using the word *sow*. It made me feel as though I wasn't talking about a wild animal, but rather a pig. It was the same way I'd heard rural landowners around Peace River refer to bears growing up—"sow" for a female and "boar" for a male. Black bears were considered, by some, a pest species, especially in areas where people raised cattle or grew grain crops. Black bears gorged on grain fields—they loved oats—and could easily trample and damage crops. They raided beehives and fruit trees and broke into chicken coops. In the 1970s, the provincial government's stance was simple: Destroy bears before they become a problem. Conservation officers like Allen set up baited leg snares and killed bears on the regular. Landowners often did the same with black bears. See a bear, kill a bear.

Much had changed over the decades, however, with conservation officers encouraging landowners to mitigate food sources on their properties—properly disposing of livestock carcasses, securing grain bins, and putting electric fences around their apiaries.

Until now, I'd never regarded a bear as a "pest"—but then again, I'd never had to live so close to one.

"Yeah, the bears can become a real problem, especially on these long days up in the tower," Laura told me. "I used to keep water bottles filled with sand up in the tower. And when a bear would wander too close, I'd chuck the bottles down to try to scare it off."

She'd tried different strategies, including banging the outside Plexiglas walls of the cupola. One summer, Laura told me, she filled water balloons, hauled them up to the cupola in a bucket on the rope pulley system, and launched them down at problem bears.

"Did it work?" I asked, laughing.

"Well, it did for some of the younger bears. Bears get freaked out by new things," she said. "But they're also curious and smart enough to learn pretty quick what's actually a risk to them."

"Yeah, I just found that out this morning," I sighed. "This bear didn't give a damn about the air horn."

"Good luck," Laura said to me before we hung up.

I glanced back over my shoulder to check on the bears and saw that they'd climbed down. I hoped they'd stay away, although I knew in my gut they wouldn't. These were habituated bears, dangerously unafraid of people.

Habituated bears were *bad* bears, no questions asked.

A few hours later, I heard the voice of my neighbour to the north, a tower in the High Level district, calling in a fire over the two-way radio.

"High Level fire centre, this is Watt Tower with a pre-smoke," he said.

I spun to my north and scanned the flat expanse. I could see, without any obstruction, nearly one hundred kilometres into the distance. My eye located a bright-white smoke. *Yes. Wait. No.* I realized it was the pulp mill outside the town of High Level.

Then I saw it, a grey tuft, as subtle as a pencil eraser smudge. *Yes, that's it.* I peered through the rifle spotting scope, attached to the Fire Finder, and swung the compass around to record my bearing on the smoke: 5 degrees, 0 minutes, bang on.

I switched my two-way radio over to Channel 99, the radio channel used only by lookouts for sharing information with one another on potential wildfires.

"Watt Tower, this is Hawk Tower on 99," I said. "I've got your smoke at 5 degrees 0 minutes. It's a long shot from here."

"Hawk Tower, that's copied," came a deep voice that sounded as though it was born for radio. "The air tankers are already on their way, but I appreciate your help."

"Copy that, Hawk clear."

I poured myself a cup of coffee and continued to scan the forest for new ignitions.

Then I saw the bears from a bird's-eye view. They'd returned to their favourite spot on the southern grassy slope, metres away from the electric fence. I glanced down. Holly was beneath the tower, splayed out on her side, snoozing in the afternoon sun. Could she not scent the bears? Did she not care they were so close? Maybe I *did* wish she'd bark and help drive them off.

"HEY!" I shouted down at the bears from the open window. "GET OUT OF HERE!"

The cubs jumped back a few steps then looked up at the sky.

I did as my neighbour had advised me to do and pounded the outside of the cupola with my hand. "I SAID, GET OUT OF HERE!" I screamed at the top of my lungs, banging the walls.

They scurried back into the forest like rats.

I called up my friend Justin, a lookout who manned a tower northwest of the town of Peace River, over a hundred kilometres away from me. A seasoned outdoorsman and hunter, he'd grown up on a farm outside Manning, a small town north of Peace River. He'd hunted a few black bears over the years, not for trophy but for meat, and did his own butchering work, skinning the hide, rendering the fat, and grinding up the meat to make sausages. On one occasion he'd shot an elk and had to track it through the bush, following a blood trail. When he turned a corner, he saw that a large black bear had claimed the elk carcass. The bear charged at him. His rifle ready and loaded, Justin dropped the animal with two shots. "He was in bad shape," Justin told me. "The bear had an arrow blunt sticking out of its jaw. It was starving to death. The blunt was so deep it was preventing him from swallowing," he said. "No kidding he wanted to claim that elk for himself—I don't blame the guy."

"Whitecreek Tower," Justin said, picking up the phone.

"Okay, I get it now—I understand why people call bears 'pests,'" I complained. "How am I supposed to keep alert for wildfires with these bears always around?"

He chuckled. "Bears are gonna do what bears wanna do. But it sounds as though you're running out of options with this female. You've got those rubber slugs your dad gave you, right? Might be time to fire off a few into her backside and show her you're not messing around."

I was hesitant to rely on the shotgun. I'd never felt totally comfortable with a firearm, even though I'd been shooting the .22 since I was a kid. It wasn't that I doubted my ability. I had a naturally good shot. My brother used to call me a "sniper" when we aimed at old tin cans at the gun range. But targeting a live animal was another thing. My dad had made it very clear to me that I had to target the bear's fleshy rump.

"If you shoot her at close range in the gut—that could cause internal damage to the organs," he explained. "If you're going to take the shot, better make sure it's a good one."

The following morning, I stood ankle deep in the garden, hoeing apart clumps of dirt. I looked up and the bears were back, grazing on the slope as if nothing had happened. With resignation, I thought of the shotgun, locked away in the case, under the bed. I hesitated. *Not yet.*

I had one last trick up my sleeve. In my rookie tower year, a lifer told me about the days before electric bear fences, when folks would urinate along the perimeter of their yard as if staking territory. "It was easier for men, of course," he said with a chuckle. "But some gals would just pee in a bucket and pour it around the perimeter," he told me. "Lookouts swore by it."

"What the heck," I muttered to myself, unbuttoning my pants.

I felt every bit as ridiculous as I must've looked, but also, I had nothing to lose.

I dropped my pants and squatted in plain sight of the bears. As soon as the stream of urine hit the ground, it was absolutely clear I'd struck a nerve with the mother bear.

I'd communicated to the bear, in a very animal way, *Fuck off*.

HUFF!

The bear dropped its head and stomped the ground with its two front paws. It lowered its head and opened its jaw. There was a notable shift in the energy between us. Up until that point, the bear had conceded to my aggressions against it; but now something had shifted in its demeanour. The mother bear glared at me and broke into a slow, confident stride. I yanked up my pants and slowly backed up towards the cabin.

"Hey now, Bear," I hollered down feebly. But it was too late for peace offerings. The bear stopped and watched me intently, the same way Holly did when stalking a ground squirrel.

I had the instinctive feeling something had switched in the bear's brain. Had I become prey?

Inside the cabin, my hands shook as I pulled out the twelve-gauge shotgun from the camouflage cloth case. Holly eyed the gun and tucked her tail between her legs, gazing up at me with fearful eyes that seemed to question, *Is that really necessary?* I loaded two cartridges into the magazine.

When I emerged from the cabin, Holly close behind me, the bears were back in their preferred spot.

I walked up to the fence and aimed the shotgun. The cubs, a few paces back from their mother, jolted at the sight of the gun, as though I'd grown a long black arm.

Holly dropped her head and turned back for the cabin.

I locked eyes with the sow. It was fair game, I told myself, I'd given the bear plenty of warning. I lined up the shot, targeting its large black rump.

My index finger wrapped around the trigger.

I took a deep breath in and, on the exhale, squeezed. The gun bucked and the bear yanked its head up at the sound. It didn't move a muscle.

"Shit."

I'd missed. It could be challenging to shoot downslope, especially with a projectile as light as a rubber bullet. I'd probably flinched the moment before I pulled the trigger, a nervous habit that had followed me from childhood. "Don't anticipate it," Brendan would say.

The cubs bolted for the forest, scrambling up a huge old spruce on the edge of the clearing, their claws ratcheting into the scaly bark. They shot up the tree, one after the other, using the large branches as paw holds, and stared down at their mother, then over at me. I deflected a surge of guilt and tried again, pumping the action, loading another rubber slug into the magazine, my brother's words in my ear, *You gotta remember to breathe.*

BOOM! The slug made contact. The mother bear jumped and beelined for the bush. The cubs scrambled down the spruce and took off after her. I stared hard at the edge of the forest, heart thudding in my chest. The firearm weighed heavy in my arms. I called Holly over to reassure her, but the dog looked away and wouldn't come to my side until the shotgun was out of sight.

Ten

Brendan and I wouldn't ever speak directly about our estrangement, nor about the letter I had written him more than ten years before. There were some topics we'd learned to avoid entirely to "keep the peace," as my mother would say.

I bit my tongue when the topic of oil and gas came up at the dinner table.

"Holy fuck it's been a good month," my brother would crow. "Production is really picking up."

What I wanted to ask him, but didn't:

"*Great*, but at what environmental cost?"

It frustrated me that Brendan didn't seem to care about the negative impacts of extractive industries on the environment and Indigenous communities. There was no shortage of evidence. In 2011, heavy rains damaged a pipeline that ran north of Peace River, which caused a leakage of 4.5 million litres of oil into more than three hectares of beaver ponds and muskeg only ten kilometres north of the community of Little Buffalo. It was the second-largest oil spill in Alberta's history. Residents became sick with nausea, burning eyes, and headaches. It would take two years for the company, Plains Midstream Canada, to be found guilty for negligence.

The list of oil spills in northern Alberta was long and ongoing. First Nations communities were often on the front lines of these environmental disasters.

June 2012. 500,000 litres of oil leaked into the Red Deer River.
April 2014. 70,000 litres of oil spilled near the town of
Slave Lake.
July 2015. 5 million litres of oil escaped a faulty pipeline
south of Fort McMurray.
June 2016. 380,000 litres of oil flowed into a creek northeast
of Grande Cache, a grizzly bear recovery zone.
April 2018. 290,000 litres of crude oil emulsion leaked from
a pipeline northeast of Zama City.

Companies, including Enbridge, Canadian Natural Resources, and Nexen Energy, would be slapped by the Alberta Energy Regulator with million-dollar fines—a pittance, really, considering what their CEOs earned every year—but that wouldn't stop the flow of production.

I wrote extensively about the harms of extractive industries on the environment and Indigenous communities, publishing my book *Women Who Dig* in the spring of 2018—but I couldn't even have the conversation with my own brother about the negative impacts of his work. Our relationship felt far too fragile, the wounds of estrangement too fresh. I was afraid to trigger a fight.

In the fall of 2018, I was invited to give a keynote speech at MacEwan University in Edmonton about my research in Comitancillo, Guatemala, where Maya Mam farmers were fighting against Goldcorp, a Canadian-owned mining company, that was operating without community consent. During the question-and-answer that followed, one student stood up and pointed out the parallel with Indigenous communities in northern Alberta who are facing higher rates of cancer because of toxic spills into watersheds that were contaminating drinking water.

I looked up and saw my brother, seated a row back from the student, staring down at me. Because we rarely spoke, I wasn't sure how he learned about the event. I guessed that our mother had urged him to attend, but even so, I was touched that he'd come.

After the event, he came up to the book signing table and gave me a hug. "I'm proud of you, Treen."

My throat constricted with emotion.

"Thanks, Bren," I said, resisting the urge to cry.

I signed a book for him, floored by the fact that—even though we might not see eye to eye on things—he'd shown up for me.

At the fire tower that fourth season, my patience with the bears was running out, and it wasn't just the mother bear with yearling cubs, there were others too. Don's observation of twelve bears in a single day no longer seemed so far-fetched. From the cupola, I watched for them, as though they were tiny black ticks that I wanted to pick clean from the landscape. They followed an overgrown trail through the cutblock that connected with the road that wound down to the highway. From afar, I didn't know how to differentiate these solo travellers, and I wasn't sure if I was seeing the same bear or several different ones. In one afternoon, an enormous mother bear with three tiny cubs showed up in the cutblock. I observed them orbiting the colossal sow and thought, *Damn, that's one big mama*. Fortunately, they never drew closer.

On the ground, my encounters with the habituated mother bear of yearling cubs were becoming increasingly tense. We were both visibly stressed by the presence of the other and on the defensive. The mother bear huffed and stomped and made a strange popping sound.

"She's popping her jaw. That's a warning signal—she's not happy with you," my dad told me over the phone.

The rubber slugs were just a band-aid solution for a problem that wasn't going away. I'd become numb to the act of firing off a couple of shots into the bear's backside. I'd even fired off a round of bird-shot, a projectile made up of lead pellets, into the nearby bushes to try to scare the mother bear, but it quickly learned that neither the shots nor the slugs—even if they stung a little—were a real threat.

Aw, you're so lucky to see so many bears out there. A text came in from a friend who lived in a high-rise condo in downtown Toronto. I bristled.

It's actually a pain in the ass. I deleted the text before sending it.

I knew that my friend meant well. I also knew that I was privileged to live immersed in a wilderness that few would ever get to know so intimately. But it made me feel sharply aware of the disconnect between *saying* that we love wildlife—or the idea of them—and what it means to actually live closely with them. I guessed that my friend wouldn't love the idea of a family of raccoons, widely regarded as an urban pest, taking up residence on her condo balcony, for example. Even less so if those raccoons could physically harm her.

All too often we want wildlife on our own, fixed, human terms, safely observable through zoo enclosures, or from a Jeep on a safari, or a comedic reel on social media. We desire the raw, exhilarating feeling that proximity to wild creatures offers, but in reality, we don't always want them as neighbours. We don't want to be inconvenienced or threatened by them. I found myself longing for the protection of those glass enclosures that keep people and bears separate.

I explained to my friend that there were no conservation officers coming to rescue me from the presence of the aggressive mother bear. I had to delineate the boundary with the bear over and over again, which was exhausting. I felt as though I was running out of options.

Honestly, I wish I could go for a walk, or concentrate on my pottery without the fear of a bear encounter, I texted back to my friend. *I'd be a lot happier if they just stayed away.*

By mid-May, my nerves were badly frayed. Brutally hot weather persisted and I lost count of the number of days I spent on high and extreme fire hazard.

On May 11, I called in the Battle River Fire, a lightning-caused wildfire that ignited about sixty kilometres to my southwest. The black braid of smoke transformed into an apocalyptic giant, evacuating the lookout to my south. Every time I climbed, I saw the towering smoke columns of the Battle River Fire glaring back at me. And to my north, that small smudge of smoke that my neighbour, Watt Tower, had called in had blown up in the sixty-kilometre-per-hour winds, jumping the guard that firefighters had established around the perimeter of the fire, quadrupling in size. I paced the cupola like a caged animal. Fire managers were worried that the fire to my north, the Chuckegg Creek Fire, was going to burn over the town of High Level.

"Am I going to get evacuated?" I asked the duty officer, the wildfire ranger in charge of operations in Peace River, over the phone.

"We've got a plan in place, Trina," he told me. "But honestly, I'd be more worried about the bears than the fires, by the sounds of it."

A week earlier, I'd finally alerted my supervisor about the habituated sow and cubs. If I had to load a lead slug into the chamber and defend myself, I wanted to make sure my employers knew that I'd exhausted every other option.

On May 29, I witnessed the Chuckegg Creek Fire jump the fire perimeter and take off like a wild horse. Looking north from my cupola, I watched as the smoke columns rolled violently, rising higher into the atmosphere. The fire was throwing hot, burning embers hundreds of metres ahead of the front, which ignited hot spot fires. Smaller columns mushroomed up before my eyes, threading themselves into the body of the wildfire, *one, two, three, four, five*. I counted over twenty. With shaky hands, I shot a video of the firestorm on my cellphone, a fire bigger than the city of Edmonton.

Oh my god. Oh my god. Oh my god.

The Chuckegg was burning so furiously hot that it had produced what scientists call cumulonimbus flammagenitus, or "pyrocumulus," an extreme manifestation of a storm cloud, capable of generating high winds and lightning and igniting new wildfires.

I didn't want to take my eyes off the fire, but I couldn't turn my back on the other area of responsibility around my tower. I did a quick lap around the cupola.

"Oh, you've got to be kidding me," I muttered.

The mother and cubs were back, defiantly ambling along the fenceline. Something in me finally snapped. I angrily picked up the phone and called the duty officer.

"The habituated sow is *back*," I said to him, exasperated.

"We've got a patrol heading up your way," said the duty officer, referring to a firefighting crew on a flight patrol, scanning for new ignitions. "I'll let them know you've got a problem bear on your hands."

A bright-red helicopter came thundering from the south, flying over my tower, sending the bears scampering back into the forest. The helicopter circled, flying low over the treetops, the pilot and crew searching for the mother bear and cubs. Driving off problem bears with a helicopter is a fairly common tactic used by tree planting operations, or oil and gas workers' camps in the forest, and it was obvious the pilot had done it before. The pilot pivoted the machine 180 degrees and dropped over a stand of fifteen-metre spruce, and I realized they must've found the bears hiding in a tree. I imagined the mother and cubs scrambling down, trying to flee from the deafening noise and the swirling helicopter blades. The trees shook violently.

"We've got the bears," said a male voice over the radio, the crew leader. He sounded confident, like the leader of a special-unit military operation securing the location of the enemy. "We're going to drive them south to a cutblock," he said.

The phone rang. It was the duty officer in Peace River.

"Look, if they keep coming back, we're left with only one option . . ." he said.

He didn't finish the sentence for me. He didn't need to. I knew they'd send out a ranger to put down the mother bear. *Put down*, that euphemism again. More than likely they'd kill the cubs too, on the premise that the mother had habituated them to my tower site.

"I know," I said with resignation, and hung up.

From his tower to the south, Don, the former lookout at Hawk Tower, had been listening over the radio. He texted me immediately.

Those are peaceful bears, Trina!

I felt a pang of remorse. Then I launched on the defensive.

They're actually habituated bears, Don. I typed out the text but resisted sending it. I didn't owe Don an explanation, I was only doing what he should've done years ago.

But later that evening, I lay in bed, my body like a charged wire from the day's events, and couldn't stop thinking about the mother bear and its cubs. I wrestled with the ethics of my actions, questioning my reactivity, and examining what was at the root of it: fear.

I imagined the two cubs clinging to the torso of a tree, the rotor blades of a helicopter reverberating like gunfire, and how afraid they must've been. I told myself, over and over again, that I'd done *the right thing*, when every part of my body felt as though I was harbouring a lie.

What is it about being human and the need to be in the right? As if that gives us the legitimacy to exist. As if questioning ourselves is too dangerous an act.

———

The next day, Holly and I were evacuated from Hawk Tower. It was too smoky to safely fly a helicopter, so the duty officer sent a wild-fire ranger in a four-by-four truck to get us out of there. Overnight, the Chuckegg Creek Fire had burned over sixteen homes in the farming community to the north. The fire remained twenty kilo-metres away, but the smoke rolled overhead like a heavy, oppres-sive blanket.

The highway to the south had been barricaded off by police offi-cers. We could barely see more than six metres ahead on the road through the apocalyptic smoke. There were no other vehicles, but we began to make out the ghostly forms of bears grazing in the ditches. I counted *one, two, three, four.* Then a dead bear on the shoulder of the road. It was the bloated body of a cinnamon black bear.

"People are saying they're seeing way more black bears because of these big fires," the ranger, a bearded guy in his mid-twenties, told me. "They've got nowhere else to go."

My mind slipped back to the mother bear and its two cubs. I wondered where they were now, and whether they'd return to their favourite spot on the slope, or if the helicopter had been enough to scare them away permanently.

Several days later, when the extreme fire behaviour died down, Tim, a wildfire ranger in his late sixties, drove Holly and me back out to the tower. Tim had a silver handlebar moustache and wore a big belt buckle and looked like an old country singer. He'd been a lookout for twelve years before he took a management position with Forestry, and had trained me and most of the other lookouts in Alberta. He was a natural storyteller; whenever you asked him a question, he'd answer with a story.

As he turned the four-by-four truck onto the muddy, rutted road that led to Hawk Tower, we spooked a large black bear into the bush.

"I'm pretty much at my wits' end with the bears," I sighed, explaining to Tim about the situation with the mother bear and cubs. "I don't know what I'm going to do if they come back."

Tim had grown up on a farm in bear country in northern Alberta. In the 1980s he'd been hired by Forestry to shoot black bears around the vicinity of a large wildfire. It was the government's solution to the problem of bears breaking into firefighters' food rations at camp. Tim had also encountered bears—both grizzlies and black bears—in his twelve seasons as a lookout, and today he raised a few head of cattle on an acreage north of Peace River. He had trained his dog to chase bears off just to the edge of the property, before circling back at his command.

"Black bears loved to trash the place when I was away," he recalled with a chuckle, referring to his farm. "But one day a grizzly sow showed up and began to den in a canyon half a mile from my house."

He didn't even see it at first. He found the bear's golden hairs snagged on a barbed wire fence and brought the hair samples to my dad's colleague, Lloyd, for DNA analysis. It was confirmed: a three-year-old female grizzly. When the grizzly showed up, Tim noticed that the black bears suddenly disappeared. He no longer had to deal with any damage caused by "troublemakers"—what he assumed were juvenile black bears—testing boundaries.

"I was prepared to declare war on the grizzly if it bothered any of my stuff. You know, slap it in the ass with a rubber slug," he said.

But the grizzly kept its distance, denning in the canyon, where it raised its cubs.

"I never gave the bear a name, but it stuck around for a few years and never bothered the horse or cows," he said. He tolerated the bear because its presence seemed to keep the younger, more curious black bears at bay.

Many folks in northern Alberta have a mantra when it comes to dealing with grizzly bears, a threatened species that has been illegal to hunt since 2006: "Shoot, shovel, shut up." Instead of calling con-servation officers, some landowners take matters into their own hands. See a grizzly, shoot a grizzly. A lookout who manned a tower along the BC–Alberta border once told me that if a grizzly ever wan-dered into her yard, she'd shoot the bear and chain the body up to her truck and drag it into the bush. "Who would ever know?" she cackled. The aggression in her voice had stunned me. There was something inherently hateful about the way she spoke about bears.

Tim kept quiet about the grizzly, however, though he knew the very spot where she denned.

"The experience taught me a bit more about some of the selfish reasons why we value some animals over others," said Tim. "But more so about the ebb and flow of different wildlife populations and their relationships to each other. Actually, I wish I had a better word than *relationship*—that's kind of a human term."

He accelerated the truck up the hill that led to my cabin and tower, and parked outside the bear fence. Everything at the cabin was as I'd left it, although I noticed several deep gouge marks across the shed door. The bear's claws had scraped the paint off the door.

"Didn't you leave your bear fence on?" Tim asked.

"I guess I must've forgot when I was rushing to evacuate," I said sheepishly.

"You know, Trina, that female probably dens close to your tower," said Tim, running a hand over his moustache, "and when she comes out of the den in spring, your slope is one of the first places where there's green up." He gestured at the south-facing slope, the grassy knoll that seemed to magnetically draw in the bears. "This is ideal habitat for them."

He pointed to the bear fence. "You wouldn't believe how much time and energy it took to convince people to invest in these elec-tric fences," he said. "People don't like change. But we were long overdue. Too many bears have been put down at forestry camps and lookouts over the years, and in many of those cases it could've been completely preventable."

He showed me a photo of a massive dead black bear, slumped over a porch window at a lookout in the Swan Hills region. The bear had been hanging out at the tower site for weeks, and when a ranger drove up to the site to deliver groceries, the bear charged. The ranger hurried into the cabin for safety, while the lookout grabbed his rifle. He shot the bear as it was clawing its way through the porch window screen.

"The site didn't have an electric fence," said Tim, shaking his head in frustration. "Who knows if it would've changed the outcome, but it sure as heck wouldn't have hurt."

I stared at the image of the dead bear and was reminded of the carcass on the side of the highway. I didn't want it to come to that. *There has to be a better way*, I thought.

Eleven

As if the mother bear knew what loaded question weighed on my mind—was I capable of ending its life?—it didn't come back with its cubs for the rest of the season.

In July, I absent-mindedly glanced out the window, half expecting to see their shaggy black coats, their doglike faces tearing at grass, but the slope was void of them. The bumblebees swarmed the wildflowers, but the hugeness of the bears was distinctly missing. Their absence grew into a presence that haunted me. I hated the feeling that my actions—and my emotional reaction—had altered the landscape and the bears were no longer a part of it. With the bears gone, I poured my energy into my pottery, wedging mounds of clay on a canvas board and sculpting them into mugs and bowls and pondering the events that had transpired between us.

For the rest of the season, I witnessed the forests smoulder and burn. Thousands of acres of trees and muskeg and wildlife habitat smouldering from the two colossal wildfires, to my southwest and north, one that would burn an area three times the size of Calgary. On the days the winds blew at fifty kilometres an hour, the Chuckegg Creek Fire spread at the rate of fourteen metres a minute. I thought often of the wildlife inevitably caught in the wake of the fire.

I suspected the mother bear and cubs wouldn't have roamed that far north, but no doubt dozens of bears would've been affected by the burn. Could they scent the smoke, or feel the wall of radiant heat approaching? I imagined that some of the bears, particularly young cubs, might not have been so lucky. Sensing threat, some probably climbed trees and held on for dear life as the head of the fire swallowed them whole. Thousands of small mammals would've perished in the flames. A friend who worked in forestry reclamation would later post on social media images of what remained in the ashes: the skeleton of a marten, the skull of a beaver, a handful of teeth that measured eight centimetres long—no doubt belonging to a bear.

Wildfire plays an important ecological role in the boreal forest, the heat releasing the seeds of coniferous trees, like spruce and pine, and recycling old forest into new forest, creating habitat for moose and deer—and predator species like bears and wolves. Bears and other wild species in the boreal forest have learned to evolve with wildfires—they benefit from it. Fire promotes the growth of pioneer species, such as fireweed, and wild berries, which bears gorge on. But the Chuckegg Creek Fire was one of those wildfires that has scientists today worried: fires that are burning so devastatingly hot that they scorch everything—trees, plants, wildlife, and even organic matter and micro-organisms in the soil—preventing healthy regrowth. Historically, large-scale wildfires altered the landscape every 100 to 150 years in the boreal ecosystem; however, wildfires today are burning at a much higher frequency.

The Chuckegg burned within twenty-five kilometres of my cabin, displacing wildlife to the areas of cover surrounding the perimeter of the fire, including north and east of my tower. Conservation officers would receive an unusually high number of reports of bears feeding along Highway 35, or wandering into the nearby farming communities, rooting through somebody's compost bin or raiding apple trees and raspberry bushes.

I found myself empathizing with the bears affected by the massive wildfires. I thought of the story my father told me about the relocated grizzly bear who'd made his way back home. It isn't easy being a bear in an unfamiliar territory that other bears already call home.

Where else were the bears supposed to go? Pushed out by the fire, bears and other wild species, displaced like climate refugees, are led by their noses—and hunger—to food sources created by us. Dead livestock, ripening fruit, grain spilling out of bins, the scent of bacon wafting through an open kitchen window. Wildfires weren't necessarily a direct threat to the bears and other large mammals themselves, but the resulting loss of habitat forced them elsewhere, into new territory where they'd face their greatest risk of mortality yet: humans.

Of all the risks that black bears face in their lives—of dying from disease, such as trichinosis, or starvation during seasons when the berry crop fails, or being preyed on by grizzly bears or larger black bears, or taken down by a pack of wolves—the number one cause of death involves people.

Before the season was over, in mid-August, my younger cousin Oscar hiked the ten-kilometre road from the highway to my tower for an overnight visit. Oscar had grown up in Nova Scotia but had spent the last couple of summers in northern Alberta working as a wildland firefighter, bunking fifty kilometres south at the fire base in Manning. Although he wanted to visit on his days off, Oscar admitted to me that he was nervous to hike alone through dense bear country to reach the tower. I'd told him stories about my harrowing encounters with the habituated mother bear.

After parking at the trailhead, he power-walked along the grassy road, boisterously singing around the corners to announce himself to the bears. About five kilometres in, Oscar was startled to look over and lock eyes with an enormous black bear hunkered down off the trail in the bush.

"It was staring at me from the shade of the trees," he told me, breathless, when he arrived. "It stayed absolutely still like it hadn't been seen. It was practically camouflaged by the forest. My body didn't know how to react. It was like my worst fear had been confirmed."

Oscar confessed that it was the same kind of fear he felt about being attacked by a shark while cold-water surfing in the Atlantic Ocean near his hometown of Halifax. Great white sharks swim along the bottom of the ocean and look up towards the surface for prey. Dressed in a black neoprene wetsuit, surfers run the risk of being mistaken for a seal bobbing on the water's surface.

"There's a very low probability of being attacked by a shark, but if the shark wanted to attack me, there'd also be a low rate of survival," Oscar rationalized.

He edged slowly past the bear and, once clear, lengthened his six-foot-two stride. He kept glancing back over his shoulder, petrified that the animal would come charging him.

But nothing happened.

Rattled by the close encounter, Oscar was nervous about hiking back out the following afternoon, but without any other choice, he packed up his bag and set off. Two hours later, my cousin called me from the highway. Only a kilometre away from his car, Oscar recounted, he saw two black forms scampering after one another as if playing a game of tag.

"At first, I thought they were wolves from a distance," he said. "But as I got closer, I could see that, clearly, they were small bears."

Immediately, I thought of them. The sibling cubs: the bigger bear with the blond mask around its eyes and the smaller one with the crescent moon markings on its chest. The mother bear would've weaned them by late June, chasing them off to carve out their own habitats in the forest, and perhaps opted to mate again. *It has to be them*, I thought.

I remembered my father telling me that siblings, after being weaned by their mother, would often stick together and face the forest as two. Sometimes they'd even den together for a third winter. Being two presented an advantage. Together, they could hold ground against larger, more dominant bears. The sibling relationship in any species—solitary or social—is one of the most formative for learning how to be and survive in the world.

Brendan and I hadn't yet regained our closeness, even as I'd grown to love his children and witnessed his ongoing commitment to sobriety. However, we couldn't part ways. We were the people on the face of the earth most genetically like each other. Even while we were estranged, he'd always been omnipresent, buried beneath my every thought. Sometimes, when I looked in the mirror, I saw my brother staring back at me.

During long days in the tower, I began to re-examine the story I'd told myself about my brother for so many years: that he was an addict, that he'd inevitably hurt me again. I read a book by psychotherapist and addictions specialist Gabor Maté, called *In the Realm of Hungry Ghosts*, that explores the way society stigmatizes, even dehumanizes, those living and struggling with drug and alcohol addictions. During the worst years of my brother's addiction, before our falling-out, the words I'd used to describe him included *monster* and *animal*. I viewed my brother through a lens of fear. I didn't see him so much as human, but rather as a beast that could harm me.

I began to learn that addiction isn't about individual strength, or will, nor a reflection of moral character. It's a chronic, relapsing

disease of the brain, writes Maté. Research shows that the pro-
longed use of cocaine can physically alter neurological pathways in
the brain, including the ability to make sound decisions, cope with
elevated stress, and even feel pleasure. In the short term, getting
high on coke produces euphoria—a blast of energy and alertness,
a feeling of being sharply awake and alive in the world. But frequent use of cocaine, studies show, can lead to a reduced production of dopamine—a neurotransmitter that's linked to feelings of
happiness and pleasure—and, as a result, anxiety and depression.
A "cocaine comedown" or "crash," as it's called, results in extreme
exhaustion, as the body recovers from the high. It is a state that
can last for several days, causing fatigue, mood swings, and suicidal ideation.

Even if Brendan was self-aware and recognizing the ways
cocaine was destroying the relationships in his life—and I'm sure
that he was—the disease of addiction was making it exceedingly
difficult for him to change his behaviours. I reflected back on the
AA meeting we'd attended together and how I'd judged him so
harshly. I'd felt he'd been lying to me as a means to manipulate me.
But in hindsight, maybe my brother was trying to show me that
he desperately wanted to change, even when every cell in his body
was screaming for him to use again.

I learned that Brendan was hardly alone. Crack cocaine is the
most-consumed illegal substance in Canada, with ten percent of
Canadians reporting they've used the drug in their lifetime. Men
are far more likely than women to use. Men who work in the trades,
including the oil and gas industry, are even more susceptible to drug
addiction. Across the country, scientists who analyze urban waste
water have found increasing levels of cocaine.

Maté writes that addiction "originates in a human being's desperate attempt to solve a problem: the problem of emotional pain,
of overwhelming stress, of lost connection, of loss of control, of

a deep discomfort with the self." I began to empathize with the young man he'd been when he'd first started using. How he'd lost his hockey identity—his lifelong dream—and had to find a new way forward, a new sense of belonging. How he always struggled with endings.

The previous winter, I'd met one of Brendan's colleagues while selling my books and pottery at a farmers' market in Peace River. The middle-aged man approached my table, hands stuffed in the pockets of his blue jeans. He smiled shyly at me.

"I know your brother," he said. "He brags about you at work all the time."

I laughed nervously, surprised by the man's words.

He pointed to his wife's table, where she was selling handmade organic soaps and essential oils made from lavender and wild sage. He didn't particularly enjoy working in the oil and gas industry, he confessed, but it allowed his wife to do what she loved.

"You and your brother look alike," he commented.

"Yeah, we get that a lot," I replied.

"Me and the guys like to tease him at work. He's a funny guy—he's always pulling pranks at work, trying to get a laugh out of everyone." The man paused. "But you know, I can tell he's a sensitive guy."

"I know."

As I reflected back on the decade we'd spent apart, I began to feel increasingly compassionate for the loneliness—and shame—my brother must've been contending with. The Latin root of *compassion* is *passion*, which means "to suffer," paired with the prefix *com*, meaning "together." *To suffer together.*

But my brother had suffered alone, as I had suffered without him.

"I'm proud of you for staying clean," I told him awkwardly during a visit in Edmonton, shortly after the encounter with his colleague, unsure how he'd respond. "I know it can't be easy," I added.

He wouldn't look me in the eye, but nodded his head.

"Treen, all those years you spent travelling and living abroad—I worried that you'd never come home."

I choked back tears. I couldn't look Brendan in the eye, but I began to see him differently. Not as an addict, or someone who could hurt me, but rather as someone who carried shame for his actions. Someone who was afraid of being alone.

All those years I'd mourned the loss of my older brother, my protector, I'd failed to understand how he'd needed protection too.

Twelve

As the fire season waned, I began to question the story I was telling myself about the bear as aggressive, dangerous—a threat. A problem bear, a pest, an inconvenience.

Don had lived for a decade with the bears without incident or harm. How had he done it? My approach had seemingly worked; the bears were gone—for now, anyway—but I wondered about the cost.

I'd interpreted every behaviour—even their lack of fear of me—as dominant and aggressive. What had my fear prevented me from seeing and contextualizing? I sensed that I was missing something essential about the bears and why they'd chosen to live in proximity to humans.

I began to see the flaws in mutual avoidance as a strategy to coexist. It felt a bit like a misnomer, or yet another euphemism to placate what had really been going on. I'd turned myself into the aggressor in an attempt to make the bear afraid. What was even remotely *mutual* about that? The exchange between us wasn't about mutualism, but antagonism.

The only consensus we'd come to was a deepening fear of the other.

Furthermore, I knew it would only be a matter of time before another problem bear ambled beyond the boundaries I'd erected in my own mind. The problem with a concept like mutual avoidance is that, if you're just scaring the bear away, you never have the opportunity to learn how to read one another's behaviour. You never have to learn how to manage conflict.

Even the terminology and concept of the "problem bear" seemed problematic in itself, a colonial way of thinking that implies nature and wildlife should get out of the way of the human agenda, or progress. For years, I'd criticized how the Alberta oil sands and other extractive industries had destroyed native habitat, contaminated the environment, and displaced wildlife from the landscape. How were my actions, standing on the hillside with the shotgun in my hands, or radioing for a helicopter to chase them away, any different? I'd come very close to pulling the trigger on that bear. I was startled by my own capacity for violence.

Maybe the real problem wasn't the mother bear's lack of fear of people, but my own fear that was preventing me from seeing the larger story.

By late summer, the bear activity around the fire tower waned. I wouldn't see any sign of the habituated mother, nor of her weaned cubs. Instead, that *big mama* of three younger cubs—the same family I'd seen in June—began to appear every day in the cutblock.

The mother bear was huge, at least a hundred pounds heavier than the one I'd gone head-to-head with, its belly practically dragging on the ground. While it fed on the purple aster and the last of the raspberries, so ripe they fell off the stem, the cubs were an explosion of activity, tumbling in games of play and chase, sneaking up on one another, and rocketing up the fifteen-metre poplars. And then one day the cubs were only two. The odds were not stacked in favour of their survival. One in three black bear cubs in North America will not survive past its first year, facing the risks of malnutrition or being preyed upon by wolves, cougars, or even male bears.

During mating season in June and July, males can become so charged up on testosterone that they'll kill a female's cubs to mate with it. Referred to by biologists as "sexually selective infanticide," the theory is that male bears kill the cubs so the mother will no longer lactate, and then go back into estrus, or heat.

Late one evening, while digging up carrots from my garden, I saw the big mama and cubs closer than usual. The family had stepped beyond the willows into the clearing, the no-go zone I'd tried to delineate with the habituated mother bear and its yearling cubs. I hesitated, wondering, should I scare them away?

The two surviving cubs pounced on the heads of late season dandelions with bravado. One of the cubs tiptoed up behind its sibling and nipped it square on the rump. The cub bawled, bounced a few steps back, then turned to swat a tiny paw at its sibling. I laughed, recalling the same way my brother used to tease and egg me on when we were kids.

The big mama did not look up at me. Mosquitoes swarmed the bear in a halo of light. One of the cubs sprinted to the mother's side and disappeared beneath its shaggy fur. Suddenly, the mother collapsed into the grass, rolled over on its back, and opened its hind legs like a frog. The cub climbed up on its mother's belly and began gnawing at one of its six engorged teats. In a hurry, the second cub galloped over and seized a nipple. Their heads worked up and down as they fed. The mother lay back. They were so close that I could hear the rhythmic sound of the cubs drinking their mother's milk. A faint motor-like hum, a steady purr of contentment.

I stood there in awe, mesmerized, carrots dangling from my hand, only metres away from the family. That the bear tolerated me there, watching it nurse, defied the dominant belief I'd been taught that bears are afraid of people. The mother bear beetling on its back, legs splayed wide open. The cubs, feasting on its milk.

I was suddenly conscious that I was breaking the rules I'd established with the bears. The mother bear had set foot beyond the clearing, the line I'd drawn, if only in my own mind.

I thought of the shotgun, tucked away in my closet, loaded, with the safety on.

I watched the bear family, suddenly so vulnerable in their natural state, and the thought of shooting at them, blowing the air horn, or even raising my voice to frighten them away felt morally wrong. It would be akin to walking into a holy place and screaming some obscenity. It was out of the question.

Without warning, the large mother bear sat upright, sending the cubs tumbling off its chest. The bear heaved itself up on all fours and sprinted away from the cubs, as if it couldn't stand them nursing a moment longer. *Get off me already!* the bear's language seemed to convey. I laughed, reminded of friends who'd confessed to me about the discomfort of breastfeeding, or their eagerness to wean their babies off their milk. There seemed to be something very relatable about the mother bear's response to the cubs.

I didn't say a word or utter a sound in the presence of the family—and there was no need. The mother bear and cubs didn't stay long, grazing only a few minutes longer before ambling into the forest. The intimacy of the encounter struck me like a bell that reverberated for days after.

Since the birth of his daughter, Brendan had circled back to another great love in his life: hockey. When my nephew was four years old, Brendan and Amanda bought a miniature pair of hockey skates, the smallest size they could find in the city. My brother taught Max how to take tiny steps forward on the ice, how to use his arms to balance his weight. The boy took to the ice like a natural. Max flew glee-fully around my brother in wide loops. Later, Brendan found small hockey gloves and placed a stick in the boy's hands. He taught him how to move with the puck and cradle it with his stick. Max shone on the ice, exuding the same joy my brother had experienced when he was that age.

"Never give up!" he'd cry to his young son as he skated along-side him.

"Never give up!" the boy parroted in a tiny, shrill voice.

Over the previous winter, I'd gone to watch one of Max's hockey practices in Edmonton. The boy was now six years old. Brendan volunteered as a coach for his team, organizing practices and skill-building exercises for the kids. I stood at rink level, watching them from behind the glass. My brother looked confident and relaxed on the ice, a hockey stick in hand, a whistle around his neck. He didn't see me standing there; he was too focused on Max and his team-mates, who looked comically out of proportion in their too-big gear and green-and-blue jerseys. I noticed that Max wore a 29 on the back of his jersey—the same number my brother had used before he stopped playing the sport. Like my brother, Max was one of the smallest players on the team, but also one of the most agile. He han-dled the puck with such natural ease.

Brendan was running the players through a practice drill. In heats of three, they passed the puck to one another and took a shot on the goalie, who appeared miniature against the huge net. Brendan praised the kids, hollering words of encouragement. "Good effort!" "Nice shot!" "Way to take it top net!" The children responded by hus-tling harder, pumping their small arms as they charged the net. Some of them lost control, skating too fast, and tumbled into their team-mates, who fell down like dominoes. "Shake it off, get back up, you'll get it next time!" my brother called, gently tapping a gloved hand to their helmets as they whizzed by, shepherding the kids back into the lineup. My eyes pricked with unexpected tears.

Maybe it was the resonant familiarity of the habitat—the cold air, the bright lights reflecting off the rink, the scent of sweat and damp gear, the sound of blades cutting and carving into the ice— but I felt the sudden urge to press my face up against the glass the same way I had when I was a kid, watching my brother like a hawk, cheering him on until my throat was hoarse.

Instead, I placed an outstretched hand against the cool pane. My brother glanced up, seeing me there, and offered a gloved wave.

"Hey Bren." I mouthed the words as he skated by in a blur.

PART III

BOUNDARIES

Thirteen

"Most of us grew up not knowing bears. We knew what we thought we knew about bears. But we didn't know the bears themselves," Kevin Van Tighem, author of *Bears Without Fear*, told me.

We sat across from one another at the Cinnamon Bear Café in Coleman, Alberta, a small town nestled in the Crowsnest Pass. It was a bitterly cold day in January. Outside, the mountains, caked with snow, rose up jagged against a clear blue sky.

I nodded at Kevin's words, considering my own history with bears. Unlike many others, I *had* grown up with a deeper familiarity with bears. The image of the orphaned, blue-eyed bear cub in my basement sprung to mind. I'd been confronted by the bears who lived nearby at Hawk Tower, but I'd regarded them, generally, as strangers. I didn't really know them—not as individuals.

A week earlier, I'd driven over a thousand kilometres south from Peace River to attend a writers' residency in the adjacent community of Blairmore. I hadn't stopped thinking about the bears I'd encountered and tried to drive off the summer before: the defiant mother bear, the independent sibling cubs, the big mama who nursed its tiny cubs alongside my cabin.

I was already familiar with Kevin's work. As a former ranger and superintendent of Banff National Park, he wrote regularly on the environment for *Alberta Views*, a magazine about social issues and politics. I wanted to ask him about bear behaviour and try to understand where, perhaps, I'd gone wrong at Hawk Tower. At my request, he agreed to meet with me. It just so happened that we were both in the Crowsnest Pass at the same time.

"The grizzly bear was the symbol of the wild, wild West, the predatory beast with sharp claws," said Kevin. "But the black bear was always the clown, the one that people fed. Walt Disney made them into a funny beast. We always saw the black bear as the goofy little brother and the grizzly bear as the older, more dangerous one."

Yet it was a large black bear, not a grizzly, that Kevin would remember in one of the most frightening bear encounters he'd experienced as a park ranger. While hiking, he attempted to dominate a black bear off the trail, which incited the bear to react, repeatedly charging him. "He was a real bugger. He was not going to back off," Kevin recalled of the harrowing encounter. "But it was my fault. I'd showed aggression to the bear, and he told me that he wasn't bluffed enough and suddenly I realized how vulnerable I was." Fortunately, the bear eventually showed mercy on that day; Kevin was able to slowly back away, without physical harm.

I knew that Kevin had a deeply personal history with bear attacks. His sister, Patricia, was severely mauled and disfigured by a mother grizzly bear defending a Bighorn sheep carcass in Waterton National Park in 1983, and had required multiple facial reconstruction surgeries after the incident. The attack provoked a lifelong struggle with depression and suicidal ideation, which Patricia wrote about in her book *The Bear's Embrace*. In 2005, she took her own life.

I asked Kevin if it made sense to be fearful of bears, or if, as my predecessor Don had suggested, they were inherently peaceful.

Fear of bears is natural, Kevin told me. To an extent, it's even healthy. "We're hard-wired to be afraid of bears," he said.

Early humans had few defences against bears. Fear was a survival tool for our species—it kept us alive. But with the development of modern firearms, "fear became a force for extirpation," Kevin wrote in *Bears Without Fear*. In the colonization of the Americas, much like the story of the buffalo, bears were picked clean off the landscape, killed for their hides, for sport, and because it was easier to live without the fear of them. Thousands of plains grizzly bears once grazed in herds on the prairies of North America. The state of California flies the image of a grizzly bear on its flag, and yet the last one was killed over a century ago. Today they're considered locally extinct in Manitoba and Saskatchewan. In Alberta, there are fewer than a thousand grizzlies left, although, due to their threatened status and a moratorium on hunting, their population is growing in the southern parts of the province, slowly expanding eastwards.

Black bears, who have a faster reproductive cycle than their grizzly cousins, keeping their young for only eighteen months compared with two or three years, are not and have never been considered a threatened species. Their population is estimated at forty thousand in Alberta, based on what Kevin calls "mystery math"; their numbers are not tracked by biologists and the same number has been used for decades now. Black bears don't have any protections in the province, other than that it's illegal to kill a mother with cubs, and a bear younger than a year old.

"We could afford to make more mistakes with black bears," Kevin said. "During the years when I was coming up through the ranks in national parks, if there was a problem black bear, you shot it," said Kevin. "If it was a grizzly bear, you relocated it somewhere to give it another chance. Black bears really are like second-class citizens in Alberta. They're just not a valued species."

I told Kevin about my struggles to deter the bears at the fire tower and asked him about his thoughts on using aversion tactics, such as rubber bullets, to demarcate space.

"It depends on the bear," he said. "You can get a bear with a bad attitude, you know, just a grump, or a bear that's been abused, and different rules are going to apply. But I'm from the school of thought that I don't try to deter a bear unless I see that there's a food reward," Kevin said, referring to bears that get into human-created food sources, such as a garbage bin, apple tree, or chicken coop.

Part of the problem, he told me, is that people don't often communicate well with bears.

"I've got emotional intelligence, but I always seem to read people wrong," said Kevin. "Well, if you can do that with people, you can do that with another species."

I nodded and thought of the defiant mother bear with yearling cubs.

"What does mutual avoidance mean to you?" I asked him.

In the context of the twentieth century, Kevin said, before the invention of bear spray, it made sense as a management strategy. Keeping people afraid of bears and bears afraid of people was the best way to keep them separate and prevent conflict. Herrero and wildlife managers were often responding to garbage- and food-habituated bears that had been frequently hazed and bullied; these bears were more aggressive towards people.

"The paradigm of mutual avoidance may have had its time, but it really simply isn't possible now," said Kevin.

For one, it's impracticable to keep people and bears separate. People live everywhere on the landscape and recreate "everywhere else," said Kevin, shaking his head. "I'm actually feeling sort of 'old man curmudgeonly,' because there's no privacy out there anymore. All of these secret places we used to visit, somebody has written up on social media and suddenly everybody is taking selfies there. It's impossible for a bear to not be around people."

"So what are we supposed to do, then?" I asked him.

"We need a different paradigm," Kevin told me. "And that's where I come to the idea of *mutual respect*, where we coexist, we spend time in each other's company, but we find ways to do it where we're not causing problems for the other."

Kevin's words followed me back to northern Alberta as I contemplated the fire tower season ahead. But in late February, before the bears would emerge from their dens, a different threat—a deadly, microscopic predator—entered the collective consciousness.

The COVID-19 virus.

Fourteen

"Oh, they're doing it," my mother said from the living room, eyes glued to the premier's six o'clock address on the television. "They're actually closing down the schools."

I sat down next to her on the couch. My dad watched from the kitchen, where he was making dinner, while Brendan, dressed in his work coveralls, paced back and forth.

"This is gonna be a nightmare for parents," my brother grumbled. "What do they expect us to do?"

In early March 2020, the emergence of the COVID-19 pandemic found the four of us living together at my parents' house in Peace River. That same week, I was supposed to fly to Geneva, Switzerland, to speak about my book at a conference on Gender Equality and Food Security, then travel on to Germany to participate in the Frankfurt Book Fair. I was ecstatic for both opportunities, but as the cases of COVID-19 rose in Italy and crossed the border into Switzerland, I'd abruptly cancelled my plane tickets.

Brendan was still employed in the Peace River oil sands and stayed in my parents' basement while he worked his fourteen-day shifts, rising at 4 a.m. to work out at the gym before donning his coveralls and heading out in the dark to reach work for 5 a.m. All day long he drove the gravel roads to check on the well-sites he was responsible for: measuring production, trucking out the waste water used in the process of extracting the heavy oil, and performing light maintenance on the drilling machinery. Those two-week shifts away from his family were hard on him.

He FaceTimed with his children every night at the kitchen table, propping his iPad up against a bowl of salad or pasta. The small voices of my niece and nephew chimed in our dinner conversations.

"Eat your trees," he said coaxingly to my niece in a drawn-out, sugary tone, and her small, chubby hand reached for a piece of steamed broccoli.

It couldn't have been easy for him to be away, especially when Brianna and Max were so young. But he needed the money and the money was good—really, really good. My brother had his eye on buying an acre of land outside Edmonton, where he would build a home for his family. I'd never seen him happier or more excited about the future.

However, with international borders closing and travel grinding to a halt following the World Health Organization's declaration of a global pandemic on March 11, 2020, worldwide demand for oil was on the verge of plunging to record lows. There was soon talk of layoffs at Brendan's company. I didn't hear the news from him; rather, my mother shared it with me to explain his sudden change in mood at the dinner table. He'd become quick to temper and typically disappeared into his bedroom after wolfing down his food.

I thought of the activists who'd dangled off the High Level Bridge in Edmonton thirteen years earlier, unfurling the banner that read STOP THE TAR SANDS. Who knew that it would take a virus, a global pandemic, to bring industry to a dead crawl? While a part of me silently cheered, the other part of me worried for my brother. What would he do if he got laid off? The CEOs of oil companies would weather the recession in their urban kingdoms, but Brendan was part of a dispensable labour force.

I passed the days of the early COVID lockdown running along the Peace River with Holly, as trumpeter swans flew low, honking and flapping their enormous wings overhead. I listened to the sound of the ice on the river groaning and shearing off in heavy slabs. We hiked through the valley where I'd ridden my horse as a girl and scanned the dead grass for crocuses, the first wildflower to emerge in spring. I stumbled upon a bear den dug in a stand of aspen on a south-facing slope. That night, I dreamt that I witnessed a generous stream of black bears emerging from the den, as though the number of bears beneath the earth was infinite.

Brendan came and went from the city to Peace River. The oil and gas industry had been designated an essential service in Alberta, with workers allowed to travel from out of province to work at camps in the North. Ironically, the provincial government had simultaneously suspended an array of environmental monitoring requirements for Alberta's entire energy industry. Companies no longer had to detect leaks for methane, a potent greenhouse gas, nor undertake soil and groundwater tests, nor measure surface water samples from wetlands for potential contamination. Oil sands operators ceased all wildlife monitoring efforts, including research programs and population estimates for various species. Reclamation projects were also shut down. The government justified the cessation of environmental monitoring as a benefit to public safety, but critics said it was just an excuse to grant concessions to resource extraction companies. Camps, with workers packed together like sardines, posed a far greater risk of spreading the virus.

Brendan's comings and goings between Peace River and Edmonton set me on edge. Our parents, who were in their late sixties, were in the target category of those who were falling seriously ill from COVID-19. If Brendan was also concerned about this, he made no mention of it.

In late March, he brought my seven-year-old nephew up to Peace River.

"We're not supposed to travel outside our 'bubble,'" I pointed out to my mom.

"Well, they need help with the online schooling," she said. "Besides, he'll bring some happiness into the house."

"Well, yeah, he could also bring something *else* into the house, Mom," I huffed.

It frustrated me that my brother didn't seem to take into consideration the risks of the pandemic beyond his own family's needs, but I kept my mouth shut, not wanting to provoke a fight.

When Max came, I took the boy down to the river and he monkeyed up onto the slabs of ice that piled on the banks as the river surged with spring melt. Ever since he was four years old, we'd been wandering along the Peace River together. I loved watching him play and explore the same way my brother and I had as kids—turning over large stones, finding a piece of driftwood from the shore to use as a walking stick. His boots caked with mud and slushy ice. As we walked, I felt the tension in my shoulders, my chest, releasing. I felt my lungs opening and closing like a butterfly's wings. I thought of my friends who lived in urban centres, cloistered in condominiums and apartments, who mostly experienced the outdoors in national parks, which had closed their gates to visitors. I was grateful for the land and for my brother's son, whose shrieks of delight were a balm against the worry I felt.

On the morning of my thirty-fifth birthday, I woke up and discovered a strand of bright-red yarn tied around the doorknob, and a note in a child's writing that read: *FOLLOW*. I picked up the red yarn and followed the line through the basement, up the stairs to the front-door landing, and around another set of stairs to the kitchen. My family waited for me with pancakes on the breakfast table and a banner that read in Max's writing: *HAPPY BIRTHDAY AUNTIE!* He hugged me with his whole body. I kissed the top of his head and my eyes flooded with tears. While the world beyond had never felt so uncertain, it was a relief to be safely tethered to my brother's son and my family under the same roof.

In late April, Holly and I flew back out to Hawk Tower. When the helicopter departed, I yanked off my mask, relieved to no longer have to worry about spreading the virus. I scanned the forest around me and wondered if the bears had come out of their dens yet.

I ran along the road with the dog, reacquainting myself with the sights and sounds of the forest, carrying a can of bear spray in one hand. As we ran, I kept my eyes peeled for any signs of the bears. About three kilometres down the road, I stumbled upon a strange artifact: a wooden electrical pole eroded into the shape of an hourglass.

It was a "rub tree," a place where the bears came to scratch their backs. My dad had previously shown me footage from trail cameras set up pointed at rub trees in the Chinchaga. Bears stood up on their hind legs and arched their backs in whatever spot they'd chosen— an old spruce, or poplar, or even a power pole—to scratch and leave behind scents from their oily fur. "It's like the bears' own version of Facebook," my dad's colleague once told me. "It's how they leave messages for one another about who they are and what they're up to."

I ran my hand down the worn power pole and snapped a photo with my cellphone to send to my dad. The wood was smooth and polished, lacquered by the bears' oily fur. Why had they chosen this pole? How long had they been coming here to carve their desire into the wood?

I noticed a set of large bear tracks at the base of the pole, and tufts of black hair that had snagged and caught on the wood. I plucked the coarse, oily hairs and held them up to my nose. They smelled of musk, a scent beyond my knowing.

I looked down into Holly's eyes and felt a kind of inadequacy, wanting to journey into her olfactory world, but I was without a map. What did she know about the bears that I didn't? I thought of the trail camera I'd borrowed from a friend. This would be the perfect place to set it up and peer through a window into the world of *Ursus*.

I tucked the long black hairs into my pocket and ran back to the cabin. Later, I pressed them between the pages of a book for safekeeping.

A week after our arrival at Hawk Tower, the phone rang from up in the cupola. It was the new neighbour at Bison Tower, the lookout to my southeast. Marina had worked twelve seasons at a fire tower outside Lac La Biche, a town located three hundred kilometres south of Fort McMurray. She'd grown up beside the ocean in the presence of old-growth forests on Vancouver Island, and every spring she migrated east to Alberta to work at the tower. She composed songs at the lookout and performed in a folk band during the winter, travelling to Australia to tour at music festivals.

Only this year, she hadn't planned to return to the fire tower. The previous fall, Marina received word from the Lac La Biche fire manager that her tower was one of twenty-six that would be permanently closed due to government cutbacks. She saw it as a sign to transition away from wildfire. But then COVID-19 struck and hijacked her plans of reintegrating into society. We were friends on Instagram and I tipped her off that the lookout at Bison had quit, last minute, and the position had opened up. With twelve seasons under her belt, Marina was hired on the spot.

"I couldn't think of a better place to weather a pandemic," she said.

I nodded, as I scanned the leafless forest around me, and felt a pang of guilt thinking about my parents and brother navigating the complexities of COVID. I was relieved to be back, but my fear of living with the virus had shifted to fear of living with the bears, I confessed.

"I've never encountered a problem bear in my twelve seasons as a lookout," Marina said contemplatively.

She told me the story of an incident during her rookie year. She woke early one morning to the sound of something scratching at the front door. It was a slight, scuttling noise, so she assumed it was a squirrel. Marina got out of bed to investigate, opened the front door, and there, on the other side of the screen, standing bipedal, was a black bear staring back at her.

"I remember the sound of my teeth chattering," she told me. "And the way the bear's fur was slicked with morning dew. It reminded me of sunlight reflecting off the surface of a black lake."

She stared at the bear for several long seconds with only a fine wire screen separating them. Then, very slowly, Marina closed the door.

"I'm pretty sure that bear was just as terrified as I was," she told me with a laugh.

Through the cabin window, she watched the bear rocket back into the bush.

"I've found that bears are naturally curious—not aggressive," she said. "Maybe you can learn how to make peace with the bears." She hesitated before adding, "You know, the forest often knows what we need to heal, but we have to be paying attention."

"Maybe," I said, although I wasn't yet convinced.

I heard the bear before I saw it. The sound of a branch breaking, of pawed feet stirring leaves on the forest floor. It was early May and the aspen stood like broomsticks, empty of leaves. I looked down from the fire tower. It should've been easy to locate the source of the sound, a pedantic shuffle through the leaves, indicating the maker was something with a long stride. Something not small. Something not in a hurry.

Bear. *There.*

A small, shaggy black bear was moving along a shadow cast by a huge spruce tree. From above, it appeared like a gymnast walking the high beam. The bear seemed to be using the cover of shadow to remain hidden. It strolled to the edge of the forest and collapsed, as though exhausted, and draped its front paws over a decaying log, as if contemplating its next move.

I lifted my binoculars to get a closer look at its face. The head was small. Big ears sprouted from its skull, almost rabbit-like. I noticed the sharp geometry of its hindquarters. A skinny bear. A spring bear. Bears lose nearly one-third of their body mass in the den over the winter.

As the bear lifted its nose to scent the air, I noticed the birthmark on its chest: two white crescent moons. It came to me as a small shock that I recognized the small bear, the same way one might recognize the younger sibling of a friend after many years apart. The yearling cub was no longer a cub, but a two-and-a-half-year-old bear.

I was relieved to see it had survived. Had it denned with its sibling? I scanned the bushes for another bear, but it appeared very much alone. The bear had come back on nearly the same day to the exact same spot to which its mother had led it. Only last year, the dandelion leaves had already sprouted. This spring was far cooler than last year's hot, dry conditions.

The bear gazed out at the dead, half-frozen grass.

"Soon," I whispered down to it.

The small bear heaved itself up on all fours and stepped into the clearing as if toeing the frigid waters of a lake. Out of the forest, it appeared exposed and vulnerable.

A flock of robins startled up into the nearby trees and the bear skittered back, as if afraid. No kidding it was scared, I thought, reflecting back on the many ways I'd tried to deter them. The air horn. The rubber bullets. The birdshot. I felt a pang of regret.

The bear paused at the boundary of the forest, its nose tilted skyward, as though reassessing the risk.

"You're okay," I whispered.

It tried again, tentatively walking into the open, beneath the boughs of noisy robins. It didn't stay longer than a minute or two. An hour later, I saw the bear balanced in the branches of an old poplar—the same tree they'd climbed the spring before—feasting on tender green buds.

My eyes became habituated to look for the bear, if only fragments of it, nearly camouflaged by the landscape. I scanned for variations of the colour black, glowing onyx in the morning light, sooty beneath an overcast sky, not black but blue after the sun had dropped below the horizon. I always saw colour before my mind registered *bear*. The shy bear would not show itself fully to me, however. I spied triangular ears bobbing above the budding alders. A small, pointed snout protruding from a yellow curtain of tall, cured grass. A mound feeding on small purple spears of fireweed in the cutblock.

When I stitched together these fragmented sightings, I formed the image of the young bear in my imagination, one that seemed to me cautious, even fearful of overstepping boundaries, and yet also very much at home in the way it navigated the landscape. I recognized the bear was following a pattern, one I'd seen before, the same schedule of feeding that the mother bear had followed the previous season. First, the fireweed in the cutblock. Then, the balsam poplar buds high up in the trees. Next, the dandelions on the slope. This observation felt like a small marvel to me. Nothing about the bear's behaviour was random. Biologists call this "site fidelity," when an animal returns to the same location every year to feed, mate, and den. I thought of my brother and me, the way we'd both wandered back home to Peace River.

I speculated that the bear was female, based on what I'd recently read about black bear behaviour. Whereas males tend to roam widely, taking more risks to seek out breeding grounds, females stay close to the places where they are born, where the food resources are familiar, a strategy for reproductive survival.

I sensed that I could not live beside the creature for much longer and refer to it so generally: bear. For the bear was not just any black bear. The bear was its own bear, just as I was my own person. And I was not like most of the women I knew in my life. Thirty-five. Solitary. No offspring. Habitually living alone in the woods for half a year. I'd spent nearly two of the past five years alone with my dog in the boreal forest. I did not represent all women any more than the small bear represented all bears.

Osa. Spanish, feminine of *Oso*, for bear. The name surfaced in my mind and stuck.

A part of me felt hesitant to name the bear. To name the bear was to project myself onto it as though it was one of the velveteen dolls I dressed up and played with as a child. My father always instilled in us, as kids, the danger of anthropomorphizing wild animals. "Bears are *not* your friends," he reiterated. He pointed out the inaccuracies of Walt Disney films and their romanticized portrayal of animals. In *Brother Bear*, for example, a male bear adopts an orphaned cub. "In the wild, males are known to prey on cubs," he explained.

Anthropomorphize is a verb that derives from the Greek words *anthropos* ("human") and *morphe* ("form"), meaning to attribute human traits, emotions, or desires to non-humans. It's a bit of a sinful word amongst Western biologists and scientists, whose methods rely on observable evidence, studying what they can see, weigh, measure, and count.

Wildlife managers have always been more comfortable assigning numbers to bears rather than names. Problem bears, for example, receive identification numbers, and their information is entered into a database. Years ago, my dad told me, officers would tranquilize a bear and spray-paint a neon-coloured number onto its side. Today they use plastic ear tags, or radio collars and GPS trackers. Numbers create a kind of distance between people and wildlife, a buffer zone that prevents us from caring too much about the individual. It's easier to take out a number than a name, after all.

What's the loss of one black bear when there's forty thousand more out there?

Naming the small bear—a bear who ebbed and flowed so unobtrusively around my tower, a bear who asked nothing of me—now felt necessary. If I saw a human neighbour as frequently as I saw the bear, I would eventually stop them in the street and ask for their name.

Language, writes Robin Wall Kimmerer in *Braiding Sweetgrass*, is "a mirror for seeing the animacy of the world, the life that pulses through all things." She points out how the English language tends to rob the natural world of agency. "In English, we never refer to a member of our family, or indeed to any person, as *it*. That would be a profound act of disrespect. *It* robs a person of selfhood and kinship, reducing a person to a mere thing."

By not naming the bear, by referring to the bear as *it*, I could not move any closer to understanding the bear. Objectifying nature and wildlife puts "a barrier between us," writes Kimmerer. "Saying it makes a living land into 'natural resources.'" If a bear is an *it*, we can pull the trigger, we can bulldoze down habitat. If the bear is a *her*, we may think twice.

"Those of us that have been taught through the Western system and come out as biologists, we need to be deprogrammed because we have such an objectified view of nature," Kevin had admitted to me over the winter. "We're not supposed to identify with bears? Well, why not? I think you should name more of your bears. People might then care more about them."

I thought back to the orphaned bear cub in the basement, the way my naive biology allowed me to empathize with the bear—to feel connected to her—without fear or question.

Every time I saw the young bear feeding in the grass that lengthened in the light, I whispered her name. *Osa*.

Fifteen

In mid-April, the company Brendan worked for shut down oil production at multiple well-sites outside Peace River. In less than three months, thirteen thousand workers in the Canadian oil and gas industry, my brother included, had lost their jobs.

"Some good news," my mother told me over the phone a month later. "One of Bren's former colleagues helped him find a job up in Fort McMurray. It's a sixty-day contract," she said quickly. I sensed the anxiety beneath the surface of her words. Brendan would be living in an isolated man camp rather than commuting from the safety of their home in Peace River. "He's leaving next week—you should call him," she added, less a suggestion and more a plea.

I hung up the phone with my mother and told myself I'd call Brendan later that evening. But after climbing down from the tower, I found myself distracted by watching Osa grazing on the grass that had grown into a thick mane and forgot about the news of my brother.

The following week, Brendan and his colleague drove to Fort McMurray via Highway 63, a 443-kilometre road that connects Edmonton to the province's biggest oil sands projects, a notoriously dangerous stretch of pavement known variably as Hell's Highway, the Highway of Death, or Suicide 63 due to the high number of accidents on it. Until 2012, most of the highway had remained a single-lane artery feeding thousands of workers and essential goods up to the oil sands. But it wasn't only the design of the road, critics said, it was the drivers too. It was oil workers, coming off month-long shifts, desperate to get the hell out of Dodge, bank accounts brimming with overtime pay, feet heavy on the pedal. "'Who's the most sober [to drive]?'" read a sub-headline in an article about Highway 63 published in *The Globe and Mail* in 2016. It was the same year seven people died in a head-on collision in February and, in May, nearly eighty thousand people were stuck in traffic, bumper to bumper, as they fled the raging wildfires that prompted the evacuation of the entire city. Since that year, Fort McMurray's town council had begun lobbying the Alberta government to commit to twinning the entirety of Highway 63 to reduce the number of accidents and fatalities.

Brendan and his colleague were working a number of back-to-back shutdown shifts—the routine temporary closures of sites to disassemble and inspect machinery and perform necessary maintenance. Workers can make a killing by banking long hours of overtime during shutdown. But there was also a steep cost: He'd spend nearly two months straight away from his partner and kids.

Brendan called me, shortly after he arrived, from a workers' camp outside Fort Mac. Between the two of us, he was the one who reached out more frequently; he was one of the only people I knew who was more inclined to call than to text. The afternoon was expiring, the sun descending towards the western horizon, and I was wrapping up a shift in the tower. I saw my brother's name pop up on my cellphone and hesitated before answering. I always hesitated when he called. It took a lot of energy listening to my brother. Often, I wasn't sure if he was really listening to me, and I worried about what he might have to say, or need from me. Or maybe it was just an old avoidance reflex from the previous decade.

"Hey Treen!" boomed Brendan's familiar voice.

As I listened to my brother, a swarm of sandhill cranes—massive migratory birds with a wingspan measuring two metres—circled above. Their call, a distinct trill, always reminded me of something prehistoric, as though they were less bird and more dinosaur. They'd travelled from as far south as Florida.

"It's a dry camp, thank god," he said, referring to the policy of "no drugs, no alcohol" being tolerated. "But guys have their ways of sneaking shit in."

He and his colleagues lived in row upon row of ATCO trailers, long shoeboxes that looked as though they were built out of white Lego blocks. My brother was doing everything he could to put his head down and retreat to his room after meals, he said. COVID-19 safety measures only intensified the cramped conditions: The camp gymnasium was closed, he grumbled. Lifting weights had always been a coping mechanism for Brendan, a way to let off stream, to feel good in his own skin. "Fuck this pandemic," he said. "I'm fucking *over* it."

Looking out on the forest around me, I felt a shot of sympathy for Brendan. I loathed what his work demanded of him—to endure the stressful and isolating conditions, the risk of contracting and spreading the virus, all for the flow of production and profit of a resource poisoning the waterways and communities surrounding it. I hated that he'd become so much a part of it, a far cry from our relationship with the land when we were kids.

"Honestly, I'm not sure how you do it, Treen," he said.

"What's that?" I asked.

"The isolation," he said. "Being alone in the bush for so many days."

I paused and considered his words. Both of our jobs required a long stretch of time living and working alone, and yet most days I didn't feel alone at the fire tower. I felt connected to the forest and the voices of my colleagues, even though I didn't know what some of them even looked like. From my perspective, my living conditions were utopian by comparison; I was surrounded by trees whose leaves whispered in the wind, by a garden of flowers that I coaxed from the soil—by the promise of glimpsing Osa and the shiver of pleasure I felt every time I saw her.

The idea of my brother's situation at the oil workers' camp, of brushing shoulders with and sleeping in compartmentalized rooms next to strangers who'd travelled from every corner of the country to earn a buck, felt far, far lonelier to me. I wasn't sure what to say to him.

"Don't focus on the end date—it can be too overwhelming," I told him. "Just take it day by day." I paused, adding, "When I'm having a shitty day, I try to remind myself that bad weather always passes. Somehow that helps."

He FaceTimed with his partner and the kids multiple times a day, he told me. He'd posted previously taken photographs of my niece and nephew on his Instagram account with captions that read:

Miss you to the moon and back!
My world and my everything! Miss them so very much!

After we hung up, I looked to my east and thought of my brother, several hundred kilometres of forest and formidable swamps between us, me in Peace River and him in Fort McMurray.

I thought of my brother, the boy who had never really learned how to be alone, and worried about how the isolating toll of his work could affect his mental health.

The rains came in late May and soaked the boreal forest like a great relief. Beyond the fire tower, cases of COVID-19 in Alberta—and around the world—continued to rise. Fortunately, it wasn't going to be a repeat of the dry, hot conditions that catalyzed the previous year's catastrophic wildfire season in Alberta which had resulted in multiple community evacuations.

Designated on low fire alert, I spent long hours sowing vegetable and flower seeds in the garden beds, baking bread, and sculpting bowls and mugs from clay. The rains flooded the ponds and boreal chorus frogs sang in the millions, their mating chorus so strong that I could hear them from kilometres away. The northern flicker, a woodpecker, drummed his love song on the tin roof of my outhouse, while the piercing call of the white-throated sparrow rose above it all.

I was not alone. The grass exploded and Osa was hard at work, feasting on the hairy shoots. I was also hard at work, watching her, writing down observations of her in a journal, on sticky notes that I put up on the walls of my cabin. Her nature was so different from her mother's—calm but alert, and tentative, whereas her mother had been bold and domineering the year before, unafraid to claim the slope and defend it. Intuitively, I felt safer in Osa's company. Perhaps because she was young and small, she needed to be more cautious in the world. She lifted her snout to read the sky. Her large, dew-slicked nose quivered.

Osa knew something I did not. She scented the change that was coming.

Then, one day, she vanished.

I could not explain her sudden disappearance, but the trail camera I'd mounted, facing the rub pole, seemed to hold clues. On most evenings, after I climbed down from the tower, Holly and I ran to the rub pole, where I swapped out the SD card and jogged back to the cabin to download the images. I was thrilled to see at least two different bears at the pole. One of the bears stood over seven feet tall on his hind legs. The other remained on fours, rubbing her side into the pole. I noticed a slight sway of the back. Her face looked familiar to me.

I saw the same bear later that evening through the cabin window as I was boiling water for tea. The dusky light painted the forest, the bear, even the dandelions with dark-blue strokes. I tiptoed to the edge of the fence, trying to conceal my body behind the outhouse. I felt a strange excitement to recognize the bear almost immediately as the mother bear—Osa's mother. Her distinct sway-back. Her confident, wide-legged stance. She grazed at the far edge of the forest and I sensed she knew I was there, although she did not look up at me. I felt a bodily unease with the mother bear, unlike the way I felt with Osa, and I wasn't sure if I'd ever lose that feeling with her. But on that evening, I decided to leave her alone.

As I retreated to the cabin, my eye snagged on an unusual shape, only metres away from her. I gasped. Camouflaged in dead grass was the ghostly form of a large cinnamon-coloured black bear, much larger than Osa's mother. His back longer, the shoulder muscle more pronounced. I noticed a blond streak of fur on his shoulder, shimmering in the dying light.

The cinnamon bear fed and slowly inched closer towards Osa's mother. This was the first time I'd ever seen two adult bears interacting so closely.

Osa's mother yanked up her head as though the other bear had crossed a line, and the fur on her neck and upper back stood erect. She opened her jaw wide and made the same popping sound I'd heard the summer before. *You're too close*, she seemed to signal to the cinnamon bear. I knew that June was breeding season for many species in the boreal forest, including black bears, and it occurred to me that he was likely trying to mate with her. The bears were engaging in a courting ritual.

I felt as though I had accidentally intruded on an intimate moment between lovers, but neither bear seemed to care that I was there, gawking down at them. Osa's mother turned broadside to the male, showing him the length of her body, and they circled one another. I listened to their shuffled footsteps through the grass, punctuated by huffing breaths, and wondered what they were saying to each other.

Finally, Osa's mother made up her mind. She turned and ambled off into the bush as if to say, *Not today*. The cinnamon bear took his rejection quietly, tearing at a few blades of grass. He paused, granting her the space she demanded, before following the scent of her footsteps into the night.

The cool, wet spring made for uneventful afternoons in the fire tower. I diligently climbed the ladder every day and sat in the office chair with a book, my boots propped up on the edge of the open window. I'd read for several minutes then look up, scan the horizon for any sign of smoke—nothing, zilch, *nada*—then sink back into my book. Marina texted me audio files of the songs she was writing from Bison Tower. I closed my eyes and listened, imagining her strumming her acoustic guitar, or plucking away at her banjo, in her cupola eighty kilometres southeast. Her voice was a smooth tonic.

> *You are just a river holding back, tethered by a dam*
> *Animals are waiting, thirsty in the night*

"How are the bears?" she'd ask when we spoke on the phone.

"Some days I feel like I'm living in a David Attenborough nature doc," I answered with a laugh. "Or maybe like a soap opera about the love lives of black bears."

I'd begun to observe, from up in the tower and down on the ground, a steady stream of jaded and wounded lovers. I noticed bears with hobbles and limps, torn fur, and fresh scars written across their muzzles, above their eyes, tattooed by both desire and denial.

Black bears are polygamous. Both males and females will mate with multiple bears through a single breeding season to increase their chances of reproductive success. Sperm from multiple males helps to stimulate the release of a female's eggs and fertilize them. Females can produce cubs, in the same litter, sired by different males.

"Females go into estrus," my dad said, explaining to me the hormonal process that signals females are ready to mate. "But it's a short window of time that they're willing to breed, so the males will follow them around for weeks, hoping to get lucky."

One afternoon in mid-June, while weeding around the green onions that poked through the soil, I observed a humongous black bear, one I'd never seen before, striding down the middle of the road as if he owned it. The forestry radio, projected through a speaker mounted on the outside of the cabin, squawked with the afternoon weather forecast.

The wildfire danger is now low in the Peace River Forest Area. So far this season, there have been twenty-two wildfires in the Peace River Forest Area, all of which have been extinguished.

But the bear took no notice of the noise. Beyond the perimeter of the electric fence, he did not walk but stiff-leg-stomped the ground like a bowlegged cowboy. I noticed the vast space between his ears, the hugeness of his skull, and the pronounced shoulder muscle. He was enormous—especially for a spring bear. I couldn't imagine how big he'd get by the end of the summer.

Osa was nowhere to be seen, and I didn't blame her. I didn't want to be seen either. I crouched down low, knowing very well he could smell everything about me right down to the scent of deodorant I'd used that morning—cool cucumber—and the turkey sandwich I'd just eaten for lunch. I glanced back at Holly, who was pancaked on her side on the concrete sidewalk, dozing in the sun. Not a care in the world that a five-hundred-pound bear prowled nearby.

The Goliath stopped to feed on a mane of dandelions with his two front legs splayed out into a wide tripod, and razed the weeds with several aggressive chomps, his teeth flashing. I froze like a fawn in the grass, hoping not to be found. A part of me felt I should sneak back into the cabin, that perhaps it wasn't safe, even behind the protection of the electric fence. But I could not resist the urge to stay and take in his enormousness.

The bear approached the base of the huge spruce, the same tree Osa and her sibling had climbed last summer when I blasted their mother's backside with rubber bullets. He sniffed the scaly bark and hoisted himself upright, unfolding his long body like a magic trick. The bear began to rub his back vigorously against the trunk of the tree, one paw reaching back, digging into the bark. I gasped as he revealed a strange birthmark, a circle of white fur hidden on his upper chest. An emblazoned O. He thrust back his head and gyrated, whole body, against the tree.

I texted my dad a blurry cellphone image of the bear against the spruce.

I'm going to call him Oscar for that incredible O.

Wow! my dad texted back within seconds. *I've never seen anything like that before. What a gorgeous bear Oscar is.*

I grinned at my dad's use of "Oscar," that he'd broken his own rule of not anthropomorphizing the bears.

Several days later, in the midst of cooking dinner, I noticed movement in the cutblock through the window. Something was bobbing above the sea of green leaves. It was the velvety rack of a bull moose whose antlers were just growing back. Males drop their antlers every winter and the hardened bone grows back in the spring. I paused, watching the moose browse on the foliage, the young aspen shaking. Suddenly, the moose took off as if being chased by something. I heard the thin limbs snapping under his powerful legs and hooves. Then I spied a flash of black fur, a huge black bear galloping after the bull. I knew it was Oscar. I rushed to the opposite window, spatula in hand, watching the chase unfold. Oscar must've snuck up on the moose, hopeful to ambush a female with a newborn calf.

Black bears prey on ungulate calves and fawns—mule and white-tailed deer, and elk—in the spring. But only the boldest of bears would go after a moose calf. Female moose are known as the fiercest protectors in the boreal forest. They'll charge hard and fast and stomp out any potential threat with their enormous legs and hooves. But Oscar wasn't just any black bear—he was a megalith of a bear, on par with an adult grizzly.

The chase wouldn't last long, however. The moose crashed away through the willows and Oscar skidded to a halt.

I stared hard at the bear. I couldn't help but think that if he was bold enough to go after a bull moose, there would be absolutely nothing stopping him from going after me. I'd read enough about bear attacks to have a pretty good idea of how it would unfold if Oscar's brain switched into prey mode. He'd knock me to the ground and go for the soft spot on the back of my neck. Or, at the very least, that's how I hoped it would go. Fast. Far less agonizing than the alternative: being disembowelled and eaten alive. Justin, my neighbouring lookout, had once watched a black bear sneak up on a fawn bedded down in the grass and tear into its belly. Herrero makes note of this behaviour in his book, too, the way that, in some predatory attacks, bears will go for the internal organs. It's why my dad always recommended that, if playing dead against a defensive attack, you should go into fetal position, or lie flat on your stomach with your legs spread wide, making it difficult for the bear to flip you over. Protect the neck. Protect the vital organs.

When Oscar heaved his huge body out of the forest, my blood stopped. I couldn't look away from this boulder of a bear. The skin on his fleshy rump jiggled as he stomped. Oscar was a bear who didn't give two fucks. When you're a big bear, you can choose the speed at which you move in the world.

Male black bears can lose up to 30 percent of their body weight during hibernation, emerging from the den on low fat reserves, but Oscar didn't seem focused on food. Levels of serum testosterone in black bears are at their highest in March and April—along with testicular size—before bears even emerge from the den. Oscar had a particular urge to attend to.

He hoisted himself up on his back legs, revealing the full length of his body. Six feet, maybe seven feet tall, his shoulders slumped and sagging. The posture made him look like an old man standing naked in front of a mirror.

I hid by the side of the outhouse and stared down at the full-frontal view of the gorilla-man-bear. Oscar leaned back against the rough bark and began to rub, up and down, back and forth. His loose flesh shook. My spine tingled. It felt like a fantasy to be granted this strange vantage point, witnessing a dominant male bear embody his desire. There was an orgasmic quality to his movement.

It was, in fact, a kind of dating trick up Oscar's sleeve. The urge to rub and grind against every hard surface he could find increased his chance of breeding success.

A study at the University of Alberta found that the higher incidence of male grizzly bears marking, or rubbing against trees, correlates with a higher chance of breeding and siring offspring. For four years, scientists collected hair samples left behind on bear rub sites—trees, power line poles, and fence posts—in the Rocky Mountains for DNA analysis. Using data previously collected from more than two thousand grizzlies in the area, researchers mapped out a family tree. They discovered that the males that scratched and marked more frequently, depositing their hormone-rich scents, often had more mates, and more offspring with a greater chance of survival.

As I watched Oscar increasing his chances of mating, I considered my own choices and odds for what biologists refer to as "reproductive success." I was doing the very opposite of him. As a woman in her mid-thirties, I'd been choosing to live alone in the forest, removing myself from civilization, from letting my scent be trailed by potential mates in grocery store aisles and café lineups, from parties and potlucks, from swiping left or right on dating apps. My choices seemed to indicate that I wasn't motivated to find a mate, although I knew that wasn't true. Some days, I desired deeper conversation, to be seen and held and wanted by another whom I cared about. But my longing felt seasonal. Half of the year I wanted to live in my own company and write books and make art, while the rest of the year I craved companionship.

The previous autumn, after the fire season wrapped up, I'd spent time with Eric, a friend I'd met at Muskeg Tower in my second season as a lookout. Originally from Prince Edward Island, he'd worked over seven seasons as a firefighter at the base in Manning. I was always drawn to Eric's warm presence and his big, exuberant laugh, and felt safe in his company. Last October we'd gone camping in the Rocky Mountains in his old 4Runner, which he'd rigged up with a platform for sleeping and a cooking area that folded down onto the tailgate. At night, the temperature dropped below zero, the windshield froze, and we held on to one another under layers of blankets, Holly curled up at our feet.

We both knew the loneliness and stress of seasonal work, of the constant coming and going, and how the unpredictability of working in wildfire affected our personal lives. As a firefighter, Eric spent three-week shifts living at workers' camps in northern Alberta, or even tenting on the front lines of large-scale wildfires.

He could be exported anywhere in North America at a moment's notice, to help quell the flames of another fire threatening another community. The word *export* made me think of the firefighters as more like machinery and less as men and women. Not so different, perhaps, from the way the oil and gas industry viewed workers like my brother.

Eric and I found solace in one another's company while knowing it was a relationship that wouldn't last. I was nine years older than him. We never spoke about our friendship, or whether we wanted more from one another, but I felt the mutual care and affection between us.

The previous October, he'd picked me up at my parents' place to spend an evening camping along the Peace River. Brendan stood at the living room window and watched Eric pull up to the house in his old 4Runner.

"Whoa, that guy's got flow," he said with a chuckle, watching him get out of the SUV.

"Okay, can you not stand there so obviously," I said, pulling him away from the window. I suddenly felt as though I were sixteen years old and we'd never left home. "Seriously, please don't embarrass me."

"He kinda looks like a pirate, Treen," he mused with a playful grin.

"Oh my god, Bren, stop," and I laughed because he wasn't wrong.

Despite our political differences, I never felt judged by my brother for the personal choices I made—or didn't make—in my life. He seemed to accept my unconventional lifestyle and that I chose not to have a long-term partner. My mother, on the other hand, made it more than clear that she wished I would find a man and have babies.

"Don't listen to Mom," Bren would groan. "Keep doing your own thing, Treen. Besides, you're probably going to write a bestseller at some point and become rich and famous."

I laughed. "I don't want to be famous. I would like to be able to pay my rent, though."

"But seriously, Treen, I know you're going to make it."

"Thanks, Bren."

"Don't ever settle—not that you would. But I hope you find someone like I found A," he said. "She's my whole world."

My brother's partner, Amanda, was everything he was not. She was the surface of the ocean on a calm day, while Brendan was like a tsunami. She held her cards close to her chest, whereas my brother wore his heart on his sleeve. She appeared to accept Brendan as he was, with his boisterous personality and emotions that filled the house—and his wild complexity.

I knew I couldn't spend the length of the summer cowering behind the electric fence. I had to force myself to overcome my fear of meeting a bear on the grassy road that led from my tower. In late June, I set out on the trail with Holly, a canister of bear spray in my hand and a hunting knife looped through my belt. My dad had always reminded me, "What good is bear spray if it's stuck at the bottom of your backpack?" An encounter with a bear could happen quickly—I wanted to be ready. I carried the knife because I couldn't quite forget the stories of bear attacks in Herrero's book. If a bear knocked me down, a knife could be a last resort: A puncture to the nose or eye could be enough to fight the animal off.

It was evident that bears had staked the road as their own. Every power pole was carved with the initials of males vying for mating rights. I dodged heaps of fresh, steaming scat, rich with clover, and slowed down to holler, "HEY BEAR!" to announce myself around every corner. With every step, I felt my body relaxing into the forest.

One afternoon, when I was halfway to the rub pole, Oscar emerged from a stand of alders along the road—a mountain barricading the path forward. The bear was less than six metres away. I stopped abruptly with Holly flanking me.

"Oh, h-i-i," I stammered.

He swivelled on his haunches and stomped into the bush.

"Thank *god*," I whispered to Holly, who looked up at me and wagged her tail.

I'd barely taken a step forward when Oscar re-emerged, as if he'd changed his mind, like maybe we weren't as threatening as he'd thought. Now the bear was less than five metres away, well within range of a blast of bear spray. I'd activated it once before at the gun range. The bear spray would deliver a projectile blast up to ten metres away.

Oscar stood broadside to us. He lifted his huge skull to scent the air. I wondered if he could smell my fear.

"We're just passing by . . ." I offered him, feeling my kneecaps trembling as though my legs would give out at any moment.

There was no barrier here between us. No glass enclosure, no electric bear fence, no protection of being in a vehicle or cabin. I wasn't carrying a firearm. Holly stood by my side, fur on her back raised, ears perked, eyes fixed on Oscar.

I could smell him, a very particular fermented odour. It stung the nostrils, although it wasn't entirely unpleasant. People often remarked to me that "bears stink like garbage." But he didn't smell like waste; rather, the scent reminded me of being a girl and galloping my horse through the alfalfa pastures on a hot summer day, the sweat rising from Pepper's neck.

The dominant male stared hard at me.

I remembered what I'd seen Osa's mother do with the cinnamon male, and shifted my body slightly away from him so I wasn't facing him head-on. I lowered my eyes. Holly stayed quiet but alert at my side. I held the canister of bear spray at the ready and flicked off the plastic safety on the trigger.

After what was probably only sixty seconds—the longest minute of my life—Oscar scented the air and, as though our scent was displeasing to him, or, as with the bull moose, we weren't worth his energy, he let out a guttural *HUFF* and stomped back into the forest.

Adrenalin rose up my spine. The close encounter with the bear was like a powerful drug. I could feel every cell in my body singing, every hair on my body upright and tingling. The feeling reminded me of learning to surf on Haida Gwaii and the sensation of a wave surging beneath me. Maybe it was the same way Brendan felt when he was younger, riding that six-metre swell to shore. One could get hooked on such a rush.

We could have turned around and gone back to the cabin, but the close encounter emboldened me and I surprised myself by continuing along to the rub pole. Walking at first, to ensure Oscar was gone and we weren't being followed, then jogging the last kilometre.

Marina's words came to mind, her observation that bears aren't inherently aggressive, but rather curious. Oscar had probably scented us along the trail and up at the cabin during the past few weeks and wanted to get a closer look. Not unlike the way I had installed the camera on the rub pole to peer into the patterns of the black bears and wildlife around my fire tower. Maybe Oscar and I were both voyeurs.

I pocketed the SD card from the trail camera and raked my fingers down the surface of the rub pole. I leaned in and breathed in the scent of Oscar and the large cinnamon male and Osa's mother and the other bears I hadn't yet learned to identify.

Later, I scrolled through the images captured on the trail camera. The cinnamon bear arching his back into the pole. A streak of a grey wolf running by. The back end of a white-tailed deer. Oscar, standing up on his back feet, working his back into the pole, revealing that alarmingly beautiful white O. And less than two hours later, the blurry image of a woman running by, eyes fixed on the camera.

Seeing myself in the images, alongside the bears, made me feel brave and wildly connected to the land. Slowly, I was opening myself up to learning a new way to communicate with the bears while negotiating the distance between us.

As the days crawled nearer to the summer solstice, the longest day of the year, my sightings of the bears doubled. The breeding season was *on*. In a single day I tallied up twelve sightings of nine different bears circling the forest around my cabin. It was like *parque central*, the town squares I'd visited while working in Latin America, where young people came to check one another out, socialize, and hold hands and make out with their lovers. The bears came to my tower to flirt and hook up.

I texted Don, the former lookout who'd spent a decade at Hawk Tower.

I get it now. The area around the tower is like a breeding ground for the bears.

It was a way of apologizing for last year. I shouldn't have doubted him.

I never once had a bear bother me in ten years, Trina, he responded. *If you leave them alone, they leave you alone.*

Swarm was not the right word to describe their presence at the fire tower, but it would be more bizarre to look out the window and *not* see a bear. I tried to make sense of their lusty storylines. It was like following a soap opera: who's mating with whom, who's giving whom the cold shoulder, who's ditched their former partner for the new female.

What kind of strange love life had I stumbled into? Who had I become? A woman living alone in the forest with her dog, narrating the love lives of black bears.

I texted a photo of Oscar to Marina with a caption that read, *My new love life?*

Your boyfriend is hot ;) she wrote back.

I laughed.

Osa had begun to reappear, but only in the early mornings and late evenings when the clearing was void of other bears.

Watching the patterns of the bears' courtship rituals, their heightened awareness of one another, made me question why Western biologists categorized bears as solitary, or asocial. On the contrary, they seemed highly attuned to each other's behaviours and movements, in constant communication: ears perked, noses lifted high, carefully mouthing leaves and the tips of willows, leaving behind their saliva as a kind of love letter to one another.

But why here? I wondered. Why had they chosen this very spot?

I shared my observations with Kevin, and he told me that it reminded him of a previous study by Stephen Herrero and David Hamer in Banff National Park, one that had documented cases of grizzly bear pairs travelling up to isolated summits or ridges as a kind of breeding strategy. The researchers observed male grizzlies blocking females from descending and therefore isolating them from any competition. They hypothesized that females judged the behaviour of males as a test of vigour, a way of determining with whom they'd mate.

Any lingering uncertainty or doubt that bears could feel with the same intensity as a person had entirely evaporated from my mind. I was witnessing emotions that ranged, day to day, hour to hour, from desire to wariness to frustration to jealousy to contentment.

One evening, I sat next to the bear fence and observed Osa's mother drive off a larger male bear. She walked parallel to the slope and, without any warning, barrelled down the hill to charge the large male. He hopped up into the arms of an old aspen and clung there improbably like a huge black burl. Osa's mother huffed and stomped

below. Then, as if satisfied that her message had been received—
get lost—she backed off and gave him space to descend.

The following day, from up in the cupola, I watched Oscar
stomping down the road towards the hill. He was in a visibly sour
mood, swinging his head back and forth and popping his jaw. He
exploded into a run, throwing his front body at the base of a spruce
then swatting at the tree. I heard the sound of claws ratcheting
through the rough bark. It was a throwback to adolescence and
watching some drunk guy at a house party whose girlfriend has just
dumped him punch his fist through the wall. Oscar did two laps of
the yard, then stomped off into the bush.

But before midnight, the sun low in the sky, I saw the familiar curve of his mountainous back alongside a smaller female. He
appeared to have found what he was looking for. Oscar and his companion seemed relaxed in one another's presence, two lovers on a
romantic date, heads obscured by and feasting in the fireweed that
was on the brink of blossoming.

Sixteen

After nearly sixty days of my second summer at Hawk Tower, I was becoming a strange version of myself alone with the bears. They roamed beneath my every thought. In the mornings, I woke and rushed to every window in the cabin—bedroom, office, living room, kitchen—plastering myself against the glass pane as I looked for them.

I scanned the slope, the cutblock, the edge of the old growth, their favoured game trails, looking for their bright black fur, or for the sun illuminating the cinnamon bear, who glowed like a dandelion flower gone to seed. I scanned for any sign of movement. Sometimes I spent long minutes holding my breath, as though underwater, focusing my eye on what looked like a bear but turned out to be a charred black log in the cutblock, or the strange geometry of a shadow cast by a particular bush or tree. Once, I'd watched a small bear in the arms of a poplar for well over an hour, only to realize I'd mistakenly been staring at a patch of black, rotting bark.

"How are you?" my friends called to ask, and instead of talking about myself, I spoke of the bears.

Just a gentle reminder, texted my friend Natalka, a biologist. *You are not a bear.*

I was losing my ability to relate to my friends, who were living in the thick of a pandemic, raising children, managing full-time jobs, attending to the front lines of health care. Some days, I forgot entirely about COVID-19, my brother and parents. Tiptoeing after three-, four-, five-hundred-pound predators in wool socks because hard-soled boots made enough sound for a bear to hear and look up. If I said these things out loud to my friends, they'd say, "You've gone too far. You're going to get yourself eaten like the 'Grizzly Man,'" referring to Timothy Treadwell, a man who camped alongside Alaskan brown bears in Katmai National Park for thirteen years. After Treadwell was viciously mauled and eaten by an old bear, his life was immortalized in a documentary made by Werner Herzog. Treadwell kept pushing the boundaries that existed between him and the bears, trying to prove, perhaps, that they weren't the savage predators Western media had made them out to be. But Treadwell's decision to pitch his tent in a densely treed bear corridor would be his last one.

A friend sent me a link to an article about a woman from North Carolina named Kay Grayson, whom locals called the Black Bear Lady. Grayson hand-fed a community of black bears dog food for nearly thirty years, claiming to defend them against poachers. She grew so comfortable with the bears' presence that she allowed different individuals entry into her home, singing to them, "It's okay, it's okay, it's okay." Grayson even reportedly plucked out her false teeth so as not to threaten her bear companions, and she invited an old female whom she called Betty Sue to sleep in her trailer. But in 2015, Grayson's friends noticed she'd gone silent, prompting authorities to investigate her rural residence, where they found evidence of her death: piles of bear scat with the remains of human bones, those belonging to the Bear Lady. At first glance, it appeared that the bears who Grayson claimed loved her had killed her. But later, a medical examiner found no sign of trauma to her bones that would indicate an attack. Investigators theorized that the woman died of natural causes and, following her death, the bears fed on her physical remains.

I was both horrified and fascinated by the story of the Black Bear Lady, which represented a stark violation of boundaries between people and bears. To me, the act of feeding the bears dog kibble in order to draw them in and build relationships with them was reprehensible, and yet a part of me could empathize with the woman's desire for proximity.

"Be careful out there," my friends would say, and I resisted replying, "You too," because they were statistically more likely to be in a fatal car accident than I was to be mauled by a bear. Annoyed as I was, I knew there was logic to their worry. I could be *that* statistic, one of those unlucky victims of the one, or two fatal attacks that occur in Canada every year. I didn't tell my friends that I regularly contemplated the ways I might be aggressively shredded and dismembered by a bear, even as I tried to get closer to them.

"I need to go," I'd say quickly, excusing myself from a phone call. "Someone is outside."

"Someone?" a friend asked. "Don't you mean some*thing*?"

My language for understanding and relating to the bears had shifted, I realized. A bear was no longer a thing in my mind, akin to a four-legged table. Nor was she a bloodthirsty predator, a nuisance to manage, an "other" to fear. The bear was not some*thing* I had power over, or the right to control. The bear was her own person.

"There's always a bear outside," Marina said teasingly. "One day we're going to stop hearing you on the radio and the only logical explanation will be that you've turned into a bear."

I laughed. Why did her words feel like a kind of compliment?

A friend texted that he wanted to drive north and hike in to the tower to see me. I weighed the pros and cons. Maybe a visit with a friend could be a good thing, I mused. I could feel myself getting "bushed," the word we use to describe the emotional state of one who spends too much time alone in the forest. But then I thought of the bears and wondered if my friend would carry a firearm. I felt protective of the kind of truce I'd forged with the bears. I didn't want my friend, his unfamiliar scent and unpredictable behaviours, to upset the equilibrium, so I told him I wasn't in the mood for visitors.

My brother texted me a photo of a mother black bear and her two cubs, grazing on dandelions at the edge of a well-site. Brendan had finished up his sixty days in Fort Mac and had taken another contract up in Red Earth, a town several hours north of Slave Lake. Fourteen days on, six off. "It's not so bad," he wrote. "I get to see the kids more often."

The mother bear looked young, maybe only a couple of years older than Osa. She was skinny. The two cubs were cubs of the year, born that January. *I thought you'd appreciate this*, he texted. *Pretty cute eh.*

So sweet, I wrote back. *I'm falling in love with the bears here.*

LOL. Be careful out there, eh, Treen? he wrote. *Good thing you've got the twelve gauge*, he added.

I don't think it will come to that, I wrote. *These bears are pretty chill.*

The last thing I wanted to do was pull the trigger on Osa, or Oscar, or even Osa's mother.

Well, don't let your guard down. They're not your friends, Treen. They're wild animals that could seriously mess you up.

I didn't want to get into a debate with my brother over text, but I felt the love and care behind his words. It was possible he worried about me out at the fire tower just as much as I worried about him working long stints in the oil sands and living at camp. We were facing risks of different kinds.

Don't worry, Bren, I wrote. *I'll be careful.*

My friends teased me that I'd become like the woman in Marian Engel's classic, award-winning novel *Bear,* a story about a woman who falls in love with a bear. They sent me erotic passages from the famed scene that describes a bear performing cunnilingus on the protagonist, Lou, flicking his "eel tongue."

We laughed, but out of curiosity I had a copy of the novel delivered to my fire tower with the monthly food supplies. I burrowed into the pages of *Bear* and instantly fell in love with the story of Lou, an archivist who spends a summer on a remote island in northern Ontario. There, she develops an intimate bond with a captive brown bear. As the story unfolds, Lou liberates the animal from his chains and the bear liberates Lou from her loneliness. "They lived sweetly and intensely together," wrote Engel of Lou and the bear. "She knew that her flesh, her hair, her teeth and her fingernails smelled of bear, and this smell was very sweet to her."

Lou swam and bathed in the lake with the bear, she ate with the bear, and even slept with him. She began to resent the flow of summer tourists who flocked to the beaches and crowded the shorelines. Lou was conscious that her relationship with the bear would be perceived by others as strange or unnatural. A local caretaker, Homer, checked in on her regularly, and observed, from afar, the burgeoning intimacy between woman and bear. Lou knew he was watching.

"You stink of bear," he commented to Lou during a visit.

"I guess I do," she responded. "There's no way of living with him except living close to him."

I paused when I read these words. Reread the sentence over and over again. There was no other way of living with the bears except living close to them. Is that what I was doing here?

Homer's response to Lou was equally as memorable.

"People get funny when they're too much alone."

When Lou tried to make love to the bear, the bear reminded her, you've gone too far, bloodying and scarring her back with his long, dagger-like claws. I was aware that the boundaries between the bears and me had shifted once again, from mutual avoidance to tolerance and now to a curiosity that bordered on fascination. Maybe even infatuation.

The bears came at night, when I was asleep, flowing by the cabin in the tall grass. The number of bear sightings at Hawk Tower had more than quadrupled from the previous year and I wasn't entirely sure why, though I speculated it was because some of the resident females were in estrus, or heat, and thus attracting a stream of male suitors. Some evenings I lay in bed, half-awake, and it sounded as though the bears were right outside my bedroom window, tearing clumps of grass, molars grinding. I dreamt of them frequently and intensely.

I dreamt that the clearing between the forest and the cabin— the space between us—was overtaken by a carnivorous jungle. There was no fence, no buffer, no barrier between us.

I dreamt of a man who could turn himself into a bear and charge, and then, when I cried out for help, the people in my dream wouldn't believe the man was also a bear.

I dreamt that a charging bear knocked me over and I did not fight back. I lay in fetal position and felt a warm liquid on my neck and I wasn't sure whether it was the bear's saliva or my own blood.

I dreamt that my brother and I were young bears searching for a den. He crawled through a broken basement window in an abandoned house. He looked back over his shoulder at me. "Are you coming?"

On a windless day from up in the tower, I heard the sound of a branch breaking. My eyes travelled down to the familiar spot where the bears often emerged. It was indistinct to the unknowing eye, just a slight opening into a curtain of deciduous foliage, now fat and frothy.

I saw that the maker of sound was Osa's mother. She waded into the long grass and the crown of yellow dandelions, moving to the very spot where I'd been that morning, as I attempted to photograph a hummingbird moth, a small, furry pollinator with a curled proboscis. The moth was lightning quick. The bear was colossally slow. She glanced back at the trail from which she'd travelled. Her ears perked up like a dog's.

More leaves rustling. Another branch snapped.

A large black bear appeared at the edge of the bush, then stepped out fully into the clearing. I didn't recognize his long black muzzle. His jaw was slightly ajar, as though leering at Osa's mother. She greeted him with several huffs of breath. The male stepped towards her and she turned the length of her body towards him.

No one moved. I held my breath.

Osa's mother made a wide arc around him into the bush and the male followed beyond. I heard the sound of their footsteps, crushing fallen leaves. Then, silence. I stopped breathing, listening intensely. Then—was that a *grunt*?

When a female bear is at her most receptive, she'll allow the male to mount her. Copulation can last from several minutes to upwards of an hour, with the couple pausing to bite or nuzzle one another. Some bear specialists refer to bear mating as "fluttering" based on the fluttering, thrusting motions made by the male when ejaculation occurs. *Fluttering.* Such an odd way to describe the mating ritual between six, seven hundred pounds' worth of predator, I couldn't help but think. The word felt more apt to refer to the lovemaking of hummingbird moths than bears.

Several minutes later, Osa's mother emerged again, solo, and resumed her previous grazing. She seemed unbothered by whatever had happened in the bush.

The male came crashing back to the edge of the forest, mouth wide open now, his long pink tongue dangling. The bear was breathing the same way my dog panted after chasing a rabbit through the bush—whole body heaving. Suddenly, he collapsed onto his side in the long, cool grass, resting his head.

The bear looked undeniably human. Drained of energy, all the tension gone from his charged, live-wire body. He lay there as Osa's mother continued to feed in the long grass, lifting his heavy paw every so often to swat away the flies swarming around his face.

"Look at the bear," Lou pondered in the pages of Engel's *Bear*, "dozing and drowsing there, thinking his own thoughts. Like a dog, like a groundhog, like a man: big."

He does *look like a man*, I thought. He looked much the same as any lover.

Then Osa's mother did something that surprised me. She stepped closer to the male, closer and closer, until she was less than a metre away from the sleeping bear-man. She stayed for less than a minute, grazing, leaning into him. I knew there was a high chance that I was projecting onto the bear, but there was a tenderness between them, the submissive male, the willing female. After a minute or so, she plodded away along the road.

The male heaved himself upright, slouched, watching her go. He yawned and scratched his genitalia. He wasted no energy on grazing, knowing perhaps that sexual desire is brief in a female bear's world. Osa's mother would be in estrus for a night, maybe another day. The male would follow her and mate with her for as long as she'd tolerate him. Then she'd redraw the boundaries between them. Soon she'd have a different imperative, something that didn't involve him.

———

One evening, a large bear with a slender face appeared below in the cutblock. I recognized the big mother of three cubs immediately. It was the same bear I'd watched nurse her two surviving cubs the previous summer. I decided to call her Big Mama. I spied a flash of black fur through the aspen leaves and a small face stared back at me. A second cub emerged from behind her. They were triple the size they were last year, now yearling cubs. The cubs couldn't take their eyes off me. Did they remember my scent? I wondered. They'd grown bigger than Holly, although a shy, tentative energy remained in their movements. They darted closer to Big Mama, clinging to her legs, then turned themselves into a vanishing act. *POOF!* One of the cubs slipped through a curtain of young aspen. The second dared to look back at me, elfish with her triangular face, a pointed muzzle, and huge ears. Within seconds, she was gone.

The following evening, I glanced out the window and my eye caught the shape of something small and black in the limbs of a fifteen-metre poplar. A yearling cub, crouched in the tree's branches. I grabbed my binoculars and rushed outside the cabin to get a closer look. I spotted a second bear perched in a tree nearby. Big Mama's cubs. Dense new growth in the cutblock obscured my view beneath the trees. Something wasn't right. What kind of threat would send the cubs so high up into the safety of the trees?

One of the cubs scratched the tree with her front legs, as though agitated. Then, as if standing on her tiptoes, she peered down, her spine arched like a black alley cat's, fur standing upright, fixed on whatever was happening below. Where was Big Mama?

My mind worked through various scenarios. Maybe it was one of the hulking male bears scenting after the cubs in an effort to mate with their mother. They would've scampered away at the scent and sound of Oscar stomping towards them. Maybe the resident wolf pack, led by a greyish female with a white-tipped tail, was trying to isolate a cub. I imagined the alpha and her pack circling below, leering up at the small bears. On the ground, they'd be an easy meal for a wolf pack.

An hour passed. The light dimmed, but the cubs didn't budge.

Whatever, *whoever*, lurked down below was holding them captive.

I felt as though I should come to the cubs' defence, and considered two scenarios: Fire off the shotgun, hoping it would be enough to scare off whatever animal was below, or arm myself with bear spray and wade through the thick willows and confront whatever dangerous force was preventing the cubs from climbing down.

I called Justin.

"I'm worried about the cubs," I confessed to him. "I feel like I want to intervene."

There was a pause on the other end of the line.

"Hello?" I thought the line had gone dead.

"Be careful," he said finally. "What you're saying is dangerous. For you. And for the bears."

I felt a shot of embarrassment. He must've thought, *She's bushed. She's gone crazy out there.* I backpedalled, quickly, to reassure him.

"I know, I know," I said in a single breath. "I'm not actually going to *do* anything . . . I'm just *saying* . . ."

I hung up the phone, feeling misunderstood and frustrated with myself for revealing too much. He wouldn't understand. He hadn't spent the last seventy-some days entirely alone with a steady stream of black bears. I was the daughter of a biologist and hunter, taught to appreciate that nutrients and energy carry through the ecosystem, and knew not to interfere with the natural laws of predator and prey. Death was a part of life.

And yet, it didn't seem fair. The odds of survival were stacked against the cubs.

I reminded myself that whatever was happening beyond the trees, that which I couldn't see, didn't require anything of me. That the cubs didn't need me. The bears didn't need me.

I realized the boundary between me and the bears wasn't electrified. It wasn't a fixed line. The boundary was more porous than I could have imagined, fluid and ever shifting, influenced by my ability to identify them as individuals—and to empathize in a way I hadn't before.

After midnight, a large bear slowly emerged from the cutblock into the clearing around the cabin. I recognized the slender face of Big Mama, her fur glowing more blue than black. A gargantuan-sized bear followed closely behind her like a boulder. It must be Oscar, I thought. They were peaceful together. Nothing in their behaviour seemed stressed or anxious.

The cubs watched from above.

I realized my stupidity. It was Big Mama who told the cubs to climb. The mother bear hadn't treed the cubs for their protection, but rather to signal to them their independence. She was hungry in a way that had nothing to do with them.

How close I came, I thought, watching her go. I had not intervened, but something in the way I understood the bears, related to them, cared about them, had fundamentally shifted.

When I woke the next morning, the cubs had vanished. The trees stood empty, their leaves trembling in the yellow light.

Seventeen

Osa turned crepuscular, moving and foraging under the cover of dark to avoid the larger, more dominant bears. At night, I left the window open and woke to the sounds of footsteps shuffling through the long grass and teeth tearing at vegetation. These rustling sounds were so slight they wove themselves into my dreams. In my dreams, I was no longer frightened of the bears. I shed my fears like they shed their heavy winter coats. Maybe they could scent it: *She's no longer afraid*.

In the morning, Osa would be gone. But she and the other bears left behind proof that they'd been there, metres away from where I slept. I gazed down from the tower at the pathways through the tall grass that undulated and intersected, shining silver where their heavy feet pummelled the foliage, widening where they had lain down on their bellies to feed. I wouldn't have ever noticed these subtle lines before. Signs of the bears would be so easy to overlook if one wasn't paying attention. But now they felt as obvious as fresh tracks in snow.

In early July, my brother texted me a shaky cellphone video of a lynx along a gravel road in Red Earth. In the video, I could hear the sound of Brendan's truck idling as he filmed the wild cat, only a few metres away in the ditch. The lynx stared at my brother—more phantom than cat, grey with long, black-tipped ears and oval eyes that seemed to penetrate the soul. I'd heard stories before that lynx could be intensely curious.

"Hey kitty kitty," my brother crooned in the video.

WOW, I texted back, the hairs on my arms standing erect. I wrote in a hurry, *That gave me* chills!

Pretty cool to see one so close!!! Brendan texted back.

He was days away from finishing up his shift in Red Earth, eager to get back to his family in Edmonton. He'd sent the video of the lynx to Amanda to show the kids, and I wondered if they felt something of the same awe I'd felt for our father. The way my brother's work put him in proximity with wildlife species that city kids would see only on television or at the zoo.

I wondered if these rare, close encounters with the wild reminded my brother of our childhood in Peace River, the animals our father brought home—the injured barred owl, the pack of coyote pups, and the orphaned black bear cub—and what they inspired in our imaginations.

Could he remember the breath of the elk on the back of his neck?

I thought of the boy who flushed grouse up out of the long grass and who tread lightly in the footsteps of my father as they stalked the edges of grain fields while hunting mule deer.

The following day, Osa appeared at the edge of the clearing in broad daylight, which struck me as unusual. It was as if she wanted to be seen by other bears. I wondered if her body was undergoing estrus. At three and a half years old, it was unlikely she'd mate—most female black bears don't give birth until their fifth year—but it wasn't out of the question, either. A study from the Cold Lake region, in northeastern Alberta, found that bears in food-rich environments could produce cubs as early as their fourth year.

Only an hour later, Oscar strolled up the slope, edging towards Osa. He turned his enormous body sideways to hers, leaving a wide continent of space between himself and the small, skittish bear. Then, slowly, he moved in a zigzag pattern towards her.

Osa's rabbity head shot upright, a tuft of grass dangling from her mouth. She crow-hopped, scampering like a young cub, back into the bush.

"Not today, big guy," I called down cheekily to Oscar. He cranked his head to look back up at me as if to reply, *Wait and see*, before following the small bear into the forest.

In the heat of July, the bears surrendered to the shade of the forest. They disappeared entirely, leaving me to wonder whether I'd dreamt everything I'd witnessed during the mating season. I checked my records to make sure I wasn't crazy: I'd had over fifty sightings and encounters with the bears within two and a half months. Some days, while up in the fire tower, lazily scanning the horizon for smoke— in a season when few wildfires would ignite and burn—I'd catch sight of black ears, or a humped back, travelling through the green labyrinth in the cutblock below. But they'd vanish as soon as they appeared, absorbed by the lush vegetation.

A helicopter arrived mid-July to drop off my monthly supply of groceries, including a package from Marina with a note that read: *gifts from below the surface*. I unwrapped the package to find a brick of dark clay that she'd harvested from the edge of her garden. "I saw your beautiful pottery and I wondered what would happen if I gave you some of this clay from my tower site," Marina wrote.

I took out my pottery tools and wired off a large slab, then wedged the mound against a wooden board covered with canvas, kneading the clay intuitively. As I worked, my mind was emptied of thought. The colour of the clay was a shade I had never seen before, neither grey nor green, but somewhere in between.

Holly snuffled at the screen porch door. Hands slathered with wild clay, I went to let her back inside, and as I opened the door, my gaze fixed on an unexpected form on the other side of the electric fence, only metres away. A bear grazing in a patch of pink Indian paintbrush. The bear wasn't black, blond, or cinnamon; he was unlike any other bear I'd seen before. His large head, the colour of dark chocolate, contrasted with the rest of him, his fur shimmering the same shade as the last light over a field of wheat. The bear appeared more myth than mammal. I stood dumbly on the porch, shocked by his beauty. And then it dawned on me: It was the same cinnamon bear who'd attempted to mate with Osa's mother. He was shedding out his lush winter coat, revealing an entirely different shade beneath.

I decided to call him Canelo, "cinnamon" in Spanish.

Like a magician, Canelo disappeared as suddenly as he'd appeared, leaving me on the porch, without language, every hair on my body standing up as though struck by lightning.

Hardly anything burned that summer in northwestern Alberta. I called in a one-tree wonder, a wildfire caused by a lightning strike to a single tree, about fifteen kilometres to my south. The thin strand of smoke rose up out of a stand of scraggly black spruce. The firefighting crew was so excited for my detection that the leader sounded practically exuberant when he said, "Confirmed wildfire," over the radio.

The temperature and dew point dropped in the mornings and evenings, the days shortened, and the fire season was practically extinguished. Overhead, the geese sounded their departure south and I knew that the sandhill cranes would soon follow in chaotic, swarming droves. The season was coming full circle. Frost bit the slope in early August and the cranberries grew fat on the bushes. Piles of fuchsia-stained bear scat dotted the road. The rains had been generous to the forest, and the wild berries had been generous to the bears. But by the end of the summer, only one bear remained nearby.

I watched Osa's incremental fattening, the sharp edges of her fleshing out. I wondered if the small bear had allowed Oscar to mate with her. Would she give birth to cubs over the winter?

Motherhood is never a certainty for a bear. Conception depends on what my dad and other biologists would refer to as a bear's "resources," her fat reserves, determined by environmental factors and food availability. In June, when bears mate, the male's sperm fertilizes the eggs in the uterus, and the eggs form into tiny balls of cells called blastocysts. These small blastocysts are suspended and free-floating, remaining dormant in the female's womb for the rest of the summer as she forages. Come November, when she burrows beneath the earth, she asks herself, Can I survive motherhood? And the body answers. If the bear has packed on enough flesh and fat, her body will signal to the blastocysts to implant into the uterine wall and start growing. But if it has been a difficult year to gather the necessary food resources—due to drought, or habitat loss as a consequence of wildfires or deforestation—the female can sense *not now* and reabsorbs the blastocysts into her body. This extraordinary biological process, one that's allowed bears to evolve over tens of thousands of years, is referred to as "delayed implantation."

I'd been delaying motherhood for most of my adult life. I never felt the drive to be a mother in the same way as some of my female friends described it, though many of them had doubts of their own.

One of my oldest childhood friends, a mother of three, told me that the environmental costs of motherhood weighed on her. "It feels selfish, this desire to procreate," she said. "And it scares me to think of what we might go through in the future. But life is also brief and beautiful. The drive is deep in us—it's about love. I want to believe that my children will be adaptable."

Brendan seemed to feel that same drive—a new sense of purpose.

In early August, he'd started back on with the same company he'd previously worked for in the Peace River oil sands. The oil economy was already rebounding from the crash months earlier, and the well-sites that had been shut down were operational once again. My brother was ecstatic to be back working in the small town where we'd grown up, where his colleagues weren't strangers, they were men and women with whom he'd bonded. I imagined he felt safer working in Peace River than in the unfamiliar territory of Fort Mac or Red Earth.

One morning he posted on Instagram a photograph of the sunrise over a forest of black spruce.

Back in the patch not a bad morning view tho!!!!

It was one of those views you can only find in the North, a view that had defined our childhood, where the sky is the same shade of fluorescent orange as a worker's safety vest and a neon-pink sign that reads NO VACANCY, and the gnarled black spruce rise up like teeth. The colour of the skies, as visceral as the fresh blood that spills out while field dressing a moose. An unforgettable intensity of colour.

I knew, because I'd seen the same sunrise that morning. I climbed the tower hours before my shift began to put myself closer to the light, and texted my brother a photograph of the view, a different vantage point on the same explosion of colours. I felt enormous relief that Brendan had survived the long shifts in Fort Mac and Red Earth and had safely returned to our family's home in Peace River. I imagined him driving down the long gravel roads, veins that connected him to the well-sites he was responsible for, as I watched on from the tower.

The two of us, separate, and yet bound by the same feelings of being sharply awake in the presence of light.

At the end of the season, Osa was no longer the skinny, skittish bear whom I observed on that day in early May. She had been only fur and bones, her face small and cub-like; now, in late August, her bony edges were smooth and round as a blueberry. Her lush fur shone like obsidian. She travelled along the edge of the forest with confidence.

The distance between us had shortened over the length of the summer. Did I trust the bear? I wasn't sure. I did believe that Osa had come to know my scent and predict my set of behaviours, which had made it safer for us to live alongside one another. By respecting one another's boundaries—not as a fixed line, nor a standoff, but an evolving, ever-shifting territory between us—we were learning how to share space and coexist.

In early September, I packed my belongings and swept out the cabin, preparing to leave my post for the winter. On my final evening, I heard the rustle of grass outside my bedroom window. It was Osa, grazing on the last of the verdant green on the slope.

I tiptoed outside, leaving the dog in the cabin, and sank down on my haunches, making myself small. I watched the bear twenty metres downslope. There was no longer a barrier between us because I'd loosened the wires of the electric fence and pushed them down to the ground, in preparation for leaving.

It didn't take long for Osa to detect my scent. She hoisted her body upright on her hind legs, lifting her blond snout to the air, standing in the tall grass. She revealed the birthmark of two crescent moons on her chest. As much as I wanted to draw closer, I knew that to coexist with the bear—to respect the bear—was to accept there were certain boundaries beyond which I would never be able to reach.

She stood there for several seconds, assessing the risk. How did I smell to her now that I was no longer afraid? As if determining that I wasn't a threat, she dropped back to the ground and refocused on her task of feasting on the grass. To me, the moment felt symbolic of a kind of goodbye or farewell—but what use does a bear, preparing for a long winter underground, have for such human sentiment?

I sat there, listening to the rustle and tear of grass, to the sound of Osa doing what she must do. What a miracle, I thought, that she'd survived the odds against her, that she'd grown into such a beautifully robust bear—and what a miracle to be here, watching her.

"See you in the spring, Osa," I whispered.

Eighteen

For months, while I'd been negotiating space with the bears, my family, friends, and community had been forced to adapt to the new terms of living with the COVID-19 virus. Only a few days after I landed back in Peace River, in late September 2020, the Alberta government issued another social lockdown.

I'd hoped to visit my brother's family in Edmonton and spend time with my niece and nephew, but I hunkered down on the outskirts of Peace River. I wasn't sure what to do, where to go, so I stayed in the North and rented a room in an old farmhouse belonging to a childhood friend, Skyla, who worked as a social worker. Skyla's house was built on a quarter section of deciduous bush surrounded by an ocean of grain and canola fields. The patch of forest was an anomaly. Deforestation along the Peace River valley, due to agricultural expansion, was staggeringly evident. Two-metre piles of uprooted trees lay in rows, waiting to be burned over the winter. The wind blew dust across the gravel road, across the fields of crops, whistling through the wheat that was ready to be harvested.

The old farmhouse and the forested land was a refuge through the winter. Holly and I hiked into the patch of bush behind the house and I was elated to discover that the story of bear was written everywhere. Claw marks dug into an aspen, revealing the green membrane of the tree. *Fresh*, I thought, intrigued. I ran my fingers over the scarred wood as though reading Braille and toed warm piles of ochre scat containing undigested wheat. I wanted to believe that the bear who lived here was watching us, scenting us, as we explored the forest that she called home. Holly spooked a female moose up from where she'd been bedded down in a thick tangle of wild rose bushes. The moose crashed through the forest. Seconds later, a bull moose stood up, only metres away. I froze on the spot, stunned by our proximity to the gigantic bull, who could pulverize us with his powerful hooves. But he wasn't interested in a woman and her dog. Mating season—the rut—was *on*. He high-kneed it through the bush, chasing the one he desired.

I thought longingly of my friend Eric. He was currently driving his 4Runner from Prince Edward Island to Alberta, fuelling up at gas stations and living out of the back of his truck to avoid any social interactions. Feeling starved for human intimacy, I'd asked Skyla if Eric could stay with us for a few days, and since he was travelling alone, and self-sufficient, she was okay with it. He planned to reach northern Alberta by the following week.

Shortly after moving in, I stood at the kitchen sink, filling up the kettle, when I noticed two black triangles flashing through the tall wheat in the neighbour's field. *I* know *that colour*, I thought excitedly. As water rushed from the tap, I watched the bear's head bob above the height of the mature wheat. She palmed the seed boughs into her mouth, appearing and disappearing behind the curtain of golden wheat. I let out an ecstatic giggle.

"The bears have followed you from the fire tower," Skyla would later muse to me.

I grabbed my camera, slipped on my rubber boots, and stepped outside, the cold October air piercing my skin. I climbed up onto the old wooden fence that ran parallel to the wheat field and straddled the top rung. Balanced there, I photographed the industriously feeding black bear, several hundred metres away. It was as if the bear was magnetic. *Just a little bit closer*.

When I crested a small knoll, she was waiting for me, standing up on her hind legs, the top half of her body above the wheat, paws dangling. The bear and I stared at one another.

With urgency, she collapsed back onto all fours and scampered into the forest behind the farmhouse. "Sorry, bear," I said to her. I felt guilty about scaring her off, realizing that I'd displaced her from foraging when she was at a critical time of fattening up. Then again, fear was probably the wisest survival strategy for a bear who lived on the edge of farmland. Here, bears would face a range of human attitudes, from tolerance to fear to resentment to violence. There was no predicting how a person might respond to a bear feeding in a wheat field, but I guessed that a woman straddling a fence post with a camera in hand wasn't the norm.

That same afternoon, while out walking the dog along the gravel road, I crossed paths with a neighbour who lived at the top of the valley. Her house looked out into the grassy hills, dotted with aspen and wild rose bushes—ideal bear habitat. A small creek slithered along at the valley bottom.

"I can never remember a year seeing so many black bears," she told me. "We had to call Fish and Wildlife officers to deal with three different bears."

"Oh?"

Conservation officers eventually came to set up a culvert trap on her property.

"One morning I heard a loud banging noise. I went out to check the trap and, sure enough, there was a bear inside. A cinnamon bear. And boy, was he angry. He was slamming against the walls of the trap with his front paws. There was blood spattered everywhere."

I said nothing.

"The officers relocated the bears," she told me. "Well, at least I *think* they were relocated."

"Why do you think they kept coming back to your yard?"

"We do have a crabapple tree," she said sheepishly, adding, "We're going to get a dog."

A few days later, Justin called me. He lived in Grimshaw, a neighbouring town to the west of Peace River. Justin told me that he'd heard from his relatives, farmers from a town to the north, that it had been a bad year for black bears getting into their crops. His uncle had already shot six bears who were feeding in his oat field.

"Bears can do a lot of damage to an oat crop," Justin explained. "They often lie down as they feed and trample down the crops, so the thresher can't move along the rows."

But *six bears*. There had to be a better way, I thought.

While scrolling absent-mindedly on Instagram, I came across a photograph, a selfie, taken by a young woman and her partner affectionately cuddling the head of what, at first glance, looked like a large black dog. I scrolled down before my brain registered what I'd seen. *Wait.* I scrolled back up. It was a black bear—a dead black bear. The woman was smiling dreamily in the selfie, as though the bear was a teddy bear, a pet, a baby. She was from a Mennonite farming community to the north of my fire tower and had posted a series of images taken on her family's farm: an older woman hunched over, harvesting rows of carrots, an older man driving a tractor. And a selfie hugging the large, square head of a dead bear. Dead, no longer a threat, or nuisance, or loss to profit. Happy selfie because the problem was solved. Hashtag, problem bear. Hashtag, pest control. Hashtag, God's country.

52 likes.

Never mind that our houses were built in the wild habitat and corridors of bears. Never mind that we'd eroded their natural foodscape, bulldozed over their dens, fragmented their preferred travel routes. Never mind that we pushed them away with rubber bullets, bear bangers, pots and pans, culvert traps, and drugged relocations and then lured them back with poorly managed garbage, dead livestock, birdseed, grain fields, and apple trees.

I searched the facial features of the dead bear, trying to determine whether I recognized him. His head was smaller than Oscar's but larger than Osa's. I wasn't opposed to the ethical hunting of black bears for meat and sustenance. Justin preferred to hunt during the fall, when the bears had grown fat on berries; he used all parts of the animal, rendering the fat and grinding up the meat to make sausages. My dad always told me that bear lard made for the "tastiest pie crust."

Some First Nations wouldn't hunt bears because of their likeness to people; it was taboo, akin to killing a family member. The Kitasoo/Xai'xais and Gitga'at First Nations recently lobbied the BC government to ban the hunting of black bears in their territories, located in the Great Bear Rainforest. Black bears carry the recessive gene that causes the rare Kermode bear, or "spirit bear"—or *moksgm'ol* in the Tsimshian language: black bears with ghostly white fur. Trophy hunting of grizzly bears in the region was banned in 2012, with a province-wide moratorium going into effect in 2017.

But I'd read about other First Nations cultures, including the Champagne and Aishihik First Nations in southwestern Yukon, who adhered to certain protocols of respect when killing or hunting a bear, including placing the head in a high place. It was a sign of respect for a species with whom people had long shared the same salmon-bearing rivers and lakes. They treated the deceased body of a bear with the same love and care that they would a family member, and wouldn't speak aloud the word *bear* for fear of insulting him. Instead, they spoke: *Grandfather. Brother. Sister.* They often placed the bear's skull in the arms of a towering poplar tree.

The image of the dead bear's head posted to social media signalled, to me, the extreme opposite. The dead, stony-eyed bear. The maniacal happy grins. It reminded me of the trophy hunting industry, which harvested parts of the animal, not for sustenance, but for material show: the head, the claws, and the hide.

In Alberta, a licence to hunt black bears, for resident hunters, costs only $20.99. On the government's website, it's advertised like a "two for one" pizza deal: *Buy one licence for a bear and you can get the second one free!* A licence to shoot elk, a rarer and hence more valued species, is double the cost. Non-resident hunters, typically those from the US or Europe, paid hunting outfitters—registered hunting businesses that guide clients to shoot wildlife—thousands of dollars for the privilege of pulling the trigger on black bears.

Most hunters value bear hide—a souvenir of their achievement—over meat. Several years earlier, the lookout to my south had discovered a dead, bloated black bear rotting on the road that led to her cabin. The bear had been shot, skinned, and dumped. There wasn't anything illegal about it.

Historically, people have hunted black bears through various methods: along traplines, relying on "spot and stalk," or sighting and tracking a bear, setting up hunting blinds, hunting with dogs, or luring bears in through baited barrels, or bait stations. The latter is used almost exclusively by hunting outfitters who want to guarantee their clients a "trophy bear."

In Alberta, baiting for the purpose of bear hunting was made legal in 1987. At a bait station, outfitters set up hunting blinds—tree stands or ground blinds—to conceal the hunter as they wait for bears. The blinds are located within a clear shot of the bait barrels (often only metres away), which are chained to the ground or to nearby trees and stocked with a food source: grain, stale bread, or old doughnuts and pastries. With holes punched in the bottom to enable the bears to paw at the food, the barrels act like slow feeders of sorts. Popcorn was fast becoming the preferred baiting source by outfitters, Justin told me.

"It's cheap, and easy to carry into baiting sites in large quantities," he explained. "They melt honey and molasses into the popcorn, which attracts the bears. And the bears can't take a large quantity of the popcorn and go." Justin despised the practice of bear baiting. "It's not hunting. And it gives the rest of us a bad name," he grumbled. Justin preferred a spot and stalk method, carefully tracking the animal and opting for the bow and arrow versus the rifle. It required him to get closer to the animal without being seen or scented.

The Alberta government justifies the practice of baiting to hunt black bears by insisting that it allows hunters to "be more selective in choosing a bear to harvest," and that it creates "close-range shot opportunities for a more humane harvest." But what is even remotely humane about habituating a bear to an anthropogenic food source and then pulling the trigger?

"They say it's to make the hunt more productive," Kevin told me over the phone. "Well, you know, there's only a ten percent success rate on elk. Maybe we should bait them too? But that would never happen. Black bears are the game animal that we seem to respect the least in Alberta," he said, pointing out how some viewed them as nothing more than "gophers," while others, often Americans or Europeans, who lived in places where bears had long been exterminated from the landscape, paid thousands of dollars to kill a bear for trophy.

He was morally opposed to the hunting of grizzly bears or black bears, regardless of the method used. They were too much "like us," he confessed. They were too *human*. I'd heard other people say the same thing, including my own father. I remembered him telling me that a dead, skinned bear appears incredibly human-like, the bones in the paws resembling those of human hands. I reflected back on Kevin's notion that "most people don't know bears," and I wondered how that influences the way we do—or don't—practise respect for the species.

Before the Thanksgiving weekend in early October, Eric pulled up the gravel driveway to the old farmhouse in his red 4Runner and I ran outside to greet him. Holly loped ahead.

"Hey, Holly girl!" Eric sang, bending his six-foot frame down to her level, vigorously rubbing her ears. He looked up at me, his long hair tied back in a low ponytail, his face tanned from a summer of working outside, felling trees and milling the wood into long planks to build a cabin on his parents' land in Prince Edward Island. He wore a faded blue jean jacket with a sheepskin collar and the same pair of worn leather Red Wing workboots he'd used on the fire line. The pandemic had found Eric stuck out east, without a seasonal job. He'd been eager to make his way west again, and would spend the winter trying to get a job with BC Wildfire.

"My turn," I said.

"Hey, Trina girl," he exclaimed, and enveloped me in his arms, picking me up off the ground the way he always did.

"Holy shit, it's been too long," I crooned, my legs dangling mid-air.

We made dinner together and it felt like a relief to be sharing space with the kind of friend you don't have to explain yourself to. I stood at the stove, stirring the sauce with a wooden spoon that he'd carved for me out of birch, years ago. Eric's presence softened something in my chest, a knot of anxiety or loneliness. I think he felt similarly. As seasonal workers, we were accustomed to living on the fringe of society—both single, without kids, and without a set plan in the off-season—although the pandemic amplified the sense of isolation.

Before sunset, Eric and I hiked along the trail through the bush, and I pointed out the spot where Holly had flushed the pair of mating moose and the aspen tree the bear had dug into.

"You got pretty close to those bears this summer, eh," he said. "But not as close as Lou, I hope," he added teasingly, referencing Engel's book *Bear*. At my urging, he'd read the book this past summer.

"That's between me and the bears," I said with a smirk.

Eric was calm and observant. The kind of guy who didn't feel the urgency to fill silence with unnecessary talk. I hadn't seen the bear since the day I'd photographed her in the field, but I liked to think she was bedded down nearby, listening to our boots crunching through the carpet of leaf fall.

"Man, I missed the North," Eric said.

That evening, we lay next to one another in my bed, Eric propped up on a pillow reading *Lonesome Dove*, a Western novel that follows the lives of two aging Texas Rangers on their final adventure across the American wilderness.

"Read me a little?" I asked, and he obliged. It was an old ritual we'd shared over the years since we met at Muskeg Tower, when he was a leader and would read aloud to his crew while they were gathered beneath my tower, waiting to get called to a wildfire. His crew fondly nicknamed him Dad because of it. There was, indeed, something very "old soul" about Eric. He was curious, even philosophical, about the world and his place within it. He read books and wanted to discuss them, and took apart the engine of his 4Runner to teach himself about mechanics, and wanted to study Brazilian jiu-jitsu, a martial art.

Eric narrated the characters' voices with his best Texan drawl, which made me laugh.

In previous fire seasons, when I'd hear him on the radio, working on a fire with his crew, I'd always feel comforted by the sound of my friend. Under the covers, I threaded my legs into his and felt the warmth of his long body parallel to mine.

———

My mother called and invited Eric and me over for Thanksgiving dinner. "It will be really small," she said. "And we can try to social-distance."

I hesitated.

"I mean, we're really not supposed to be gathering right now, Mom," I said. "Who's all coming?"

"Your brother, Amanda, and the kids," she said. "Oh, and Bren invited a friend from work."

"Geez, Mom, really?"

"He's all *alone*, Trina."

"It's like Bren thinks that the rules don't apply to him," I huffed, but I agreed to go. After a summer in the bush, I was desperate to see my family.

On the drive to my parents' house, I warned Eric about Brendan. "Just a heads-up that my family can be a little . . . volatile," I said. "It's my brother, really. We have totally opposing views on things. So don't be surprised if something comes up."

Eric glanced over at me from the driver's seat.

"That sounds pretty typical for any family," he said sympathetically.

"I guess so."

It occurred to me that I hadn't brought a friend to a family dinner in over a decade. Maybe I was overthinking it. For many years, I'd braced myself for conflict. It was a habit that was hard to kick, expecting the worst from my brother. Maybe I was being unfair to him.

"Auntie!" cried my nephew when we came in the front door, and my heart expanded at the sight of him and my niece. They had both grown since I'd seen them last, six months earlier. They hugged my torso and legs and smiled shyly up at Eric.

My brother shook Eric's hand and welcomed him and we sat down at the long table to eat.

His colleague, Greg, was about the same age as Brendan, in his late thirties. Greg lived with his wife and two kids in Edmonton and, like my brother, made the commute up north to Peace River every couple of weeks. He wore a black I ❤ CANADIAN OIL AND GAS hoodie.

The logo caught my eye. Since I'd left the tower and re-entered society in September, I'd been noticing it everywhere in northern Alberta. It had been created by a group calling themselves Canada Action, which aimed "to take action in support of our vital natural resource sector" and to curb "misinformation" and negative press about Alberta's oil sands. Apparently, oil and gas companies in the province had bought up thousands of sweatshirts, T-shirts, and bumper stickers from Canada Action to distribute to their staff. The logo had become an unofficial uniform to unite what one writer at *Maclean's* magazine called "petroleum patriots."

Since the early 2010s, Indigenous communities and environmental groups in Canada had been making headway against major oil and gas projects in the country, rising up against the proposed pipelines that would risk contaminating their ancestral territories. Protests and lawsuits were leading to major delays or to projects being entirely shut down, including the Northern Gateway pipeline, which aimed to transport diluted bitumen—a by-product of crude oil—from Alberta to a port in Kitimat, BC. The deepwater port would allow for the expedient shipping of oil to Asian markets. But in 2016, Prime Minister Justin Trudeau promised to ban oil tanker traffic in northern BC, with the moratorium being passed in 2018, effectively killing the Northern Gateway project.

In February 2020, solidarity protests involving both Indigenous and settler communities, called Shut Down Canada, sprang up across the country against the Coastal GasLink pipeline, which would transport natural gas from reserves in northern BC to the port in Kitimat. The hereditary chiefs of the Wet'suwet'en, a First Nations community in northeastern BC, were adamantly opposed to the project, and for two years had erected camps to block construction. After the RCMP raided and dismantled the Wet'suwet'en's camps and arrested land defenders, nationwide protesters targeted railways, erecting blockades to halt passenger services and cargo freight operations in Canada. Indigenous and environmental groups were sending industry and government a message loud and clear: LAND BACK. Return control of ancestral territories to their original stewards.

I knew that Greg's sweater with the I ❤ CANADIAN OIL AND GAS logo wasn't about staff appreciation. It was about fostering a rise in populism, emphasizing the idea of "the people" in opposition to "the elite," or those with a more liberal perspective, and it was a way to symbolize togetherness of those in favour of pipelines and petroleum projects. The Alberta government was, in part, fuelling these divisions. Just before the pandemic broke out, Premier Jason Kenney had created what became known as the energy "war room"—the Canadian Energy Centre (CEC)—allocating $30 million in public funding to establish a fully staffed headquarters in Calgary dedicated to rebut "every lie told by the green left" about Alberta's oil sands industry.

The I ❤ CANADIAN OIL AND GAS logo had become a favoured companion to other popular bumper stickers: *FUCK TRUDEAU*, or, worse, the silhouette of a naked girl with two long braids being pulled by hands behind her, the word *Greta* tattooed on her lower back. The decal, designed and printed by an Alberta energy company, was an obvious attack on the Swedish environmental activist Greta Thunberg, who'd inspired a movement of young people to protest against industrial emissions and climate change.

When I first saw the Greta logo, I felt sick. She was a child, for god's sake. What the logo was endorsing was child *rape*. But I could hardly say I was surprised. It was a flashback to my girlhood in Peace River and the embodied fear and feeling of being objectified and silenced. At that time, my brother had sheltered me from the worst of it. Being his "little sister" had offered some level of protection from cruel or predatory behaviour from guys. But now he worked for an industry with a well-earned reputation for hostility, even violence, towards girls and women. I later wrote an impassioned response to the Greta logo on my Facebook page, linking to the company's website, and while my brother never commented, his childhood friend and colleague in the oil sands did. "As a father of two daughters, this absolutely disgusts me," he wrote beneath my post. "But this shouldn't be a reflection of the industry, itself."

I braced myself for the topic of oil and gas to come up at Thanksgiving dinner, probably instigated by my brother, but no one uttered a word about pipelines and protests. Maybe we were all weary due to the uncertainty of the pandemic and just grateful to be under the same roof. We set our political divisions aside for an evening.

I studied Brendan as he conversed with Eric. He appeared content and relaxed in the company of his partner and children, and I knew he was getting closer to his goal of buying land and building a house outside Edmonton. Last month he'd taught his daughter, only three years old, to skate for the first time. He posted a video of her, dressed up in hockey gear, passing the puck to my nephew, with the caption:

No better teacher than her big bro!

After dinner, as we were getting ready to leave, Brendan pulled me aside.

"Treen, I really like the Pirate—and I can tell you do too," he said.

"Shhh, keep your voice down," I said. "Don't call him the Pirate."

"Okay, fine, I really like Eric. He's a good guy."

"I know, Bren. But we're just friends, honestly."

"Think about it, Treen."

"Okay."

"No, seriously, promise me you'll think about it."

"Okay, okay," I said with a laugh. "I will."

The next day, Eric and I drove to Canadian Tire and I bought Max a fishing rod and kid's tackle kit. We drove out to a stocked pond outside Peace River and I taught him how to cast the line. Naturally athletic, he mastered the cast on his second try. He stood on the dock next to Eric, excitedly waiting for a bite. After an hour of reeling in slimy reeds, the boy whined, "Fishing is *boring*."

"Fishing is a lot about learning how to be patient," Eric said calmly. "Things can happen when you least expect it."

Max didn't say anything, but quietly reeled in his line and cast again. I thought of my brother's words about Eric. Eric *was* a good man, and I cared about him, although I sensed our romantic connection wouldn't endure. What I loved, however, was the feeling that my brother was looking out for me again, a form of *mutual protection* as siblings, as he'd done when I was younger. He wanted me to be with a genuinely kind and caring person.

Several days later, Eric packed up his 4Runner to journey west to British Columbia. It would be the last time I saw him before he met the woman he'd eventually marry on Vancouver Island. We hugged for a long while in the driveway and I kissed him on the cheek.

"Safe travels," I said.

"Take care, Trina."

I watched Eric go, my eyes cloudy with emotion, but I never asked him to stay.

Nineteen

In early November, snow drifted across the open fields. Grain stalks poked through the snow like beard stubble. I glided along the edge of the gravel road on cross-country skis, pushing forward, spearing my poles through the hard white crust, heading towards a long driveway that led past a stand of aspen to the old farmhouse. A truck pulled up behind me, idling. A woman was at the wheel, and she rolled down her window to talk to me.

"Do you ski often along this road?" she asked.

"Well, yeah, I live here." I pointed one of my ski poles up the driveway towards the old farmhouse.

"Best be careful, because a few folks saw a black bear digging in the ditch last week," said the man in the passenger seat. "It looked like the bear was digging a den."

"Where exactly?" I asked.

"Just up ahead. There." He pointed past the turnoff to my driveway.

I stared at the slanted, snow-covered earth between the road and a stand of aspen. It was hard to imagine there was a bear nestled into the side of the ditch. Why would a bear choose to den so close to vehicle traffic and the presence of people when, less than a kilometre away, the animal could dig into the valley slopes, prime denning habitat?

Only a small buffer of trees stood between the ditch where a bear might be denned and the farmhouse. Could it be the bear I saw in the grain field last month?

"I *live* here," I said again, a bit dumbfounded. I'd heard stories of bears denning in culverts before, although they were rare.

"We just wanted to warn you," the woman said before they drove off.

I nodded with a straight face, trying to hide my excitement. They obviously had no idea who they were talking to.

The next day, I took Holly and Skyla's dog, Echo, to try to find the den. My boots crunched along the snow-packed road, while the dogs zigzagged in the ditch, following invisible scent trails. We walked to the edge of Skyla's property line where the bush ended and an ocean of grain stalks began. Not a single tree stood in this section of land. Surely, I thought, a bear wouldn't choose to den so close to a field of crops, without protection. I turned back, convinced that the people had been wrong; maybe the bear had actually been digging for roots, or chasing after a ground squirrel. Then I noticed Holly dip her snout into the snow at the edge of the road. She held it there for several long seconds the same way she would when hunting for mice who build tunnelled networks under the snow. If she had been hunting a mouse, she would've pounced with her two front paws and plunged her face deep into the snow. It was how coyotes and foxes hunted too. But Holly pulled back, as if alarmed, and retreated.

The den.

I gingerly touched my boot to the depression and the snow collapsed into a deep cavity. I gasped. I dared to nudge the edge again, and the hole widened into a gaping mouth.

The dogs circled cautiously, reaching with their noses, but wouldn't step any closer. The people had been right: A bear was curled up right under my feet. I could see my bedroom window through the stand of aspen.

I stared dumbly into the den, uncertain what to do. I wondered whether I should alert conservation authorities, or a local biologist, or the municipality, who cleared the snow off the road every few days. Was the bear safe here?

I tied a piece of black cloth around an adjacent fence pole to mark the spot and headed back to the house, where I called a friend, a biologist who had worked on a black bear study in Colorado that used radio collar technology to track females in their dens. My friend would fold and worm his six-foot-tall body into the opening, holding a long jab pole tipped with a tranquilizer needle.

"They aren't really sleeping, you know," he told me. "They're groggy and kind of looking around. Some are more awake than others."

He and his team would tranquilize the bears, pull the mothers out from their dens, along with any cubs, measure their weight and size, and tag the cubs.

"Their dens give off this sweet smell," he said. "Almost like honey."

He wondered whether the bear's choice to den in the ditch was actually an anti-predator strategy. Black bears, he said, sometimes prefer to den closer to human features on the landscape—roads, railways, houses, industrial sites—to use people as protection from other predatory species, including wolves and grizzly bears. It was true—grizzlies sometimes preyed on black bears. My father's colleague had once watched a grizzly bear digging a black bear out of her den, shovelling heaps of dirt with his large front paws, to prey on her.

"Did you hear any breathing down below?" he asked.

"I didn't get *that* close."

"Sometimes you can actually hear them snoring," he said.

I couldn't stop thinking about my friend's words. To listen to a sleeping bear—I couldn't resist.

The following day, I went back to the den and quickly spied the ventilation hole, barely wider than the mouth of a coffee mug. Hoarfrost sparkled around its edges. I crouched and lowered my ear, holding my breath, listening for a heavy exhale. My heart drummed like a male ruffed grouse, louder and faster with every beat. Then a creaking sound from below broke the silence, as though the earth was moving. I fell backwards, found my legs again, and sprinted back to the house, sure that the sound was the bear, shifting, turning over in her den.

That night, I stared out my bedroom window. The snowy branches sparkled under the throw of moonlight. Somehow I felt comforted by knowing that the bear was there, so close, burrowed into the road. As I climbed beneath the covers of my duvet, I thought of the bear, curled in her den, and my loneliness softened.

When winter hooks its claws in the North, snow encases the earth, and bears curl into the warmth of their own bodies—hidden in old tree cavities, dug into slopes, protected beneath layers of soil and snow—and feed off their fat reserves. Bears ask their body to perform evolutionary magic. Their heartbeat slows to a rate of eight to ten beats per minute. They exhale once, maybe twice, in the span of a minute. They do not eat, drink, defecate, or urinate. Bears transform into large yogis beneath the earth, yet they don't enter what's considered "true hibernation." Biologists refer to it as *torpor*. The animals rest. They wait. Their metabolism drops and they conserve and sustain their body's energy resources to endure harsh conditions when food is scarce. Bears possess the ability to practise *hetero-thermia*—Greek *hetero*, "other," and *therme*, "heat"—regulating their body temperature to match that of the surrounding environment.

Scientists believe that torpor may have allowed some mammalian species to survive mass extinction events. The oldest example of torpor has been found in the tusks of *Lystrosaurus*, a 250-million-year-old Antarctic animal that managed to survive the Great Dying, a massive global warming event triggered by volcanic eruptions that occurred 252 million years ago and decimated 96 percent of marine life and 70 percent of terrestrial species.

The black bear was imparting the most vital lesson for surviving a global pandemic: Hunker down through the discomfort. Wait it out.

Every day, I checked in on the den, observing, from afar, the ventilation hole. The dogs tentatively circled at a distance. I was envious of their ability to scent the bear. I imagined the honeyed aroma my friend spoke of. A part of me longed to crawl right in.

The size of the den hole varied with the unpredictable weather throughout December. As the temperature rose above zero, atypically warm for northern Canada, the snow cover melted, widening the mouth and exposing the surrounding dead grass. I wondered how the sudden thaw, a previously unusual occurrence in mid-winter that was becoming increasingly common in Canada's northern boreal, would affect the bear's cycle of dormancy. Would it shake her out of torpor?

Justin had recently told me a story about a local farmer discovering a black bear den along a road close to his property. The farmer lit a smouldering fire beside the den and fanned smoke into the opening to force the bear out. When the bear emerged, the man scared the bear onto his property and pulled the trigger. Perfectly legal. I worried about the same thing happening to my bear neighbour.

One evening, Skyla spotted a black truck idling along the side of the road, close to the den hole. "I thought I should let you know," she said. "Since you're 'the keeper of the den.'"

"Maybe it was just a coincidence he was parked there."

"I don't know. I kinda doubt it," Skyla said with a shrug.

I knew she was right. There wasn't any reason to park in that specific spot. Whoever was in the truck knew about the presence of the bear.

The next day, while driving to town to get groceries, I passed a green-and-white conservation truck heading back up the hill towards the farmhouse. A man in uniform was at the wheel. I whipped a U-turn and followed the truck, but the conservation officer didn't turn down the road that led to the den. I pulled over, feeling sheepish. Once again, taking it too far. Organizing my life around a mystery beneath the earth. Skyla's words echoed in my head: *keeper of the den*.

But I couldn't stop caring about the nameless bear curled beneath the earth. I didn't know how to go back to that mindset of "it's just another black bear."

In January, hoarfrost gripped the limbs of the willows by the bear den. Ice crystals clung to every living and non-living surface: branches, bark, fence post, even the electrical wires that slumped between the power poles. Even my exposed hair and eyelashes, as though I'd applied a thick coat of brilliant white mascara. The whole world had grown white, decadent fur.

I thought of the words of Cree, or Nêhiyawêwin, language consultant and knowledge keeper Jeff Wastesicoot, from Pimicikamak Cree Nation, whom I'd listened to recently as part of a webinar on Bear Teachings co-hosted by Indigenous Climate Action. "We tend to translate a little bit differently than what the English term knows about bear," said Jeff. The Nêhiyawêwin word for bear is *Maskwa*, which is derived from the word for grass, *Maskwaseek*. In Nêhiyawêwin cosmology, bears are born from the grass. "[The English language] refers to it as a carnivore . . . and the word *carnivore* provokes fear. But the law of bear isn't about fear," said Jeff. ". . . It's about respecting distances."

According to Nêhiyawêwin beliefs, bears give birth to their cubs after the first hoarfrost in January. I stared down the ventilation hole laced with crystals and wondered if the bear was a female. Was she curled around two cubs, no bigger than a pair of shoes, groping blindly for their mother's milk?

A friend had suggested I lower a GoPro into the den, but it felt, to my mind, like a violation of privacy. An invasion into the bear's mysterious domain. I didn't want to intrude upon the miraculous act her body was asking her to do.

Rest. Fast. Survive.

I'd never once see the bear, but all winter I dreamt of her as I dreamt of Osa, curled beneath the earth, cubs sliding forth from her body like a powerful river.

PART IV

COMMON GROUND

Twenty

In late April 2021, I boxed up my belongings and boarded a helicopter to fly back to Hawk Tower for my third season in the wildlife corridor. We soared over the evidence of industrial development on the landscape: a forest carved up by cutlines, access roads, wellsites, and cutblocks. The words of a ranger rang in my ears from an orientation held a few days earlier in Peace River. "We're at one hundred and fifty percent capacity for logging in our forest area," he'd said. Since the onset of the COVID-19 pandemic, the price of softwood lumber and plywood had nearly quadrupled, but the available forest for harvesting—that which wasn't already decimated by wildfires or pine beetle infestations—wasn't enough to meet demand. There wasn't enough "fibre," as the industry called it, a convenient euphemism for forest. Over the course of the hour-long flight, I counted the number of cutblocks we flew over. *One, two . . . four . . . six . . . twelve.*

A biologist friend in Peace River had warned me that the area around Hawk Tower would be logged over the course of the winter. Logging companies made their harvests when the spongy muskeg earth was frozen and they could operate heavy-duty machinery without getting stuck or causing extensive damage and erosion to the ecosystem.

"Do you mind following the road leading into the tower?" I asked the pilot through the mic on the radio headset. "I'd like to get a good look at where they've logged."

"Roger that," he said, dropping the machine lower over the trees.

I craned my head to look down through the window as the helicopter emerged into an open cutblock where nearly every tree had been felled. The logging company had harvested softwood tree species, including spruce and pine, only a few kilometres from my tower, and less than half a kilometre from the bears' rub tree. These were the trees that gave protection to the bears, rough bark to rub up against, thick branches for their cubs to climb, and roots under which they could den for the winter. According to the provincial ground rules laid out for timber companies, black bear dens were considered "sensitive sites" and the logging company would be responsible for "making a reasonable effort" to identify the dens of grizzlies and black bears and wolverines, bat hibernacula, raptor nests, and boreal toad breeding sites. For black bears, companies were required by law to leave a forested buffer of one hundred metres around located dens, although it was easy for workers to look the other way. Flagging off sensitive areas would cut into company profits.

The company had spared isolated stands of black poplars in the cutblock, but without a community of living roots holding them up, they'd be exposed to high winds and would inevitably come crashing down. "Every tree in the forest is already spoken for," my dad once told me, referring to the number of "tenures," or harvesting rights, owned by logging companies. If a stand of forest wasn't slated for harvesting today, it would be twenty, forty, sixty years down the road. I've never forgotten his words, a reminder that the forest isn't managed so much for ecosystem health as for harvesting. Even Alberta's Ministry of Forestry had been renamed

Agriculture and Forestry, as though the boreal forest were akin to a Christmas tree farm.

The extensive harvesting was, in part, what was fuelling uncontrollable mega fires every fire season. Logging companies, mandated to regenerate the harvested cutblocks within two years of cutting, typically replanted a mono crop of softwood species, like pine and spruce, which are also considered highly flammable, pyrogenic trees. They burn hot and fast, and contribute to the rapid spread of wildfires.

I looked down on the massacred forest and felt a profound sense of loss. I thought of the orphaned black bear cub that my dad had brought home when I was five years old, the same bear whose mother had been crushed in the den by logging equipment, and worried about the female bears I'd grown so fond of watching: Osa, Big Mama, and even Osa's mother.

I prayed that they were safe.

In the months leading up to my departure for Hawk Tower, old tensions between my brother and me were, once again, surfacing. We argued incessantly about COVID-19, oil and gas, pipelines, and protests. Hackles up. Claws out. Teeth bared.

On his first day in office in January 2021, US president Joe Biden had revoked the permit for the Keystone XL Pipeline, which would have covered nearly two thousand kilometres from Hardisty, Alberta, to Nebraska. The Keystone project was a cornerstone of the Alberta government's goal to triple production in the oil sands. Premier Kenney called the move a "gut punch" and characterized it as a direct attack on trade between the US and Canada.

It was obvious to me that my brother, as an oil and gas worker, was feeling increasingly vulnerable. He viewed the shutdown of the

Keystone pipeline as a personal attack on his job security and well-being. He blamed the cancelled project on the rise of anti-pipeline protests orchestrated by Indigenous communities and environmentalists alike.

"What do these people think will fuel their cars, or heat their homes at minus thirty?" he complained, shaking his head.

"People are worried about the environmental consequences, Bren, and the speed at which we're pumping out carbon into the atmosphere," I pointed out. "Climate change is real. I mean, look at these crazy fire seasons we're getting. You can't say it's not happening."

"So better we use Saudi-produced oil? At least Canadian oil is *ethical oil*," he said. "These protesters need to give their fucking heads a shake," he added, his voice rising an octave.

"Canadian oil is definitely not ethical oil, Brendan," I sputtered, thinking of Fort McKay and Fort Chipewyan, who'd been harmed by environmental contamination and high cancer rates, and the community of Little Buffalo, only an hour's drive from Peace River, that suffered the consequences of the pipeline leak and a 4.5-million-litre oil spill.

Shortly after that conversation, Brendan began sporting a black hoodie with I ❤ CANADIAN OIL AND GAS printed on the front. I felt a shot of anger every time I saw him wearing it, although I tried not to react.

I reminded myself that my brother was shouldering a great deal of responsibility for his family. He was in the process of negotiating with the bank to try to get a mortgage on a piece of residential land on the outskirts of Edmonton. He wanted his kids to be closer to the land, he'd told me, able to experience nature in the way we had as kids. Money was extremely tight, however, and he was dependent on the flow of oil. The cost of land had skyrocketed across Canada. I empathized with my brother's dilemma: to afford to purchase land meant taking on work that degraded it elsewhere. For the vast majority of his career, the oil and gas industry had been his only employer. I'm not sure he saw any real alternatives that would pay the equivalent.

The tensions between us were only intensified by the wider societal unrest growing in Alberta—and across Canada—in response to the COVID pandemic. In Peace River, a group of people who were opposed to COVID safety measures of masking, vaccinations, and social lockdowns began illegally gathering at a café called Karen's Kitchen. They organized weekly convoys of vehicles that drove up and down the streets of Peace River, honking their horns and flashing their emergency lights, with duct-taped signs that read *COVID IS A HOAX, END THE LOCKDOWN, THIS IS ABOUT TYRANNY VS. FREEDOM*. One afternoon, while driving home from the grocery store, I merged onto a road, unintentionally threading myself into the convoy. I angrily put my mask on so I wouldn't be identified with the protesters. These were the same people who stuck *FUCK TRUDEAU* stickers to their vehicle bumpers.

My brother wasn't amongst the protesters, but he didn't hide his frustrations with the mandatory public safety measures, either. He railed against the efficacy of masks to protect against the spread of the virus, and complained that my nephew wasn't allowed to play hockey and my niece couldn't practise gymnastics.

He never subscribed to the COVID IS A HOAX protest movement, nor would he refuse the vaccine, but that winter he'd occasionally come back to my parents' place after a shift at work, cough, and make a joke of it. "Uh-oh, it's COVID," he sneered. I felt as though I hardly knew Brendan in these moments. We'd both been raised by the same parents, who'd always shown empathy and care for our neighbours, friends, and community. We'd been raised by the same father, a biologist, a *scientist*. My dad never said anything, but I imagined it frustrated him. He stayed quiet, perhaps, as a means of not triggering a fight.

I can't remember when Brendan started saying, "Fuck Trudeau," but it grated on me every time he said it. "Fuck Trudeau" felt like toxic bro-code, like a handshake to indicate belonging to the growing number of Canadians who were protesting against the COVID safety measures. The saying was fast becoming a beloved slogan of the far right and populist movement in Canada, appearing on truck bumpers, written on protest signs, and commercially emblazoned on clothing, stickers, and coffee mugs. #FUCKTRUDEAU exploded on the Twittersphere.

"The COVID lockdowns need to stop," my brother said. "This is bankrupting small business owners. Do you have any idea of how hard it's been being a parent through this?"

"No, I can't pretend to know how difficult it's been for you guys," I said. "But you do realize that the measures are in place to prevent the hospitals from being overwhelmed, don't you? And maybe you're healthy, you'd be fine if you got COVID, but there are many others who are at risk of getting really sick—or, worse . . ."

"Your job hasn't been impacted by the pandemic, you sit on your ass alone in a tower all day! You have no clue how hard it's been on people," Brendan retorted. "Just wait and see how these mandates are going to affect the number of cases of mental illness and suicide."

I brushed off my brother's words. It sounded exactly like what Premier Jason Kenney was saying in the media to justify the province's more lax regulations on COVID.

Despite the progress my brother and I had made in recent years, on learning how to be in one another's lives again, the COVID-19 pandemic erected new divisions between us, ones that felt far too vast to bridge.

It was a relief to escape the intensifying social and political tensions at home and burrow back into my solitude at the fire tower.

I was desperate to see Osa again. I scanned the forest from the cupola, searching for her familiar shade of black, hoping she'd survived the winter. But on May 1, the same calendar day that she'd appeared in the last two years, her trail stood empty.

"Where *is* she?" I fretted to Justin over the phone.

"Bears are always moving according to their own rhythm," he reminded me.

"I know, but I'm worried about her."

"How's the new tower dog?" Justin asked, trying to change the subject.

In late March, only a few days before my thirty-sixth birthday, I'd picked up an eight-week-old, blue-eyed Siberian husky from a farm outside Fort St. John in northwestern British Columbia. She was a wolfish thing—dominant-spirited, inquisitive, and brave. I hoped that Holly, now twelve years old, would help to impart some bush smarts to the young dog whom I called "Sof."

In early May, while out for a walk, Holly stopped to nose at something ahead on the road. The puppy trotted up behind her to investigate, following in the older dog's footsteps. I bent down and found the dogs sniffing at a long tuft of dusty black fur. The tuft was several inches long. I knew immediately: *bear.*

The following day, Holly and I ran the three kilometres to the bears' rub pole, where I set up the trail camera for the season. I was relieved to see that the energy company still hadn't replaced the pole that the bears had whittled down into the shape of an hourglass. "That's probably the most impressive rub tree I've ever seen," my father had admitted to me over the winter. The pole stank of the bears' strong musk. I noticed a few black and blond hairs snagged in slivers of wood and guessed they belonged to Oscar and Canelo, the large cinnamon male.

A week later, a bear finally appeared in the cutblock, and my heart soared. Oscar was even larger than I remembered. As I stepped outside, Sof let out a high-pitched whine from inside the cabin. Oscar's head shot up and I wondered if he thought it was a moose or elk calf. He power-walked upslope and I retreated into the cabin. I noticed the tuft of missing fur on his ears; he must've rubbed the hair clean off. The big male sauntered up to the electric fence and touched his nose to the top wire, but the electric shock barely registered. He twitched as though it was nothing more than an irritating horsefly, then ambled off.

He and Canelo, the large cinnamon male, appeared intermittently in the cutblock over the next week, sharing the space without ever crossing paths, like shift workers.

I wondered about the females—Osa, her mother, and Big Mama. They were nowhere to be seen.

"The females are probably hiding their cubs if the males are out patrolling like that," my dad reassured me. "They'll do everything to keep their cubs safe from harm."

In late May, as I watched for smoke from the cupola, I heard the sound of a branch breaking below. Hope rose up in my chest; I knew it would be her. I glanced down from the tower and saw Osa standing at the mouth of her favourite trail, surveying the slope.

"There you are, girl," I called down to her, as if no time had passed between us.

This was the third time I'd witnessed this moment of the bear's emergence, a ritual that I'd come to anticipate with great affection. Osa craned her head to look up at me. I wondered if she could scent the addition to our family: the puppy. Glancing down, I saw that Holly and Sof were both curled up, sleeping in the shade of the cabin, seemingly unaware of the bear.

Osa was alone—there didn't seem to be any sign of a cub. I felt a pang of disappointment, but knew that I shouldn't have been surprised. She was only in her fourth year. Maybe next spring she'd emerge with cubs.

Osa walked lazily to the shade cast by the old spruce, the same tree she'd climbed as a cub, and flopped down on her belly. She appeared so content, resting there in the dappled light, closing her eyes. The bear heaved over onto her side, dozing off.

The puppy woke up and must've scented the bear, for she trotted over to the electric fence and peered down at Osa with great intrigue. Sof glanced back at Holly, who slept beneath the tower, as if to confirm, *You mean we are cool with this big, black sleeping dog?* After a few minutes Sof lost interest in the bear and curled up into a ball in the grass.

"Good *dog*," I whispered from up in the tower, a bit incredulous to be gazing down at the scene of a sleeping bear and my sleeping dogs.

I sent a photo to my father.

Wow, he wrote back. *Osa must feel very comfortable with you to fall asleep in the open like that.*

She dozed for nearly half an hour, swatting away the flies with a heavy paw, her hind leg lifting to scratch her belly. I turned down the volume on the two-way radio so as not to disturb her. My eyes welled up, watching the bear. How could I say that I cared about Osa as though she were my sister? I would hesitate to say it out loud to someone, although it was true. I was conscious that Osa wasn't there because of love, or friendship, or sentimentality, but that she felt safe enough to sleep in my presence—and in the company of my dogs—and that I felt safe with her nearby. The recognition of her vulnerability made me feel somehow *responsible* for the bear, responsible for my actions and reactions towards her. I wanted the bear to feel relaxed and safe in my company.

I assumed that Osa was back to stay, but she disappeared into the forest as suddenly as she'd come.

———

Oscar abandoned the clearing to the smaller male, Canelo. I didn't mind. I preferred the calm demeanour of the cinnamon bear. He lay down on his belly in the cool grass as he fed, a way to lower his body temperature and conserve energy.

I felt a sense of quiet normalcy, watching Canelo. I had accepted that the bears belonged on the landscape just like any other species—American robins, white-tailed deer, snowshoe hares. Species that didn't elicit the same emotional response as a bear did. Like good neighbours, or even roommates, we'd become familiar and predictable to the other. By understanding one another's needs and patterns, and the ways in which we moved on the land, we could share an overlapping domain. Although I hadn't dropped my guard or forgotten what was at stake.

The bear had grown so comfortable with my presence that he no longer wandered away when I climbed down the tower. I hand-washed my clothes in a basin using an old scrub board, then weeded the garden beds and fixed the eavestrough that had blown down in a wild thunderstorm. While I worked and went about my routine, I spoke to the cinnamon bear gently, in a singsong voice.

"Hey handsome, I see you there," I crooned. "Please don't mind me. I don't mean you any harm."

The bear did nothing but feast. A response that felt, to me, like a form of acceptance.

I thought of Don, the former lookout, who'd told me that he often talked to the bears, a behaviour I'd initially labelled as crazy. But three years later, here I was now, speaking to Canelo the same way I might speak to my dogs, having learned that it wasn't the words that mattered so much as my intonation or the intent behind them.

I'd always been taught to yell or speak gruffly with bears, but this could be interpreted as threatening, even antagonistic. Bears are responsive to voice, much like dogs. A calm voice can reassure them: You're safe where you are.

Charlie Russell, an Alberta conservationist, writes in *Grizzly Heart*, his memoir about living closely with brown bears, or grizzly bears, on the Kamchatka Peninsula in Russia—a region with the highest density of brown bears in the world—that a soft, high-pitched voice is soothing to bears and can de-escalate an aggressive encounter. His partner, Maureen, was capable of calming even the wariest of bears with her sugary tone. Russell related this observation to what he learned about Indigenous peoples in Kamchatka and their belief that women, as foragers and berry pickers, were able to more harmoniously coexist with bears than men. Women were, perhaps, less of a threat to the bears' safety, Russell posited. He marvelled at the traditional practice of ensuring an old woman would stay to watch over a cabin, knowing that the bears would respect the old woman, and therefore the cabin.

Many Indigenous cultures, I was learning, speak of a psychic connection between women and bears. In southwestern Yukon, the Southern Tutchone, an Athabaskan-speaking group, tell the story about the Woman Who Married a Bear. In the story, a young woman, while out harvesting wild rhubarb, steps over a pile of bear scat, breaking a taboo. She speaks badly of bear, yet another cultural taboo. A male bear then confronts the young woman and steals her away into the earth, where they live together and produce bear cubs. In the spring, the woman's brothers locate the den and kill the bear. But before the bear dies, he asks of his wife: Put my head in a high place. She obliges. When the woman returns to her human village, however, she grows fur and long, pointed claws and the community teases her. She and her cubs run away to fully transform into bears.

The story symbolizes the close familial kinship between bears and the Southern Tutchone peoples; there are practices of respect to follow when living with bears.

Over the winter I'd met a grizzly bear guide named Brad Josephs who'd worked on the Katmai Peninsula in Alaska for over twenty years.

"I think women make better bear guides than guys do," Brad mused.

"Why?"

He thought about it for several long seconds.

"With women, it's less about ego," he said reflectively. "So they're able to more fully meet the bear where they're at."

For Brad, it wasn't even about the words spoken. It was about what was inside a person when they encountered a bear. He'd come to believe that bears have telepathic abilities: They can intuit a person's inner thoughts. If you are angry, aggressive, or fearful of them, he said, they will pick up on it.

On the evening of the summer solstice, the longest day of the year, Canelo grazed on the northern slope, nearly immersed in the lush grass. The way the light struck his golden fur, he'd never been more beautiful to me. I sat outside in a meditative state for what felt like hours, as the mosquitoes haloed us both. If Osa was my sister, I mused, maybe Canelo was like a psychic lover—like a husband bear whom I could vow to love and respect. In that strange solstice light, a part of me longed to grow fur and long, pointed claws, and tunnel away with the bear into the earth.

In late June, the temperatures began to soar and the wildfire hazard skyrocketed. Low, bruised clouds churned and thundered to the north of the tower. One evening, after a long shift up in the cupola on extreme fire watch, I stood on my picnic table to photograph the sun, yellow as an egg yolk, setting behind the veil of the blue storm. The mosquitoes feasted on my exposed skin. A strand of lightning shot down, forty kilometres away. I felt a ripple of adrenalin, standing there, exposed, absorbing the energy of the chaotic sky.

Then I turned south and saw the bears, blended into the shadows—a mother and a tiny cub. My heart palpitated as the sky groaned and lightning pulsed in the distance. I crept towards the edge of the slope to get a better look, but I could barely make them out in the dim light. The cub scampered along the edge of the bush, darting in and out of view. The mother was buried deep in the dandelions. I tried to make out an identifying feature, but it was too dark to tell who it was.

The mother bear had probably turned nocturnal, I realized, feeding under the safety of the night to avoid interactions with me and the dogs and the male bears. I remembered my dad's words about how risk-averse mother bears of young cubs tended to be.

I tossed in my bed that night, wondering who it could be. Osa's mother? Big Mama? I hoped they'd come back the following morning. At the crack of dawn, I tiptoed back to the slope to look down, but the bears were long gone.

Several days later, after a long stint up in the sky, I longed to stretch out my cramped legs. Holly and I set out to run the grassy road that had grown swollen with sedges and clover. The puppy cried mournfully from her crate in the cabin, but she was too young to run long distances. A kilometre away from the cabin, we came around a bend and Holly halted a few paces ahead. I saw the bear at the grassy edge of the road.

"Oh, hello there," I called down to the bear, who was maybe fifteen metres away. The long grass made the bear appear small. A juvenile, I thought.

I assumed the bear would get a good scent of us, meander off, and that we'd be able to continue along. But the bear stood up on its hind legs and I realized my mistake. The bear was much larger than

I'd thought, and the chest was all black, no white blaze, so I immediately ruled out that it could be Osa.

I noticed the familiar caramel-coloured muzzle and recognized the bear as Osa's mother. Then the grass beneath her feet stirred and out popped a tiny black cub.

"Oh, shit."

I took a step back. This was my first close encounter on the road with a mother and cub. I'd broken the golden rule: Whatever you do, don't surprise a mother bear with cubs. People say that black bear mothers are harmless, but it's not always true. In the decades he spent working with bears, Charlie Russell was attacked only once, by a defensive mother black bear with a yearling cub. The bear bit his buttock, but Russell's son, a teenager, beat the bear off with a stick, and they survived the attack.

"I'm sorry, Mama," I apologized to the bear, trying to keep my voice as relaxed and non-threatening as possible. "We'll get out of your hair now."

I stepped backwards slowly and called for Holly to follow my lead, and she obliged. Later, a friend would remark to me: "Wow, there's no way my dog wouldn't have chased the cub." It was exactly how cubs could be easily separated and orphaned from their mothers, or how we might've triggered a defensive attack on the part of the mother bear.

Osa's mother gathered up our scent and collapsed back down onto all fours. She walked off into the tall grass with a stiff-legged stomp, expressing her discontent that I had displaced the family from their grazing spot. Then, not one but *three* cubs shot across the road after her.

I grinned down at Holly.

"Three cubs!"

Although my body was desperate for a good run, I turned around and headed back to the cabin to give Osa's mother and her cubs the space they deserved. Producing enough milk to sustain the three cubs would be an extraordinarily demanding task for the bear. I wouldn't run or hike on the road for the next week. It was a way of showing Osa's mother respect, a peace offering of sorts, to make up for my former aggression towards her.

A week later, early in the morning, I bent over my task of weeding a bed strewn with a tangle of poppies, peas, and dill. I looked up and saw Osa at the bottom of the slope, feasting on the tall grass. It was as if she'd never left. I wiped the dirt off my hands and crouched at the top of the hill to watch her.

"Welcome back, girl," I called out gently to the bear.

Suddenly, there was a ripple of movement in the long grass and a small cub's head surfaced above the greenery.

"Do you have a cub?" I squealed. I did a double take of the bear's rabbity ears, the distinct blond muzzle. Yes, it was definitely Osa.

Osa had a cub! I felt the same rush of joy as when I heard the news about the birth of my brother's daughter.

My mind flew back to the day Osa had dozed alone on the slope. I'd assumed she hadn't had a cub, but I realized that she'd probably cached it in a nearby tree to investigate the clearing around my tower. Biologists refer to these trees, typically mature aspen or spruce, as "sanctuary," or "babysitting trees." A recent study in Ontario found that black bears prefer to den within thirty metres of sanctuary trees, so their cubs can emerge and immediately find safety. Maybe Osa had just needed a break on that day. She'd seemed so exhausted, napping in the sun like a sleep-deprived mother. I liked this version of the story, but the truer one was that she'd probably left her cub to scout for food and assess the risk.

The cub scampered through the grass, bobbing in and out of sight. He sprinted beneath his mother's belly, making a move for a teat to nurse, and she turned on him, nipping the cub hard, as if to say, *Not now!* The cub jumped back and bawled his displeasure.

Bears deal in tough love, setting hard boundaries with their cubs to teach them the necessary survival skills. They do what they must in order to survive—and there's little room for nuance. "A bear will never lie to you," my friend Karine Genest, a polar bear guide whom I'd met over the winter, had told me recently. "They aren't like people in that way; they're easier to read. In a sense, they're more predictable to be around." The best way to learn about bear behaviour, Karine said, was to observe bears interacting with other bears, the way they express what they want and don't want with their whole bodies: their ears, position of head and jaw, their body posture, vocalizations, gait, and behaviours. With bears, there's rarely ambiguity. They won't hold back. They aren't afraid to tell you exactly what's on their mind. With people, it's often so much more difficult to know where you stand, said Karine. There's so many things that can go unsaid.

As I watched Osa with her cub, Sof trotted over and sat beside me on the hill. Osa's cub caught wind of the puppy and stood up on his hind legs. He craned his neck around, nose quivering, as though memorizing our scent: a hairless two-legged one and her wolf pup. I noticed a single white crescent moon on his chest.

I decided to call him Osito, Spanish for "Little Bear."

Twenty-One

Despite the heated arguments we'd had that spring, my brother had begged me to drive down to the city in April to see my niece and nephew before flying back to the tower.

"Cmon, Treen," he said. "You haven't seen them in ages."

It was true. The pandemic had stolen so much time from us. My niece was somehow nearly four years old. Brianna could now tip-toe across a balancing beam and do somersaults. She could string together words in complete sentences. I'd missed so much of it. She was developing a personality different from my nephew, my brother said. Brianna was more introverted in her activities, he told me, enraptured by her own imagination, playing with her dolls, and drawing and painting pictures of animals she loved: cats, dogs— even bears, he laughed.

I worried that I was missing out on bonding with my niece at a critical time in her life—that magical period when children tap into their naive biology—so I conceded to my brother's pleas. My nephew greeted me at the door. I didn't take my mask off, however, deciding that it was one safety measure I could try to follow.

"Auntie!" Max squealed, hugging my torso tightly.

Brianna ran behind him, but stopped dead in her tracks when she saw me.

The mask, I realized. It was as if she didn't recognize me. As if I'd become a stranger to her. My heart dropped a bit. It had been so many months since we'd seen each other, probably longer, even, in a child's mind.

"It's *me*," I called to her gently, briefly lowering my mask, smiling.

Brianna nodded shyly, finally recognizing me, and wrapped her arms around my thighs.

"Hey Treen!" Brendan boomed as he came to the front entrance. "Oh my god, you better take off that mask!" He frowned. "I don't want any masks in the house."

"Bren, my roommate is a social worker—she's a front-line worker," I said, muffled through the mask.

My brother's face softened at the mention of my roommate, who had grown up in the same neighbourhood that we did. He'd been in the same grade as her older sister.

He shrugged. "Okay. That makes sense."

I relaxed into the company of my brother's family, playing mini-hockey with my nephew in the basement the same way Bren and I played as kids, and colouring with my niece at the kitchen table. At dinner, the kids sat distracted with Peppa Pig on the television screen. Max poked at Brianna and she began to whine her displeasure.

"Enough fighting already!" Brendan scolded them, turning off the television. "Eat your food, please."

Brendan drew a bath for my niece and gently shampooed her hair and sponged her back as she splashed and giggled. I tried to corral my wild nephew, who jumped on his bed, laughing hysterically, hyped up on having me sleep over. As my brother towelled Brianna off, Max fired a shot at my brother's backside with a Nerf gun.

"Hey! I told you to get your pyjamas on," Brendan said sternly. "It's time for bed."

Later, with the kids tucked in and lights out, I went downstairs and sat across from my brother at the kitchen counter. Amanda, who'd recently gone back to school, was studying for an exam in their bedroom. He made me a cup of jasmine tea.

"It's so hard being a parent," he admitted. "I get so frustrated with them sometimes, Treen. They test my patience, you know? I get angry and I shouldn't."

I saw the dark half moons under Brendan's eyes and the sag in his shoulders as he leaned over the counter. With the land purchase on the horizon and the goal of starting home construction later in the fall, he was visibly exhausted.

"You need to give yourself more credit, Bren. You're doing a good job."

I didn't often praise my brother, but I meant it.

He paused and pulled anxiously on his earlobe. That unconscious shared trait of ours.

"I'm getting older," he said reflectively.

It was a rare sort of thing for my brother to say, almost philosophical—certainly, vulnerable—and I wasn't entirely clear what he meant by it. In hindsight, I wished I'd asked him to explain himself. But I thought about his words for days after, how they seemed, to me, indicative of the ways in which he'd grown and matured. I wondered if what he really meant by those three words *I'm getting older* was that he'd been through enough to know what was at stake—what really mattered and, at the end of the day, what was worth fighting for.

Proximity ignites empathy. Being in my brother's home, watching him parent, I could empathize with that which stressed him: providing for his children through the pandemic and struggling towards his goal of building a home on the land where they'd feel safe.

We were both getting older. We were both passing into a new stage of adulthood, one in which we could accept our imperfections—our contradictions. "If there is a stage at which an individual life becomes truly adult, it must be when one grasps the irony in its unfolding and accepts responsibility for a life lived in the midst of such paradox," writes Barry Lopez in *Arctic Dreams*. "One must live in the middle of contraction because if all contraction were eliminated at once life would collapse."

When I saw beyond the one-dimensional lens of my brother as an oil worker, as someone whose political beliefs I didn't agree with, I realized it's possible to love someone without agreeing with them, or even fully understanding them. My brother and I might never really know one another, but we could practise love and empathy for the other.

We could learn to lean into the paradox of that which polarized us.

In early July, temperatures soared in western Canada, surpassing seasonal averages by more than 20 degrees, and reaching record highs beyond 40 degrees Celsius. Meteorologists were calling the phenomenon a "heat dome," resulting from a high-pressure ridge which created an atmospheric lid that sealed over a region and forced hot air down.

Osa and her cub took refuge in the boughs of the old spruce, sleeping in the shade of the branches. I looked down sympathetically from the tower at them. They must've been melting under their heavy fur coats. The grass wilted under the hot sun. My rain barrels drained until they echoed bone-dry. It was so sweltering up in my Plexiglas cupola that no matter how much water I guzzled, I climbed down at the end of the day with swollen feet and hands, a symptom of heat stroke.

The heat dome was considered a once-in-a-thousand-years event; however, due to anthropogenic climate change, scientists posited that it could occur far more frequently—every five to ten years.

Even at my northern latitude, the temperature cracked 30 degrees day after day, breaking weather records that dated back to the 1960s. Farmers' crops sizzled in the fields, the extreme heat stunting the growth of perennial grasses, drying up dugouts, streams, and creek beds, and baking seeds before they'd even germinated. Millions of acres of wheat fields failed entirely. The community of Lytton, British Columbia, recorded the hottest temperature in Canada's history, 49.6 degrees Celsius, and the following day, June 30, a wildfire broke out. Fuelled by violent winds, the fire tore through the small town, razing the community to the ground. Many people barely escaped from their homes before losing everything they owned to the blaze.

The bears disappeared during the day, sleeping in the shaded forest, burrowing into the cool muskeg and peat moss. Moose swam out to the middle of the nearby pond, immersing their huge bodies in water right up to their heads, their antlers rising out of the water like floating driftwood.

I watched the forest wither under the force of extreme heat. The young, knee-high spruce seedlings turned a rusty shade. When I touched their boughs, the needles fell clean off. The spongy mosses, normally drenched with moisture, dried out so they crunched underfoot. Some of the leaves on the trembling aspen were already turning yellow, two months early. The wild blueberry plants that grew interspersed with Labrador tea in a boggy area around my tower should've produced tiny green berries by now, but the plants threw all their energy into their leaves. They were irregularly tall but void of blueberries. Not good, I thought. Dangerous, in fact. I worried what effect a failing berry crop would have on the bears.

One afternoon, Osa's mother appeared along the mouth of the road. Two of her small cubs tumbled in play, clumsily balancing on their hind legs, swatting at one another. The larger of the two cubs had a white triangle on his chest. I looked for the third cub and assumed he was hidden out of sight. The cubs began to pounce in the grass, bouncing around like popcorn in hot oil. I looked closer through binoculars. *Grasshoppers*. The heat dome had created the ideal conditions for grasshoppers to thrive. Female grasshoppers bury their eggs, which can remain dormant for many years, waiting for the heat necessary, ideally temperatures in the range of 30 degrees Celsius, to hatch. The cub with the white triangle blaze palmed a grasshopper to his mouth and munched on his catch.

The third cub did not appear.

I felt a wave of sadness, realizing that the cub had probably died. While I couldn't know the cause of death, I speculated that Osa's mother, an older bear, didn't have the fat reserves required to produce enough milk to sustain three growing cubs.

Not in the face of a once-in-a-thousand-years heat dome.

During this sweltering period, I mapped out a bear family tree in my imagination: Osa's mother, the grandmother, and her two surviving cubs, along with her daughter, Osa, and Osa's cub, Osito. Black bears, I was learning, are highly matriarchal in their movements on the landscape. Mothers carve out space in their habitats for their daughters, a way of ensuring access to food, safety, and reproductive success. They hold space for one another.

Males are not so lucky. They have to take more risks to venture out into unfamiliar territory, trying to find their place on the landscape to compete for food resources and breeding rights. Big, dominant males, like Oscar, often control a territory and will push smaller, less dominant males out.

"Bears have relationships," Kevin Van Tighem had once shared with me. "They know one another. They know who to avoid and who not to avoid. Mothers remember their daughters and sometimes actually hang out together. It's a community of animals out there."

I noticed that the two sets of mother bears had remarkably different parenting strategies. Osa's mother, a grandmother with much more experience, seemed more tolerant of her cubs' curiosity, allowing them to explore at a greater distance. The two cubs moved in a wider arc around her, seemingly egging one another on in their daredevil pursuits.

As a new mother, Osa seemed to be more cautious. She and Osito stuck together like two peas in a pod. Without a sibling for her cub to play with, Osa fulfilled the role of mother and sister. She'd playfully swat at her cub and topple him over. But mostly she grazed and Osito mimicked her, growing fat and fuzzy.

I showed my dad a photo of Osa's cub. "The cub is probably a male," he said. "Males tend to be a bit bigger. And he's a healthy-looking cub." He was significantly larger than his two cousins, having no sibling to compete with for his mother's milk.

It seemed as though Osa and her mother were using the clearing around my cabin—and the proximity to me and the dogs—as a kind of nursery, or daycare, to safely graze and watch over their young. I recalled watching Big Mama lie on her back to nurse her two cubs, only metres downslope from my cabin. At the time, I'd thought it strange, but now it all made sense to me. I wondered if the mother bears were using my presence as a protective buffer from threats to their cubs, much like the bear who'd chosen to den so close to my house over the winter. Predator species such as wolves, fishers, wolverines, and cougars wouldn't risk coming so close to the scent of a human and her dogs.

This theory, whether true or not, made me feel a bit like an Auntie to the cubs. It was an important role that I was growing into with my own brother's children.

"If something ever happens to us, would you be the guardian of the kids?" he'd asked me during my visit in April.

I'd been startled by the question, not for the responsibility of caring for the children, but for what it would mean: losing my brother. Even though being with Brendan often felt tense and loaded, after everything we'd been through together, the years we spent estranged from each other, I didn't want to consider a future without him in it.

"I hope you're not planning on going anywhere any time soon."

"Of course not, but I mean, we need to have a plan in place," he said quickly. "Mom and Dad are getting older. And, well, the kids just love you."

"You don't even need to ask," I'd said to my brother. "I would be there in a heartbeat."

"Yeah, well, if it happened, your life would look very different. You'd be back at the hockey arena every weekend," he said with a laugh.

I felt a strong maternal pull with Brianna and Max, a sense of responsibility for their care and development. I wanted to share the best parts of me with them: my life as a writer, a potter, a woman who lived with her two dogs in the woods. I hoped I could help teach them that there are different ways to live and find meaning in life. I wanted to help them build their own relationship with the land and the wild ones who dwelled there.

Over the winter, my niece and I had bundled up in parkas and snow pants and walked down to the frozen Peace River. I suggested that we pretend to be penguins and she looked up at me with a wild, happy gleam in her eye as we waddled and slid on the ice.

I taught my nephew how to make a mug out of clay. He rolled the clay into long snakes that he wound round and round to form the base of the vessel. The boy who typically vibrated with energy and athleticism sat quietly as he worked. He looked up at me and said reflectively, "I like how I feel when I'm doing this."

"How do you feel?" I asked him, and he thought for several seconds about it.

"Calm."

I had never known this kind of love before. The love my brother and I felt for the children seemed to hold the fragile, unreconciled parts of our relationship intact.

In late July, Brendan called me from his work truck. He was en route to a gas well-site outside Peace River, down the Harmon Valley road. He put me on speaker so I could hear the sounds of the truck bouncing over the potholed gravel road. I put him on speaker and I imagined that he could hear my voice echoing in the octagonal dome of the cupola.

"Hey Treen, you gotta thank your colleagues for me!" His voice blasted the phone speaker. "They just saved about a dozen of our sites from getting burnt over by a wildfire."

I'd heard the commotion over the radio the day before, when a holdover fire broke out and spread through coniferous forest south of Peace River. Holdovers could be deadly and come out of nowhere like zombie fires. Typically caused by lightning, they ignited and burned low, out of sight, smouldering deep in the peat. Under hot, windy conditions, they could take off at terrifying speeds.

Fortunately, the lookout called in the black smoke and a fire-fighting crew, staged on five-minute getaway at her fire tower, got up in the air within minutes to action the blaze. The fire had exploded to the size of thirty-four hectares—about the equivalent of fourteen football fields—within an hour. Tanker planes dropped abundant loads of retardant clay to box in the fire, and ground crews pumped water from beaver ponds to quell the flames.

"Seriously, though, you guys saved our asses out here," my brother said. "That could've been real bad for us if that fire burnt over all our sites. These wildfires are becoming fucking *insane*!"

"Yeah, well, that's why they pay us to do what we do," I replied with a shrug, inwardly beaming at my brother's words of appreciation.

I was struck by Brendan's recognition of the worsening wildfire crisis, which threatened everyone, no matter their social or political views. But also, our jobs, starkly different on paper, had suddenly overlapped in practice. I admitted that my responsibility as a lookout wasn't to protect only communities and wildlife, but also the values of resource-extractive industries: logging, mining, and, yes, even oil and gas. Even if this made me feel extremely ethically conflicted, I could acknowledge my own complicity. It was complex—we were both tangled up in the same resource-driven, capitalist system that degraded the land we loved and was fueling the climate crisis.

It reminded me of a time I'd asked Tim, the seasoned ranger and former lookout, why Alberta was one of the last places in Canada with such a robust fire tower program—when every other province had decommissioned their towers—and he'd answered me, point-blank.

"That's easy," he said, summing it up in four words. "Because we have oil."

Twenty-Two

From inside the cabin, I heard a sound that belonged but was irregular enough in the forest that when you heard it, you'd sit up and take notice. I held my breath and listened hard. The sound of a cub braying at the top of its lungs. I immediately thought of Osito and his cousins. Seconds later, a sound so loud and awful that it could only be human-made—an air horn bellowed through the forest. Hearing the air horn go off was like an alarm bell indicating: *Someone's here.* My first instinct was concern, not for whoever fired off the air horn, but for the bears.

I grabbed my climbing harness off the hook by the door and rushed outside to sprint up the ladder. The cub's panicked cry echoed up from the forest to the north of me.

From above, I saw a ripple of movement in the young aspen in the cutblock. The tightly knit trees stood at two metres high. Humans, or bears? I heard the crashing of branches, someone bushwhacking a path through dense brush. Way too noisy to be bears, I thought. Then I saw a flash of fluorescent yellow, a colour that definitely didn't belong.

"HEY!" I shouted down.

Silence. The trees stopped moving. I tried again.

"HEY!"

The aspen shook and branches crashed as the maker of sound emerged from the bush onto a trail that ran parallel to the cutblock, only metres away from the clearing of meadow around my yard.

"Hello?" A woman dressed in a yellow-and-orange safety vest sheepishly hollered up to me.

"What's going on down there?" I asked, just as a man staggered out from the bush, behind the woman. I guessed they were forestry surveyors contracted by the timber company who held the harvesting lease here.

"We had a run-in with a mother and cub!"

Mother and *cub*. Osa and Osito.

"I guess you heard the air horn," she added.

"Umm, yeah, I heard it!" I said, not masking the disapproval in my voice. "Kind of hard not to hear it when you're practically in my backyard. Those bears *live* here! The mother is a very calm bear, but you probably caught her off guard."

I could hear myself. I sounded just like Don, the former lookout at Hawk Tower, who'd scolded me the day I called for the helicopter to chase Osa and her family away. *Those bears are peaceful*, he'd texted me. I'm sure the workers were exchanging looks with one another, like, who is this crazy person alone in the bush talking about the bears like they're her friends.

"What are you doing here?" I asked.

"We parked our quad at your gate and came on foot," the woman said, motioning down the road where a locked gate kept out unwanted ATV traffic, rare as it was. "We're doing a regen survey."

A "regen," or regeneration, survey involved measuring and monitoring the progress of young tree seedlings, sowed by tree planters in the year following the logging. The timber company would measure the progress of regrowth every few years until, decades later, the area would be slated once again for logging.

"You didn't think it would be a good idea to come up to my cabin to let me know you'd be working here today?" I let the question hang.

Had they come up to introduce themselves, I could have warned them about the two sets of mother bears with cubs. The workers exchanged a few words between themselves. They didn't respond.

I saw Osa out of the corner of my eye. The young aspen parted and her black back surfaced into view as she carved out a wide path around the workers through the aspen. She was going out of her way to avoid them. The pathway would intersect with the trail and head west. Osa was steering her cub away from the people whom she did not know. *Good mama*, I thought.

"Look," I called down to the workers, not waiting for a response, "the mother and her cub are heading west right now. What's your plan?" I wanted to help them finish up their job as quickly and safely as possible.

"We need to head in that direction as well," the woman said hesitantly.

I assessed the situation. It was not wise for these workers to continue on foot in the same direction as the bears. Winds were coming from the north today and the bears might not scent them in advance. Osa could potentially consider another close encounter as threatening behaviour. If the workers continued to displace her, the bear could be pushed to react.

It occurred to me that I'd suddenly gained, quite literally, a bird's-eye view of the potential for human–bear conflict. Even if people enter a landscape with the best of intentions, they aren't aware of the resident wildlife—their patterns, behaviours, and individuals within the population—and it's easy to accidentally disturb or displace different species. If anything negative unfolded, the bears would potentially be labelled as aggressive, or problem bears, and be killed for it.

"If you have to go west, why don't you drive your quad instead? Just go around my gate," I offered as a solution. The noise of the ATV would hopefully prevent another surprise encounter between the workers and the bears. The sound would tip Osa off: *People are coming. Get the cub to safety. Climb.* That instinct was buried deep in her nature.

"That way, she can hear you coming," I added.

"Okay," the woman called up, and they returned to the gate.

I looked down and saw Osa and Osito now out on the trail, journeying west. I guessed she'd take the cub a few kilometres through the cutblock to check out one of the blueberry patches. From what I'd seen, the berries still hadn't formed on the plants, however.

I heard the quad's engine fire up, rumbling from a kilometre away, loud enough that Osa would hear it too.

In early August, a colleague forwarded me an article with the news headline: WOMAN DEAD AFTER BEAR MAULING IN NORTHERN ALBERTA. It hit like a gut punch.

On July 31, a black bear had mauled a twenty-six-year-old woman who'd been working with a tree planting crew in a remote forested region northwest of Swan Hills, Alberta, not far from where my classmates and I had camped years ago. She had been planting trees, alone, when the bear attacked. A colleague working nearby heard her cries and came running and managed to scare the bear off, but it was too late. She later died from her wounds in the helicopter that had come to rescue her.

In the days following the attack, wildlife authorities set up trail cameras and culvert traps in the vicinity where the woman was killed and took blood samples from her clothing to create a DNA profile of the bear. Of the three bears located in the area, officials determined it was an adult female responsible for the attack. Shortly after the woman's death, a bear was tracked down and euthanized.

There were hardly any details offered in the media to explain causation. The attack occurred midsummer, following weeks of extreme drought. It was just before the time when bears enter into hyperphagia, a metabolic process that catalyzes an extreme need to pack on calories in preparation for denning. I remembered my dad telling my grade ten class that there was a high density of black bears and grizzly bears in the Swan Hills. If the berry crops were stunted, it would result in bears competing for limited food resources. Could food stress, related to the heat dome, have been a factor in the bear deciding to prey on the woman?

Researchers have linked the effects of climate change to increasing numbers of encounters—and potential conflict—between people and bears in North America. Recently, a study at the University of Calgary discovered that rising temperatures are resulting in changing phenological patterns for low-lying vegetation, including earlier ripening of buffalo berries, which are an important berry for black bears and grizzly bears immediately before they den in the autumn. According to the study, by the year 2080, buffalo berries could ripen three weeks earlier than they do today, which would shorten the duration of food availability for bears.

"When you see a deficit in berries, [bears] start looking for other sources and they have to sort of scrimp and scrape to get their calorie budget up and then they start maybe crossing those lines and coming into contact with human food," John Paczkowski, a senior park ecologist, told CBC News. For bears that live close to human communities, that could mean wandering closer to people or human infrastructure—towns, oil and gas camps, and fire towers alike—to investigate the aromas of anthropogenic food sources.

Shortly after the attack, I spoke on the phone with my neighbour, Marina, about the tragic incident. She'd come back to Bison Tower for a second season, although it would be her last year as a lookout. This was her fourteenth summer of watching for wildfires.

The mauling of the young woman made me question my relationship with the bears, one I'd deemed to be peaceful. I thought I knew Osa, that I could predict her behaviours around my cabin or out on the trail, but could I really?

"Maybe the pendulum has swung too far over to the other side," I stressed to Marina. "Maybe I'm getting too relaxed around the bears."

"I don't know," she said slowly. "To me, the risk of being killed by a bear is just so extremely unlikely. Especially when you compare it with the number of bears killed by people every year. It's just night and day. Did you ever hear about the Conklin bears?"

"No—what's that?"

She told me about an incident that took place at the Conklin garbage dump, not far from her previous fire tower site in the Lac La Biche region, in August 2009. Conklin, a hamlet of less than two hundred people, was located south of Fort McMurray in northeastern Alberta. Following the peak of the oil boom in the mid-2000s, Conklin saw explosive growth of the construction of workers' camps in the vicinity. An influx of workers poured into the community, and as a result there was an increase in anthropogenic waste. In the spring of 2009, before her fire tower opened, Marina had been bunking at a forestry camp in Conklin.

"One evening, the camp boss asked if I wanted to tag along to 'see the bears' at the garbage dump because 'that's what we do here for entertainment,' he told me," she said. "I wasn't so stoked about the idea of going to check out 'dump bears,' but curiosity got the better of me."

She jumped in the camp boss's truck and they drove out to the garbage dump.

"It was absolutely bizarre," Marina recalled, when they pulled up to the scene of the Conklin dump, an unfenced, sprawling lot heaped with mountains of trash. Other vehicles were parked throughout the lot and guys, many of them oil and gas workers, stood outside, taking photographs of the feeding black bears as if it was a totally normal Friday night activity.

"I counted maybe eight or nine bears throughout the dump," she told me. "They barely even looked up at us. They just devoured the garbage and acted like we weren't even there."

The bears' fur looked dull and unhealthy. She remembered seeing one bear with his head completely immersed in a bag of Doritos.

The fence around the dump looked as though it hadn't been fixed or maintained in years.

The sight of the garbage-habituated bears haunted Marina all summer at the lookout tower. And then one morning, while listening to CBC Radio in her cabin, she heard the news. Fish and Wildlife officials had shot twelve bears at the Conklin dump after receiving complaints from PTI Conklin Lodge, a nearby housing complex that had recently sprung up to house hundreds of oil and gas workers. One of the managers had supposedly seen "five bears climbing on the decks and hanging around buildings," which prompted the decision to destroy the bears.

Government officials justified the slaughter by claiming the bears were habituated and had become a public safety concern. "We took action before there was a mauling or—heaven forbid—a death," said government spokesperson Darcy Whiteside.

Marina was devastated after hearing the news of the killings. It was considered the largest bear *cull*—that convenient euphemism again—in Alberta's recent history.

But the incident was symptomatic of the wider economic times in the province; the way oil workers' camps were popping up in northern Alberta like mushrooms after a hard rain, encroaching on wildlife habitat, and bears were just expected to get out of the way.

"I met a steel contractor one season who laughed when I told him about what happened at the Conklin dump," she said. "'Black bears are a dime a dozen around here,' the guy said."

The man told Marina that, in advance of the construction of oil workers' camps, he'd heard stories about the informal policy of companies sending out contractors to "kill any black bear they laid eyes on." In other words, eliminate the problem before it's a problem.

"He told me he'd heard that one company alone had killed twenty-five bears before clearing the forest to build their camp," Marina said. "I thought maybe the guy had been exaggerating, that number seemed insanely high."

But the stories of dead black bears in the area surrounding Marina's tower began to pile up. One day, her supervisor, a wildfire ranger, pulled up to her tower with a dead black bear in the back of his truck. He'd found the bear in a ditch, only a few kilometres away, and got out to inspect the carcass. There was a bullet wound in the bear's side, leaving him to believe the bear had been shot and dumped.

A helicopter pilot who'd worked for decades in northern Alberta had once told me about how bears that nosed too close to oil and gas camps were shot and disposed of. Workers would tie the dead bears to her longline, a system that allows a helicopter to carry objects below while in flight. The pilot flew their bodies out to remote places—vast stretches of swampy peat and muskeg—to dump. Once, she confessed, she looked down while flying, just as she pressed the button to release the bear, mid-air.

"He looked exactly like a man falling," she said.

By 2012, the number of black bears shot by Fish and Wildlife in the Lac La Biche region had tripled from the previous year. On paper, 145 bears were put down by officials, after they responded to complaints from oil and gas companies operating south of Fort McMurray. Nearly half of those deaths had occurred as a result of bears being attracted to food and garbage in oil and gas camps. Even so, no company or individual was charged or fined for negligence.

"It's just a matter of a high number of bears in the area," said Travis Davies, a spokesperson with the Canadian Association of Petroleum Producers, in the *Calgary Herald*. Conrad Fenema, Alberta Fish and Game Association president, said the shootings were justified to keep people safe from hungry, problem bears. "Can we stand in the way of progress?" he said, referring to the demand for workers' camps and oil well-sites given the boom of oil and gas. "No, but it is not as though they are an endangered species." Even Fish and Wildlife official Darcy Whiteside deflected the killings by saying, "We have an estimated 40,000 black bears [in Alberta] so this had no impact on the black bear population as a whole."

"After the killings at the Conklin dump, I saw very few bears for the next five years," Marina told me. "It's as if they could sense the forest wasn't safe for them anymore."

Throughout August, as I watched the mother bears preparing their young for hibernation, I reflected more on the concept of "habituation." Before occupying Hawk Tower, I'd believed that a bear that wasn't afraid of people was a bear to fear. But over the past several years, I'd changed my mind. I'd come to believe the opposite to be true, that it was arguably much safer to live alongside bears who weren't on edge around, or unfamiliar with, people. A scared bear was more likely to react in an unpredictable way. A scared bear, or a bear abused and antagonized by people, could be a dangerous bear. Bears who could predict the behaviour of people were less likely to cause conflicts.

Just as I could be providing protection for the mothers to raise their young, so too bears like Osa and Osa's mother, Big Mama, and Canelo, and even Oscar, could be creating a kind of protective buffer for me from wary, less predictable bears. On the other hand, it was impossible to know all the challenges these bears faced on a daily basis in order to survive. My dad often reminded me, "Even if a bear is familiar to you, you don't know what kind of day they've had. Maybe they've been bullied by humans, or by another bear. They might be in a bad mood and you don't necessarily know. You can never drop your guard in bear country."

Environmental pressures—the heat dome, for example, and the failed berry crop—could motivate a familiar bear to react differently. Similarly, the encroachment of human development into bear habitat—building roads or workers' camps, or logging activity—could lead to an increase in human–bear encounters. My dad had described the way their brain could go into a defensive, or *prey* mode like the flick of a switch. Bears and humans alike, we all have our breaking points.

In late August, I sprinted down the road with the dogs. Sof had grown over the season and the husky's innate love of running was evident. I hadn't planned to go very far, as I needed to be back at the cabin at 7 p.m. for "sked," a mandatory radio check-in for lookouts. I ran without my two-way radio, or even my cellphone, and felt faster without a load.

We loped past the beaver pond, the road edged with pungent goldenrod. The bumblebees droned lazily from flower to flower. I slowed to admire their heavy legs, loaded with yellow pollen.

They'd soon burrow underground in the soil, much like the bears. After two kilometres, the dogs and I turned around and headed back for the cabin. We'd better make it a quick one, I thought. I had to race to get back for that radio call.

Two hundred metres ahead on the road, I saw him: Oscar. *Fuck.* It was undeniably him. The big bear parked himself like a boxcar on the rail tracks. There would be no going around him.

"Shit," I said to the dogs. I clutched Sof's leash a little tighter, not yet trusting her off leash with the bears. Holly, on the other hand, paced herself a few steps ahead. I trusted the aging bush dog's instinct with my life. She wouldn't charge the bear unless she had to.

Oscar didn't look up at us, but I knew in my gut that the bear knew we were there. I double-checked the winds, bending the tops of scraggly black spruce from the south, and it was carrying our scent right to him. The Goliath suddenly turned away to scratch his ear with his hind leg. Animal behaviourists call this "displacement behaviour," when a bear feels a conflict between two motivations, such as the desire to approach an object while at the same time being fearful of that object. Oscar was trying to buy time to make a decision. Similarly, I wasn't sure what to do. I felt a flicker of panic, not for the bear, but about being late for the mandatory radio check-in. I cursed myself for not bringing a radio or cellphone. I knew very well that if I didn't answer the radio dispatcher, they'd worry that something had gone wrong and send a helicopter to investigate.

I decided to take my chances with Oscar and try to pressure him off the road. Hopefully, he'd give way and veer off into the forest.

"Hey bear!" I anxiously called up to him. I didn't want to get my hand slapped by my supervisors for missing the mandatory call. No doubt Oscar picked up on my fear.

As we advanced towards him, a pack of three, Oscar looked up and pivoted on his gargantuan haunches. He strode downslope towards us. *Twenty metres. Sixteen. Twelve.* The white O on his chest like a mouth gasping for air. His head hung low. Ears pinned. Mouth ajar.

"Fuck," I muttered as he approached. I'd pushed him too quickly. I thought of the twenty-six-year-old tree planter recently mauled by a black bear in the Swan Hills.

The dogs flanked me. I reached for the canister of bear spray on my belt. He was drawing close enough that I could detonate a blast of the pepper spray at him.

Without even thinking, I changed tactics. I began to back off, slowly, a behaviour that was enough to signal to Oscar: *We're not looking for a fight.* He ground to a halt, turned broadside, and grazed as if nothing was the matter.

I put thirty metres of space between us. The dogs and I waited. If Oscar wouldn't budge, I could always bushwhack and go the long way around, I reassured myself. I would miss the mandatory radio check-in, which could result in being reprimanded by my supervisor, but I couldn't do anything at this point but admit I'd made a critical mistake. Well, two mistakes: I'd forgotten my radio *and* I'd tried to hurry a dominant male bear.

But after five minutes, Oscar graciously slipped off into the forest. We walked cautiously by the spot where he'd departed.

"Thank you," I called out gently. "Have a nice day!"

When clear, we sprinted back to the cabin, the adrenalin of the close-range encounter propelling me forward. I grabbed my radio mic with only seconds to spare.

"Good evening, Hawk Tower, you're on high hazard tomorrow," belched the radio.

"That's copied," I panted.

The encounter with Oscar was a humble reminder: Bears don't hurry through life the way people do. I'd made the mistake of reacting and forcing my agenda on the bear. Oscar could've charged

or caused serious injury to myself and the dogs—but he hadn't.
"The bear radiated potency," Doug Peacock, author of *Grizzly Years:
In Search of the American Wilderness*, had written about a frighteningly close encounter with a grizzly bear. "He carried the physical
strength of disposition that allowed him to attack or kill most any
time he cared. But, almost always, he chose not to." Like Peacock,
I'd been floored by the bear's incredible show of tolerance, "a kind
of restraint that commands awe—a muscular act of grace." However,
the encounter with Oscar served as an important reminder that the
rules of respect were necessary to keep everyone safe. The dominant
bear taught me a valuable lesson that day: When you try to force
the hand to get what you want, it can cause greater problems.

Slow down. Check your ego. Share the road forward.

Twenty-Three

The logging activity around Hawk Tower would have another consequence for the bears, one that didn't become obvious to me until September, when I heard the steady hum of ATVs approaching. Hunters. Triple the number I'd ever recorded in previous seasons. On quads, they drove around the locked gate by the highway and followed the road to my tower.

One evening, I waved down two men who appeared to be in their late forties, each on his own quad, loaded with gear, their firearms strapped to the front rack. Though I was always intimidated in these encounters, I tried to hide my fear so that I might gain information from the men: their names, where they were from, and what species they were after. This was a tactic that I'd learned at my tower training in Hinton six years earlier, a way of reinforcing to uninvited visitors that the tower was a government facility and their presence and actions in the area would be documented. This practice began shortly after Stephanie Stewart, a lookout stationed at a fire tower overlooking the community of Hinton, disappeared in 2006. The RCMP designated it as homicide, although Stephanie's body has never been found and the case remains unsolved. Whenever strangers showed up at my tower, the story of her disappearance lurked at the back of my mind. Perhaps greater than the risk of being mauled by a bear was the risk of being vulnerable to human intruders.

As I suspected, the hunters weren't from the Métis community to the north, who knew this area intimately, and whom I rarely saw or interacted with. The men had driven up from Edmonton and had no idea where the logging road from the highway led. One of the men told me he'd been surprised to learn that "fire towers were even a thing these days."

"What are you after?" I asked.

"Moose, mostly," said one fellow. His tone was relaxed and friendly. "Elk, if we're lucky. We're just scouting out a few areas for hunting later this month."

While rifle season for moose, elk, and deer didn't start until the seventeenth, the season on black bears had been open since the first day of September.

"We saw the cutblock down by the highway and figured this might be a good area to check out," said the other man.

That was the cause of the increase in non-local hunters showing up, I realized. The recent logging activity, visible from the highway as people drove by, was creating recreational access for hunters on ATVs. The pioneer species that sprung up from cutblocks—grasses, berries, and young deciduous trees—provided food for moose, deer, and elk to browse and forage. Hunters knew this. They even relied on apps, including iHunter, *Canada's number 1 digital hunting companion*, to help locate land that had been recently disturbed by logging or wildfire.

One of the men peered closely at me. "Do you see much wildlife up here?"

"Not really. Usually I'll see a couple moose in June, but I haven't seen anything in a while now," I lied, thinking of the large bull moose whom I'd seen taking refuge in the nearby beaver pond through the heat dome.

I surprised myself with the lie. As a hunter's daughter, I wasn't opposed to the ethical hunting of wildlife, even of black bears, for meat and sustenance. In my first season at Hawk Tower, in late September, a man from the nearby Paddle Prairie Métis Settlement drove up to my tower at six o'clock in the morning, rousing me from sleep. "I'm sorry," he'd apologized. "I thought you'd closed for the season. I must've scared you," he added in a grandfatherly way. I hadn't seen any hunters from the community since; they knew the land intimately, they knew where to go and when. But I didn't recognize these men who'd driven up from the south, nor their hunting practices.

They'd said they were scouting for moose and elk, but would they hesitate to pull the trigger on Oscar or Canelo?

In particular, I worried about the mothers and their cubs. It could be so easy to assume a black bear was without cubs, especially when mothers frequently treed their young, or cached them out of sight, as a protective strategy. According to the Northern Lights Wildlife Society, a rehabilitation centre in Smithers, BC, hunting is one of the common ways that black bear cubs become orphaned.

Standing in the presence of the non-local hunters, I felt protective of the bears, as though I'd become the mother bear. I didn't want the men anywhere close to the bears, whom I'd learned to identify as individuals, as though they were beloved neighbours.

"My dogs and I will be out here until late October, so I'd sure appreciate it if you could hunt in the flats on the other side of the highway," I told them matter-of-factly.

Another lie. I was scheduled to fly out around the end of September, but I wanted to discourage them from coming back later in the season.

"Not a problem. We were just taking a look around. We'll head back down and get out of your hair."

Two weeks later, after the rifle season on moose and elk had opened, two guys in their twenties approached on ATVs, spinning their tires right up to my cabin. The way they gawked up at the fire tower like tourists made it clear to me this was their first visit.

"Oh, there *is* someone here!" I heard one of them say.

Watching their arrival through the cabin window, the hairs on my arms shot upright the same way the fur on the back of Osa's neck lifted when another bear approached. I walked out to meet them, put my hands on my hips and widened my stance. They were packing rifles and had cans of Pilsner in their cupholders.

"You're not allowed to shoot up here," I said firmly to the men. "We live up here. My dogs and I are often running along the road. I'd prefer if you hunted down below."

"Yeah, well, legally we can shoot within two hundred yards of your cabin," said a blond guy wearing a John Deere baseball hat. "This is all Crown land."

I sucked in a breath at those colonial words, *Crown land*. Spoken like he was entitled to it.

"Well, there's a cliff to the north anyway. The land drops off. There's nowhere else to go," I said, changing tactics, trying to de-escalate the tension between us. "You've got to take the main road back out to the highway."

His friend smirked and ran a hand over his beard. I was a joke to these men, I realized. They probably saw me as nothing more than a dumb blonde alone in the woods. I crossed my arms tightly across my chest to stop my hands from shaking. If they were bears, they'd have been able to smell my wariness.

"We have every right to be here," he said. "So we're going to explore a little more in the area."

They revved their engines and bulldozed their ATVs through the cutblock. I stood on the hilltop and watched them reach the cliff to the north. Realizing their mistake, they turned around and gunned it back down the road. Later, I discovered their trash, crumpled beer cans and a receipt from a liquor store in Whitecourt, Alberta, a town five hundred kilometres south.

I called my dad to tell him about the standoff with the hunters.

"Well, if they're making that much noise, you can rest assured that they're not serious hunters," my dad said. "I don't think Osa would show herself on the road."

He sensed my concern for the bears and the wildlife whom I'd grown so fond of watching, season to season, raising their young and responding to the social and environmental pressures on them. At night, I'd toggle through hundreds of images taken on the trail camera and see myself and the dogs threaded into a stream of wildlife: a mother moose with twin calves, a lone coyote, the resident grey wolf and her pack, the blurry wing of a raven, and a river of bears.

This was *common ground*, I thought.

The presence of the non-local hunters threatened to upset that balance.

Hunters, hunting outfitters, and hunting organizations alike often claim they're doing society a favour by controlling black bear populations, in particular, reducing the number of potential "problem bears" on the landscape.

In 2020, with the onset of the COVID-19 pandemic and the closure of international borders, hunting outfitters' business ground to a halt. In Saskatchewan, where hunting black bears by bait stations is also legal, Jeff Smith, a hunting outfitter, told CBC News that the number of negative encounters between people and bears was on the rise as a result of the lack of hunting activity, particularly from his American clients. Smith pointed out that, every year, around two thousand bears would be harvested. Without clients, he said, "it's fair to say the provincial forest now has two thousand more bears roaming about than normal." Hunting keeps the black bear numbers down, he told the media, because "the bear has no enemies . . . so they just keep multiplying unless they're harvested."

After a woman and her infant baby were fatally mauled by a grizzly bear at their cabin in a remote part of the Yukon on November 26, 2018, Jim Shockey, a trophy hunter, outfitter, and television personality, wrote a long, impassioned post on his Facebook page, to over 700,000 followers, that the woman and her baby's deaths were preventable. "I predicted that someone was going to get hurt if something wasn't done to deal with the grizzly bear plague," he wrote, railing against Yukon hunting regulations, which allow hunters to legally harvest one grizzly bear every three years. Shockey's comments were slammed by critics, including Don Reid, a zoologist with Wildlife Conservation Canada, who told the *Yukon News* that "I think 'plague' is an inflammatory word . . . It suggests very unusually high numbers and a great deal of damage being caused to humans . . . and neither of those is happening." Months later, the results of an autopsy of the grizzly responsible for the woman and child's deaths revealed that the bear had been starving and was incapable of surviving hibernation due to lack of body fat. The autopsy found porcupine quills—an uncommon food source for grizzlies, indicative of the bear's desperation—lodged from his mouth to his digestive system.

While there is a persistent belief that killing bears prevents human–bear conflict from occurring, research shows that the opposite could be true. Hunting does *not* decrease the likeliness of negative encounters between people and bears, and certainly not, as Shockey so arrogantly proposed, fatal ones. A 2023 study in Ontario examined the impact of increasing the number of bears that could legally be harvested through the introduction of a spring hunt, in addition to the existing fall hunt, on documented cases of human–bear conflict. The results? Researchers found that, despite more black bears being hunted, there wasn't any reduction in the number of reported human–bear conflicts. Hunting failed to solve the root cause of the conflict, which most frequently was the result of an unmanaged food source. Kill one problem bear without solving the deeper issue and another bear will follow his nose back to the source.

Even more intriguingly, the authors pointed out, in some cases the increased number of bears harvested may have led to an *increase* in conflict. Why?

Hunters and hunting outfitters alike, my dad explained, tend to target large, dominant males. *The bigger, the better*. "But the big, dominant males like Oscar are often naturally controlling a bear population. They help to keep the population in check by limiting breeding access to smaller juvenile males. So when you take these big males out, it often leads to more bears on the landscape." But, my dad pointed out, these are not necessarily the bears you want around. Large, dominant males can often be perceived as aggressors, but in reality these bears only get big for one reason alone: They've figured out how to manage conflict and relationships with people and communities. Juvenile bears, on the other hand, tend to fall into that category of "problem" or "nuisance bear." They're taking risks and testing boundaries. They often overstep. In other words, trophy hunting—*bigger is better*—isn't necessarily doing a service to society; rather, it could be interfering with the bears' natural method of controlling their own populations.

Some Indigenous groups, including the Southern Tutchone people in southwestern Yukon, specifically the Champagne and Aishihik First Nations (CAFN), have possessed this knowledge about the natural hierarchy of bears for millennia, enabling humans and bears to coexist. In Klukshu, a village situated along a salmon run, where both humans and bears have harvested migratory salmon for ten thousand years, people intentionally tolerate the presence of older, dominant bears. This is the concept of the "good bear" documented by human–bear conflict specialist Dr. Douglas Clark, a professor at the University of Saskatchewan, who studied how the CAFN took advantage of the bears' natural dominance hierarchy for their own ecological benefit. The good bears, typically older, more dominant bears, regulated the presence of juvenile bears.

Not only did these bears protect the community, Clark found, but people's tolerance of them also provided environmental benefits. Bears feast on the salmon, rich in nitrogen, and deposit their carcasses along the forested banks. Research in nearby coastal Alaska has documented that nutrients from salmon carcasses and bear scat, transferred from the marine ecosystem to the terrestrial one, boost the growth of trees and plants. In Klukshu, they could have other positive benefits, Clark's research suggests, promoting the growth of willows and, in turn, creating improved habitat for moose—the CAFN's preferred source of large-game meat. By tolerating individual bears at close range, the Southern Tutchone people have learned, over millennia, how to build a relationship with bears that is mutually beneficial. It's win-win for everyone: people and bears and the greater ecosystem they inhabit.

I was struck by the concept of the good bear, a far cry from the doctrine of mutual avoidance. From everything I'd observed at Hawk Tower, it made sense to me. Oscar was a good bear. Canelo was a good bear. Osa, and even her mother, were good bears. I'd learned to predict their behaviours; we'd established a peaceful coexistence. And while we didn't live on the banks of a salmon run, the black bears were ecologically benefiting the forest. For evidence of that, I didn't need to look further than a pile of scat, steaming, in the middle of the road, rich with the seeds of berries and plants. In the boreal forest, black bears and grizzly bears are also "good" in the sense that they're "ecosystem engineers," what biologists define as organisms that modify, maintain, and create habitat. Bears are naturally distributing seeds and promoting the growth of vegetation on landscapes disturbed by logging or human-caused and -exacerbated wildfires.

However, a colonial attitude towards black bears (and the policies that govern them, including allowing the habituation of bears to bait stations in order to shoot them) permits us to act with impunity towards them because, well, who cares about another dead black bear when there's "plenty more where that came from."

I decided to call my supervisor on that day the young, arrogant hunters who had shown up at my tower refused to leave the area. Forestry acted immediately by dispatching a firefighting crew from the base in Manning, who drove a four-by-four truck up the rutted road to reach my tower. The crew leader, dressed in a soot-stained yellow Nomex uniform, got out of the truck and walked towards the cabin. I shook his hand, relieved at their arrival.

"Those guys had me spooked," I confessed.

The crew leader told me that, just as they'd arrived at the gate by the highway, the hunters had been loading their ATVs onto a trailer hitched to their truck.

"Maybe it was just my imagination, but they had guilt written all over their faces," he said. "I think they knew why we'd shown up."

They didn't come back for the rest of the season, nor did any more hunters, though every now and then a gunshot, echoing from afar, would shatter the sound of birdsong through the forest.

Twenty-Four

On September 13, Brendan posted on Instagram several photos of the acre of land he'd bought for his family on the outskirts of Edmonton, a short distance from the North Saskatchewan River. An orange excavator sat in the middle of what used to be a farmer's field, digging into the knee-high weeds. I noticed a stand of balsam poplar trees behind where the house would be built, and was glad my niece and nephew would grow up with even a small fragment of the boreal forest in their backyard.

Although I was proud of my brother, I feared what would happen if there was another economic crash—and surely there would be— and he lost his job again. Why not purchase a smaller starter home?

That Albertan mantra: *The bigger, the better.*

My brother posted photographs of the excavator breaking soil, and a caption that read:

It's officially begun!

Though I took the more pragmatic position, Brendan's enthusiasm was irresistible. That exclamation mark symbolic of the way he'd always lived: riding the big highs of life, sinking with the lows, and very rarely anywhere finding himself in between. It was impossible not to feel a kind of mutual excitement for the future, one that, despite our differences, Brendan wanted me to be a part of. Working towards his dream of building a home was just another chapter in one of those Choose Your Own Adventure novels we devoured on camping trips as kids.

While I celebrated my own journey, the life I'd cultivated as a lookout and a writer, of making a beautiful home for myself in the woods, of observing the bears and merging into their ursine world, a part of me longed, too, for what my brother had nurtured—a family of the human kind. Brendan was demonstrating what kind of love is possible when you drop your guard, your defences, when you open yourself up to the world. He was building a shelter from the ground up, and just as when we were kids, he beckoned me inside.

By the end of the season, the rain poured down in heavy sheets. I felt the forest sigh in relief, but the heat dome had taken a serious toll.

Osa's mother appeared on the slope with only one cub—the one with the white triangle on his chest—remaining. She had lost two cubs over the last two months, and her body showed it. She looked underweight, slack in the shoulders. Her belly didn't drag as it should have. The surviving cub scampered after her and I saw that he was significantly smaller than Osa's cub.

"You're lucky to be alive," I whispered to the cub, though I wasn't sure how lucky it was to have lost two siblings.

Osa's mother crested the hill to where the helicopters landed to graze on the last of the clover. It was bold of her. Even Oscar, who had at least one-hundred-fifty pounds on her, would divert around the edges of the hilltop. It put the bears on even ground with my cabin and with me. But the matriarch didn't hesitate one bit. She turned her body broadside, showing off her distinct sway-back. I admired the silver hairs at the base of her neck. When she opened her mouth to tear at the leafy clover, I saw that her canine teeth had yellowed.

Under a microscope you can age a bear based on a cross-section of tooth the same way you age a tree by counting rings. The cementum, the outer part of the root, adds a new layer each year, made up of a thin, dark line that forms during hibernation and a light area that indicates the bear's growth during the summer. For female bears, the space between the dark lines also tells a story. The wider the space, the greater the production of calcium and growth of cementum. But tightly drawn rings are like the rings of a tree during a drought year. Instead of producing cementum, the bear poured all her calcium and energy into producing milk for her cubs.

I wondered what story of motherhood her teeth would tell. How many cubs had she raised? How many daughters did she share space with?

Ten metres away from Osa's mother, I sat down on a patio step and made myself small and non-threatening to the mother bear, feeling at peace in her presence.

I thought of the society I'd soon be returning to, one embroiled in social conflict over the COVID-19 pandemic, mandatory vaccinations, and pipelines. One scroll through Instagram was enough to make me want to toss my cellphone out the window. The anger and grief was palpable, no matter people's political or social beliefs. "People are afraid right now," my mother told me, commenting on the anti-masker and anti-vaxxer protesters who gathered in Peace River and drove the streets, and also on those who were immuno-compromised, living in fear of contracting the virus.

My brother, too, was afraid, she reminded me. Afraid of losing his job, afraid of slipping back into old habits, afraid of failing his family. Afraid to leave a volatile industry.

People are not so different from bears in that, when our territory is encroached upon, when our ideals are threatened, there's an instinct to react and lash out at one another. But such human re-activity doesn't put us any closer to addressing the root causes of social or environmental conflict—not with bears, or wildlife, and certainly not with one another. My apprehension around Brendan during the worst years of his addiction led to an estrangement that felt necessary and safe. However, my brother had changed and grown over the years, and I had to acknowledge that the self-protective distance I had created now kept me comfortably isolated and intolerant of our differences. Fear can serve us, but clinging to it can get in the way of being fully present in the world and forming meaningful relationships with wildlife—and with one another.

I'd once referred to Osa's mother as a "problem bear," but now I felt a blend of fear and awe for the black bear. Awe because she was, in fact, much more than people said about her kind. She was beautiful. A survivor of many environmental and human-caused challenges. A fierce keeper of the forest. An ecosystem engineer, regenerating logged or burnt forest with seeds and new life. She was a Grandmother, holding space for her daughter and granddaughters. I was in awe of Osa's mother because, despite the mistakes I had made and the wrongs I had committed against her, she allowed me back into her domain, tolerating me near her cubs, so that I might learn something and maybe even do better by her.

The cub bawled loudly and Osa's mother turned back, as if to encourage him up the slope. He was so small that I wasn't sure he would survive the cold months ahead.

I decided to stop referring to the bear as Osa's mother. I gave her a name that sang of the praise and respect she deserved: the Matriarch.

The leaves on the aspen gleamed golden. I could faintly hear the chorus of a chaotic flock of sandhill cranes in the distance, reminding me that *change is coming*.

My cellphone dinged with a text from my brother. A photograph of my niece kneeling in front of my old white-and-blue dollhouse that my mom could never bring herself to get rid of. In her hand was one of the small bear figurines, covered in fine velvet, dressed in a pair of jean overalls.

She's playing with the same bears that you played with when you were little, Bren wrote. *I'm telling you, Treen, she can just play alone for hours like you used to.*

I marvelled at the image of my niece and the memory of being her age and slipping away for hours into the imaginary world of those bears. I was touched by what my brother remembered.

Despite the heated arguments we'd had over the winter, fuelled by the stress of the pandemic, he still reached out with family updates and bids for connection. I didn't want to fall back into old habits of fear and mistrust, and to lose one another again. We needed one another.

In early March, Brendan had been working in Peace River, wrapping up a fourteen-day shift, when the first published copies of my book *Lookout* arrived at my parents' house.

Your books are here, Treen, he texted, and I could tell he was excited.

Don't open them without me! I texted back.

I drove from the old farmhouse down to my parents' house along the Peace River and Brendan greeted me at the door. He helped me lift the heavy boxes up onto the kitchen table and handed me a knife to slice through the packing tape. It was as if we were kids again and he was waking me up on Christmas morning at 6 a.m. His enthusiasm was infectious.

"Open it already!"

I laughed and slit open the flaps of the cardboard box. My brother pulled out a copy.

"Oh my god, Treen, a *hardcover*!" he cried, turning the book over in his hands.

My mother took a photo of us holding the book to commemorate the moment. Brendan's arm was draped casually around my shoulder. When I look closely at the photograph, I can see that my brother had tears in his eyes. He was smiling the same way he did in the photograph he'd sent me after the birth of his daughter.

On September 28, 2021, the same day I flew out of the fire tower, Brendan posted aerial images of the house foundation where his family would one day live. A house where we would celebrate Christmas together and sit around a campfire in the backyard and plant trees and look out the window to spy a lone coyote or a moose trotting by. The leaves on the aspen behind the house had ripened into a tangerine shade. I'd explore the trails through the trees with my brother's children one day. We'd stumble upon a scattering of porcupine quills and tufts of coarse fur. I'd teach them about the nutrient cycle of life and death. *Leaves grow in the sunlight. Porcupine eats leaves. Coyote eats the porcupine.*

Brendan proudly wrote:

Foundation complete! Time to build this thing!

House is looking good, Bren. Don't forget to build me a room ;) I later texted him.

For sure, Treen. And a dog run in the backyard so you can all come and stay.

PART V

SURVIVAL

Twenty-Five

Winter was a bad fever that wouldn't break. In early May 2022, snow struck the cabin at Hawk Tower at eighty kilometres an hour and drifted up to the windows. I waited out the storm with Holly and Sof, the baseboard heaters cranked and emergency supplies ready in the event of a falling tree taking down a power line. No one could reach me by helicopter or road in these conditions. It snowed for four days straight. The bears didn't budge from their dens, burrowed beneath the roots of old trees, the snow obscuring all evidence of them. I thought of Osa and her cub. Mother bear and cub—one solid organism curled in the den.

I'd spent the past winter living in a lakeside cabin in a mountain community near the British Columbia–Yukon Territory border, interviewing biologists, guides, and filmmakers about their unique relationships with all three species of bear in North America. I learned about an old grizzly bear named Numas, which means "Wise One" in the Kwak'wala language, from Sherry Moon, a bear guide and member of the Musgamagw Dzawada'enuxw First Nation. As Sherry walks through her traditional territory on the west coast of BC, she feels a deep, relational connection to her ancestors and the bears. One day she stumbled into the path of Numas, who was sleeping in the shade of a tree. Numas calmly lifted his head and looked at her, and then lowered his huge skull and went back to sleep. "It's like he knew I wasn't a threat to him and he wasn't a threat to me," she told me. "It's amazing to feel that connection with the bears."

Another guide, Krista Duncan, a member of the Kitasoo/Xai'Xais First Nation, grew up in Klemtu, BC, listening to stories from her grandmother about respecting the *mooksgm ol* (spirit bears), *ksamxsm ol* (black bears), and *medi'ik* (grizzly bears) that gathered along the streams to fish. When she decided to become a bear guide, Krista spent long hours alone in the forest, making her scent and behaviours familiar to the bears. One summer, she earned the trust of a black bear mother, who began leaving her cubs with her while she went fishing. "She basically had us babysit," she recalls. "It made me fall in love with guiding."

I was eager to return to northwestern Alberta to see Osa, the Matriarch, Oscar, Canelo, and the community of black bears around Hawk Tower.

In April, I drove nearly two thousand kilometres south to visit my brother and his family in Edmonton before the fire season. His new house was finally under construction, with the walls erected and a roof overhead. He was in the midst of wiring the electrical and hoped they'd be able to move in by the end of the summer.

"You've got to come check it out sometime, Treen," he gushed to me.

"Absolutely," I said.

But it didn't work out to go see the new house on that visit. My schedule was full of social activities with friends whom I hadn't seen since before the pandemic, and I needed to stock up on bulk foods for the coming tower season. I stayed with Brendan and his family for only a night.

"I'll come for a visit in September after the fire season wraps up," I promised him.

"No problem, Treen," my brother said.

My niece and I slept on the floor next to my nephew's bed. In the morning, we spooned down cereal at the kitchen table. Brendan came downstairs wearing his work overalls and a backwards ball cap, with his truck keys in his hand. He looked handsome, only a few months shy of his fortieth birthday. He'd just attended one of his oldest friends' surprise party. It was hard to believe the boys who used to have sleepovers in our family's basement, playing floor hockey using a rolled-up sock as a puck, were turning forty.

For the first time in years, I felt secure in my relationship with my brother, trusting that whatever hardship life threw at us, we'd be there for the other.

Brendan seemed weary, however. He was still making the five-hour drive to the Peace River oil sands to work fourteen-day shifts, but he'd recently found an exit strategy. He and his colleague Greg had started their own electrical company in Edmonton, taking on contracts with homeowners and housing developers to wire residential properties. After nearly twenty years of working contracts at isolated camps in northern Alberta, he wanted out. He didn't want to miss watching his son and daughter grow older; he wanted his family to sleep under the same roof at night.

I was elated by this news—and proud of him. Quitting the industry wasn't easy, but it was a decision, I hoped, that would be healthier for Brendan in the long run.

"Hey Treen, I'm sorry we didn't really get much of a visit, but I've got to get to the new house to put in some hours on the electrical," he said. "Have a great summer at the tower, hey?"

"No worries, Bren. It was really great to see you guys," I said, getting up from the table.

We loosely hugged and I went back to eating breakfast with the kids and heard the garage door open and then shut.

———

On the fifth day of the storm, the snow let up and the heavy blanket of ice fog cracked wide open. The dogs and I stumbled out of the cabin and gazed up at a sky the same shade as a pale-blue egg. The sun poured down on us and I knew that, within only a few hours, the snow would dissipate into a strange memory. I could already hear melted snow trickling down the eavestroughs into my rain barrels.

By the afternoon, I stood ankle deep in heavy clay soil, burying potato seeds already sprouting green arms into the garden bed. The sun roared down with such ferocity that I took off my long-sleeved shirt, squinted up at that bright, hot light, and thought: *If I was a bear, I'd come out of the den today.*

Maybe an hour later, I looked up from my work and saw a hairy black lump clinging to the white torso of an aspen, fifteen metres or so off the ground. My eye caught the wild-eyed stare of a cub. *Osito.* He pierced the bark with his claws, dug in, and hung on for dear life. Then I saw Osa, her elephantine body improbably balanced on a skinny tree several feet behind. It was like seeing an old friend after half a year apart. I imagined that she remembered my unique scent, a blend of unshaven armpit musk, lavender shampoo, the grease from a blueberry scone at the corners of my lips, the dog hair that clung to my clothes.

"Osa probably knows you better than you know yourself," a friend had remarked to me, and I wondered if he was right.

She descended slowly from the tree. I listened to the sound of her short, curled claws ratcheting into the bark, and the branches under her hairy bulk cracking clean off. Osa was no longer the small bear she was when I met her three years ago. She had developed muscle and heft. Her long black fur hung down in crimped tufts.

I knew that Osa and Osito's days together were soon coming to an end. Black bear cubs only stay with their mothers for a year and a half. Within a few short weeks, Osa would drive Osito away with tooth and claw, forcing him to move alone through the world as a subadult bear. *Wean*, derived from Old English *wenian*, "to habitu-ate and prepare," is to "un-accustom," or detach from that to which one is strongly devoted. I was bracing myself for it, knowing it was under the surface of their every interaction. A sentimental part of me hoped I wouldn't have to see Osa chasing away her only cub whom I'd grown so fond of watching, but the other part of me, the role of observer, wanted to play witness to this important stage in a black bear's life. I'd watched Osa as a cub, a subadult, and now a mother bear. The family breakup signalled a key turning point in the evolu-tion of *Ursus americanus*, a solitary species. Osa would mate again. The cub, transitioning to a subadult bear, would face the greatest chance of death in his lifetime. Osa was preparing her cub to face the forest alone.

The bears hunkered down in a day bed beneath the old spruce, low branches forming a protective umbrella over mother and cub. Over the next several days, I adapted my routine to watch them, shadowy forms through the leafless forest. Osa slouched on her back against the base of the spruce, giving her cub the last of her milk as they waited for the ground to thaw and the early risers—colts-foot, fireweed, horsetail, dandelions—to germinate on the slopes. I admired Osa's patience. After seven months of living underground, subsisting off her fat reserves and losing a third of her body weight, she was hungry in a way my body would never understand. She rested beneath the spruce like a hairy black Buddha.

"To encounter the bear, to meet it with your whole life, was to grapple with something personal," wrote Barry Lopez in *Arctic Dreams*. I couldn't think of truer words to describe what living alongside Osa had meant to me. I owed a lot to the bear. She had taught me how to look beyond myself and to consider survival from a different point of view. That Osa tolerated and trusted me nearby was no small thing. It had opened my mind to new relationships, and to fresh potential in familiar ones.

———

As the snow melted away, I wanted to spend every second I could watching Osa and her cub. I spent long hours, flat on my stomach on the hilltop, filming the bears with a new camera I'd purchased over the winter. The telephoto lens brought me even closer into their world, so close that I felt as though I could read their expressive eyes. I'd once described the bear's eyes as cold and unfeeling, but now I interpreted affection and curiosity.

Osito had grown in the den over the winter. His legs had sprouted like dandelion stems, looking comically out of proportion with his torso. It was difficult to imagine the small bear surviving alone in the forest. *Too soon*, I thought, knowing that the bears didn't need my sentimentality.

I'd heard from friends who had watched a mother black bear wean her cubs in their backyard that it could be violent. "The mother bear turned on the cubs out of the blue," my friend told me. "She bit at them and chased them up a tree. Honestly, it was pretty difficult to see."

Osa seemed to increasingly pick play fights with the cub, lunging and nipping and swatting at him with her huge paws. Osito would submissively tumble onto his back, then with a surge of confidence launch back at her. They wrestled at the foot of the road. I wondered if these sparring matches were Osa's way of toughening the cub up for his coming independence.

As May unfolded, I woke and saw them through the cabin window, sleeping beneath the huge spruce. I crept outside to hide in the grass and film. They began to play like two black dogs with their jaws wide open, white teeth flashing, mock biting one another. Osa gravitated between dominance and submission, nipping Osito, and receding as the yearling bear lunged back at her like a snapping turtle. I watched Osa slouch on her back, propped up by a log, as if she was going to nurse. She rubbed a nipple and glanced over at the cub, who did not come for her milk.

I sent the video clip to Justin, who was back at Whitecreek Tower.

"Wow," he remarked. "Osa seems damn near conflicted. Like she's torn between the decision of nursing her cub or chasing him off."

"I got that same feeling," I said.

As if exhausted by the uncertainty, the mother bear curled herself into a ball and closed her eyes while Osito frolicked with a fallen tree branch between his paws.

On the Sunday of the May long weekend, I spent the morning puttering around the cabin, drinking coffee, organizing a box of vegetable and flower seeds, and reading Suzanne Simard's *Finding the Mother Tree*, a book about her efforts to change harmful practices in the forestry sector in western Canada. I was grateful for the snow from the blizzard, lingering still in the shade of the bush, cooling the forest and preventing the fire hazard from climbing.

After delivering my one o'clock weather report over the radio, I climbed the fire tower, not rushing up the ladder, knowing that nothing would burn today. I marvelled at the low clouds rolling by. I set my camera on the Fire Finder and filmed a time lapse of the sunlight piercing through the low clouds as they passed over a grain field, six kilometres to my north.

From the cupola, the farmer's field looked like a square hole cut out of a green blanket. It was the only plot of farmland along a gravel road that ran through black spruce and beaver ponds. Last year, I'd watched the farmer cut down the trees, use pumps to drain the water from the wetlands, and set fire to the root piles. Ten years from now, a local permit officer had told me, the expanse of forest to my north would be entirely cut down and converted into grain fields. It would, no doubt, have a negative impact on the black bear population and other species who lived here in the wildlife corridor. A recent study found that agricultural zones along the Wildland Urban Interface are "hot spots" for black bears, particularly during the autumn months, as they're drawn to feed on ripe crops, increasing risk for conflict to occur between humans and bears.

I made my body very quiet for ten minutes, as the camera snapped in five-second intervals, so as not to shake the cupola and jostle the image. I closed my eyes and reflected on the idea of deforestation as a time lapse in the boreal forest. The sad reality of how it could take a century for a forest to grow, yet only a handful of hours to tear it all down.

At 2:34 p.m., the phone rang.

"Trina," my mother's voice blurted out. "You need to climb down."

"You need to climb down," echoed my father.

They were huddled around a speakerphone, calling during the middle of the day, but this fact didn't signal to me that something terrible had happened.

"I can't climb down," I told them, confused. "I'm working right now."

"You need to climb down," pleaded my mother. There was something desperate in her voice.

And then, it finally clicked: My parents knew something that I did not, they had some vital piece of information, as if they were already in the future, already a few steps ahead. My first instinct was that *you need to climb down* meant that being a hundred feet off the ground was a threat to my safety, that some apocalyptic force was careening towards me. My eyes frantically scanned the horizon for a funnel cloud or black-eyed tornado charging towards me. I braced myself for a gale force wind capable of knocking over the tower. But looking around and seeing the horizon clear, I realized they were calling about a disaster that had happened, or was currently happening, beyond what I could see.

Brendan's face surfaced in the lake of my mind.

"What happened?" I asked.

It was far worse than I could have imagined.

"Your brother took his own life."

They say wild animals shake and tremor after experiencing a traumatic event. A deer, escaping a near-death encounter with a predator, lies down in the grass to tremor the fear, releasing it right out of her system. My own body shook as I climbed one hundred rungs down. I heard my teeth chattering. My hands and feet, uncertainly placed on the ladder, not climbing but grasping.

My immediate feeling was that I did not want to leave the forest. I could not confront the reality of Brendan's death. "Whatever you do, please don't pull me out of here," I pleaded with my supervisor. "I'm okay," I said, trying to convince him of a mind sound enough to be left alone.

I climbed back up the tower like a black bear cub fleeing into the limbs of a tree for safety. I didn't know what else to do. I looked out at the forest as if searching for some sign of Brendan and saw him in the formation of a dark-blue, lenticular cloud, one sanded down by high winds, that looked like a hockey puck.

I saw him in the form of a fledgling raven flapping shakily above the trees, cawing out to his parents, who nested nearby in the arms of an old spruce. *Brendan* means "little raven" in Old Welsh. Our mother had given him the name. Our father loved ravens for their keen intelligence, playful spirit, and tenacity to survive in the North.

I gazed out on the forest, the buds on the aspen closed like clenched fists, and felt a clarity that surprised, even startled, me: My brother was gone. The knowing severed me. It cleaved me into two, the person I'd been in the moment before picking up the phone and the person I'd become after hearing the words. I had lost the person most like me—genetically and intuitively—on the face of the planet. I had lost the future I'd finally allowed myself to imagine with my brother in it.

A fearful part of me had been bracing myself for that phone call for twenty years, while the logical part of my brain couldn't grasp that he was gone. I needed proof of death. I climbed one hundred feet down and called my mother back to gather the few known facts. I needed to know *when* and *where* and *why*—knowing we'd never know—he'd gone.

My mother told me about the unanswered calls and text messages. He'd been alone in the house. The doors, locked. The friends who knocked. The empty bottle of vodka. The friends who returned, knocking louder. The web browser history on his phone that read *how to*.

It happened at seven o'clock in the morning. It would have been lightning quick. No note. No words left behind to explain *why*. He died from lack of oxygen to the brain.

After my parents got the call, they packed their bags and a box of memories of my brother: photographs, a hockey jersey, and a wooden sword that my grandfather had carved for him when he was a boy, with the etched letters that read *BRENDAN THE BRAVE*. My dad dug a hole in the backyard to plant a plum tree they'd just bought from a greenhouse the day before, and then they got in their car and drove five hours south to the city. The fact that my parents had just been hit with the most devastating news of their lives and yet they remembered to plant the sapling was not lost on me. No doubt they'd been in shock, but also, it was just the kind of people my parents were: loving, kind, responsible beyond measure. I imagined my dad kneeling in the backyard, tears streaking his face, as he buried the seedling's roots in soil.

I walked to the nearby beaver pond, which was still shrouded in a thin layer of ice, with the dogs. I noticed a dead leaf frozen on the surface of the ice. I looked into the forest. Sunlight filtered through the woods and clung to the skin of a peeling birch. The forest, the light. Everywhere I looked was a portal carrying me across a great river that separates the living from the dead.

I longed for Osa and the cub, desperate for a wild, mammalian heartbeat other than my own. Where had they disappeared to? For several days I walked as if in a trance, looking for my brother underneath every stone, every spruce bough, every stand of thick, dry grass.

"Why haven't you left yet?" family friends inquired. Maybe they judged me for not running immediately to my parents, my niece and nephew, in a moment of crisis. But I wasn't ready to leave. I wanted to be alone with the forest and my brother, whom I saw everywhere in everything.

On the fourth day after he died, I woke up from the trance, frighteningly alone.

Where was my brother?

Where were the bears?

Natalka, a friend who worked as a biologist in Peace River, called. "I'm coming," she said. "You shouldn't be alone out there."

"Okay," I said, dazed.

A helicopter dropped her off the next day. She and her colleagues had been flying a mortality survey north of my tower, scouting for a GPS radio collar on a female woodland caribou. They always knew when a caribou, a species on the brink of extirpation in northern Alberta, had died because the GPS tracker stopped moving for longer than twenty-four hours.

They arrived with a caribou head in the helicopter's basket. The dogs circled like wolves.

The pilot, my father's friend and former colleague, hugged me awkwardly and shuffled on the helipad. His son had died the year before in a heavy-duty machinery accident.

My friend brought fresh mangoes and sausage and homemade bread. She cooked meals for me and washed the dishes and turned on an episode of *Stranger Things* and sat beside me, knitting a sweater. She suggested we make a weaving together on a hand loom I'd built out of a broken scrub board. I could not fathom making something beautiful in that state of despair, but I obliged and we took turns weaving different colours of yarn and materials, a strip of tanned leather, a piece of red twisted mesh from the orange sack.

The weaving hangs in my house today.

A week after Brendan died, I slept wedged between the warmth of his children on the bedroom floor at their home in Edmonton. My mother slept in the bed, my father in my niece's room, and my sister-in-law across the hall. This physical proximity to my family, close enough that I could hear the breath of Max and Brianna next to me, and my mother snoring softly, was consoling. All of us bound together by a brutal loss. I watched the children's paper-thin eyelids fluttering as they slept, feeling both protective of and protected by them. In the morning, my niece told us she'd heard my brother's voice in the middle of the night, reassuring her that he loved her.

My sister-in-law, who is Dene, asked a family friend to come over to smudge, or purify, the house. The woman requested that we open all the windows and doors, and she went room to room, wafting sage smoke with a red-tailed hawk feather, to cleanse their home. I forced myself to go down into the basement where Brendan had died. I wished I could've been there to comfort my brother and hold his hand. I would've reminded him how far he'd come and everything he had to live for, to hang on until the storm had passed. *Bad weather passes*, I would've told him.

And, I'm proud of you.

I love you.

Later, the coroner's report would find that he'd had trace levels of cocaine in his system.

The comedown.

The crash.

A tsunami of negative thoughts and emotions flooding and muddying his brain.

Research has found that, in one of four suicide attempts, the period of time between experiencing suicidal thoughts and then acting on them could be less than five minutes.

My body descended the stairs into the basement. I thought I'd be afraid, but I was not. I needed to see and try to make sense of what would never make sense. But I did not feel my brother there, only the physical space he'd left behind. We cracked open the window. The family friend wafted the sage, a scent that reminded me of riding my horse through hills of the Peace River valley, the horse's hooves stirring through wild herbs. My nephew played a video game of NHL hockey on the big-screen TV.

Afterwards, Brianna pulled me by the hand outside to the backyard.

"Auntie, come play!"

We bounced on the trampoline and Max joined us. We rubbed our heads onto the black trampoline until our hair stood on end from the static electricity. My niece giggled and it was a sound so innocent and infectious that I joined her. I have no idea how my body was capable of laughter, but the children made me buoyant against the weight of despair. I jumped against the gravity of loss. What would I say to my brother's children? What would they ask me about him twenty years down the road?

"His brain was broken," my mother had gently explained it.

What was broken, I'd thought, was the world that we lived in. A colonial system that bred boys to deny their feelings and one in which men needed money to prove their societal worth. Where the idea of manhood in Alberta was permeated in oil, stoicism, and strength. What was broken was an industry that isolated workers and fostered a culture of hyper-masculinity. A profit scheme that hooked guys on big paycheques, booze, and drugs, and kept them coming back for more. Oil workers were just as dispensable as the wildlife—the black bears—they cleared out of the forest.

I'd always been worried I'd lose my brother in a car crash, but in Alberta, more people die by suicide than are killed in car accidents—and three out of four of those deaths are men. Men who work in the trades are exponentially more likely to die by suicide.

We would never know, for certain, what factors motivated Brendan to take his own life, but the COVID-19 pandemic had, indeed, taken a toll on people's mental health; he had been right about that. Accidental drug overdoses rose by 30 percent between 2020 and 2021 in Canada, with half of those deaths involving the use of a stimulant, including cocaine. Brendan hadn't died directly from a drug overdose, but in my mind, the drugs hadn't *not* killed him, either.

What explanation could we offer my brother's children for a loss so colossal?

he loved you he loved you he loved you he loved you

We bounced and I glanced up and saw a hawk soaring above us.

"Look up," I said to the children, who craned their heads skyward.

The hawk circled high above the three of us, as we watched incredulously in that small, square yard in the middle of the city suburbs. It was probably hunting for mice in the huge grassy field behind the house, but I told myself it was my brother.

I was somehow both a thousand years old and five years old. I slept in the same bed with my mother, our bodies racked with emotional grief that manifested as physical pain, as though we'd been trapped by a landslide, the earth pushing down on our chests, breaking our ribs. We slept with our fingers interlaced.

I opened my computer to write my brother's eulogy, but the screen was so bright I could not summon the words. It became painfully obvious to me that I hadn't really known him as an adult. For most of my adult life, I'd been attached to an early impression, an idea of my brother as the one who was always a few steps ahead. I'd wanted my brother on my own terms. Now I would have to piece together his story, so I reached out to his co-workers, his friends and fellow hockey parents, to hear about my brother in their own words.

His colleague Greg said that Brendan would call upwards of six to seven times a day as he was driving the gravel roads up north, going from well-site to well-site. Greg would always answer. "Brendan always made me laugh," he said. "His energy was contagious." A fellow hockey parent had told me how Bren would rally the boys in the dressing room before their games. He'd crank up the volume on a song the kids loved and they'd dance around the room.

"Brendan noticed things about the kids that others would miss," he told me. "Little things. Like he'd compliment one of the boys on a haircut or new hockey stick. You could tell he was trying to make them feel good about themselves."

One of Brendan's friends told me that, a few months before he died, he'd sent her a Facebook message. He'd seen her crying in her vehicle in a grocery store parking lot in Edmonton. The woman had just ended a relationship. My brother had invited her for dinner at his and Amanda's house, telling her, "I've struggled with mental health, too, and you're not alone."

More than two hundred people attended my brother's memorial. His earliest hockey teammates were there, the boys he'd grown up with, now middle-aged men. I recognized their faces as they recognized mine, the kid sister who had always watched like a hawk from the bleachers. One of the men told me it hadn't always been easy to be my brother's friend. During the worst of my brother's addiction, he'd stepped away. But recently, the friends had reunited. Brendan had been reaching out to his earliest friends. "He was really trying," he told me. "And we were all so happy to see the old Bren again."

I stood alone to read the eulogy and tried to make people smile, even laugh, at the memories of the man my brother was. That's what he would've wanted. A seat for every single person at the dinner table. *The more the merrier*.

Brendan died a month before his fortieth birthday.

I placed a puck next to him in the coffin.

I kissed his folded hands, tattooed up to the knuckles, and whispered goodbye.

Twenty-Six

Some of my friends thought I was crazy to go back to the forest imme-diately after my brother's memorial. But I longed for a safe place to process, and my cabin in the woods, alone with Osa and the bears, was the only refuge I could think of. I wanted to grieve Brendan away from the projections of others, and on my own terms. *Suicide*, I was fast learning, was a word that fired like a gunshot.

I wanted to rake my consciousness clear of thoughts in the way that being in the presence of a bear can do. I wondered if Osa had weaned the cub while I was away.

I ran to the bears' favourite rub pole several kilometres down the road. My legs felt as though they were made of hardwood. My lungs, lethargic. I came around the familiar bend in the road and was physically deflated by what I saw. The power company had replaced the bears' rub pole, whittled down into an hourglass, with a new pole. It felt like the loss of a legacy. The pole had been like a work of art, an abstract statue, or a sacred totem pole, carved by a community of black bears.

But then I ran my hand down the new wooden pole and saw that I was not the first to touch it. Someone had come before me, etch-ing their claws into the wood. Leaving their mark. A few black hairs snagged on a splinter of wood. Two paw prints where the bear stood bipedal to rub and leave their scent—their story—behind. Perhaps it wasn't the pole that mattered so much as the beaten-down memory trails through the forest that led the bears back here, year after year.

Later, I checked the images captured by the trail camera set up adjacent to the pole. The cinnamon bear, Canelo, had been there, standing up on his hind legs, back arched into the pole. I checked the date: 22/05/2022. The same day Brendan departed the world.

I wouldn't ever see the cinnamon male again.

Osa hadn't yet weaned the cub. Every day, the mother and cub wandered onto the south side of the slope, grazing together. Watching Osa helped to anchor a sorrow that had completely unmoored me. When I looked in the mirror, I could hardly recognize the woman I'd become. My face was red and swollen from crying. My appetite had vanished and I was losing weight, and yet I felt heavier than a bear before hibernating when I climbed up the ladder. My hair grew oppressively long and thick, and I felt this primal urge to take scissors to it.

I saw that Osa had rubbed a section of fur clean off her belly, a naked patch on her side as though someone had taken a wax strip to her. I empathized with the bear, desperate to moult her heavy winter fur.

My long, unkempt hair—heavy with grief—had to come off.

Many species routinely moult, or slough off their hair, feathers, fur, or wool. Some insects lose their wings. Some step right out of their exoskeleton or shell. Others roll and rub, alone or socially, as though performing a ritual.

I was the bear rubbing her forehead onto the wooden pole over and over again. Desperate to shed out.

My friend Julia, a firefighter, drove her four-by-four truck on the washed-out road to do it for me. She tied my hair into a ponytail, a long rope that reached the middle of my back. I heard the blade of the scissors chewing into the mass of hair that no longer felt like my own.

"Yes," I said with clarity. "Cut it all off."

In late June, Osa manifested on the northern slope, which was odd. The slope bordered the cutblock, where there were no mature aspen or spruce—sanctuary trees—for cubs to climb to safety. Suddenly, the realization dawned on me: Osa had weaned the cub.

I couldn't see Osito anywhere. Osa tore at clumps of dandelions, their milky stems hanging out of her mouth. I filmed her grazing amongst the yellow asters. No cub.

Now we were both alone, I thought.

"It's just you and me, girl," I said to the bear.

And then Osa stopped feeding and stood upright on her back legs, her rabbity ears perked alert, scenting the air. Before I could adjust my lens and zoom out, the bear lunged forward and bar-relled through the cutblock, the young tree saplings bending back as if made of rubber. I'd never seen Osa charge, or display aggres-sion before. I was shocked by her capacity to move so powerfully, so swiftly. A black bear can charge at speeds of up to fifteen metres per second. They can sprint, at short distances, faster than a racehorse.

Suddenly, a bear cub rocketed up a fifteen-metre poplar on the other side of the cutblock.

Osito.

Osa began to scale the tree, climbing up after her cub, driving him higher into the canopy. Three metres off the ground, she climbed back down, leaving Osito clinging to the torso of the tree at twelve metres up. When he'd descend, Osa would materialize again, as if out of thin air, chasing the cub back into the branches. For an hour, the mother and cub yo-yoed up and down the tree.

I had thought it would be distressing, watching Osa wean the cub. But in fact I felt emboldened by the bear. Osa was facing a sudden change in life the way animals do, with full body courage. With the acceptance that there was no other way. The weaning wasn't cruel. It was an act of necessary love, a way of ensuring that her species would evolve and survive.

Heat swarmed the forest in the early days of July and the bears slunk away into the cool shadows. I looked desperately for Osa. I scanned the masts of old poplars and spruce for Osito. I ran daily to the rub pole to check the trail camera, and pored over dozens of videos that had been triggered by the movement of grass blowing in the wind.

No bears.

Grief came like a beast. I cried as if I were a child again, howling for her closest companion and playmate, the one she'd always followed behind. I wept as an old woman too, the one who would grow older than her big brother. Francis Weller, author of *The Wild Edge of Sorrow*, describes grieving as stepping into an untameable, but necessary, state of derangement. "Grief is subversive, undermining the quiet agreement to behave and be in control of our emotions. It is an act of protest that declares our refusal to live numb and small," writes Weller. "There is something feral about grief, something essentially outside the ordained and sanctioned behaviours of our culture . . . We move in jangled, unsettled, and riotous ways when grief takes hold of us. It is truly an emotion that rises from the soul."

How do animals grieve? I thought of the Matriarch who'd lost two cubs the summer before. Had she mourned or ritualized their deaths? Do bears grieve their dead?

A growing body of scientific evidence supports the idea that non-human species have the capacity to grieve, or mourn, and even ritualize the loss of their relatives. Western science has been slow to broach the subject of animal grief, perhaps out of fear of losing objectivity. Since they aren't able to verbalize their experiences, we can't really know what a bear, or a chimp, or an orca whale perceives. But researchers can measure animal behaviours following a death, including loss of appetite, sleeping disturbances, or loss of sociability or increased stress.

In the spring of 2018, an orca whale named Tahlequah, or J35, gave birth to a calf who died after only half an hour. While it's not uncommon for an orca whale to carry the body of a dead calf for a day or two following their death, Tahlequah travelled over 1,600 kilometres along the coast with her dead calf, for seventeen days. "I have never seen that kind of grief," Ken Balcomb, a marine biologist and researcher with the Center for Whale Research, told the *Atlantic*. Similar behaviours have been documented in other cetacean species, including bottlenose dolphins and beluga whales. Adults keep dead bodies afloat and carry them in their mouths or on their backs.

Gorillas, chimpanzees, and macaque mothers have been documented by scientists carrying the corpses of their young for days, even weeks. Researchers in Zambia observed a female chimpanzee using a tool—a piece of dried grass—to clean the teeth of her deceased son.

Elephants have been known to gather around the bodies of the deceased, caressing their bones with their long trunks, for months, even years.

After the viewing, my mother confessed to me that she could have sat with my brother's body for days. "It wasn't enough time," she said. "I wanted more time with him."

I imagined that something animal in my mother, motivated by a deep primal urge, would've carried his body home with her, on her back, in her mouth, if she could have. She would have picked his teeth clean with a blade of grass.

What am I doing now but feeling for my brother, revisiting what's left of him day after day, running my hands over the story of his bones.

In August, I summoned the energy to reach out to the Edmonton Suicide Bereavement Association and began meeting online with a small group of strangers who'd lost their loved ones to suicide. I cried through most of our first meeting together, but they understood my anguish. We'd crossed the same river of loss. At the core of grief exists "our longing to belong," wrote Francis Weller in *The Edge of Wild Sorrow*. "This longing is wired into us by necessity. We are shaped for closeness and for intimacy with our surroundings." I felt seen by these people who were strangers yet who intimately understood how my life had changed. I was struck by the number of people grieving the loss of male relatives: husbands, fathers, cousins, brothers.

The loss of my only sibling was akin to the loss of a "keystone species," what biologists call an animal that helps hold an ecosystem together. When a keystone species, including bears, wolves, and cougars, is removed from a habitat, there's the risk of triggering a "trophic cascade," a waterfall effect on the nutrients cycling through the system.

Imagine the girl's pencil drawing of a life cycle diagram in elementary school. She erases the sketch of the bear and subsequently draws too many deer to fit on the page. But then there's so many deer and elk there's no room for plants and trees. And without the trees whose roots hold and protect the soil from running off, the soil erodes, and that affects the health of the river. Soon the girl is erasing the fish too. Even the worms in the soil disappear into eraser smudge.

Trophic cascade, caused by the loss of a keystone species, can trickle all the way down through a system to influence plant and soil matter.

What happens when the young girl erases the bear?

Does she know what she'd be erasing in herself?

Who would I have been without my brother?

The cut-off from a sibling, writes Fern Schumer Chapman in her book *Brothers, Sisters, Strangers*, "becomes a fault line, dividing a family and life into 'before' and 'after.'"

The loss of a sibling changes who we are and who we become.

As the days unfolded, I began to accept that I'd inevitably grow older than the age my brother was when he died. I'd learn to be alone in the forest without him. Only now it wasn't as it had been in the days when we were estranged—that feeling of being the only child. Now I grappled with that sense of learning to be in the forest—and the world—not away from him but with the memory of him ever present. I would move forward in life, carrying the spirit of Brendan with me. I would learn to live for the both of us.

The sounds of the forest struck me with painstaking clarity. The cry of the red-tailed hawk pierced the sky with longing. I could not remember a summer witnessing the flight path of so many hawks. A broad-winged hawk landed in the branches of an aspen and watched me.

"I see you, brother," I said.

And later, he was there on the road where I ran, feasting on a freshly killed grouse.

In late summer, I heard a slight rustle in the young trees in the cutblock. I looked down from the fire tower as a long-legged, gangly bear emerged onto the road, skinny and skittish.

Osito. I was certain it was him. I saw that he had shed his shaggy winter coat. His dew-soaked fur glistened like sunlight on a black lake.

I was grateful for the glimpse of the young subadult male, as he was destined to disperse and roam into the forest beyond. I didn't know if I'd see him again.

I saw hardly any bears for the rest of the summer, but I found myself accepting their absence. Maybe I didn't need to see the bears with the same urgency I'd once felt.

Humans are eternally questioning and searching for answers, but bears know who they are and where they belong on the landscape. As much as I'd learned over the years, I accepted that some knowing—some mystery—would always be out of my control.

The bears had taught me about the value of looking closely. My eyesight had sharpened for those subtle signs I would have once walked right by without noticing.

Once you know how to look for the mark of bear, you'll see her everywhere.

Look up. Five black stars on the torso of an aspen tree.

Look closer. See how the bears have chosen this tree. See how the bark is covered with her graffiti art. Some trees are better for climbing, for feasting, for marking than others.

Only the bears can tell you why.

When the fireweed went to seed and death came for the leaves in the forest in brilliant strokes of crimson red, Osa appeared in the clearing, embodying the energy of a dominant female—a mother, a daughter, a sister—a bear who knew what it took to survive.

I dropped the task of boxing up my belongings, left the dogs in the cabin, and went to be alone with the bear. Osa lay down on her belly to feed on the last of the clover. I walked out, beyond the electric fence, and lay down on my own belly to film her.

The heat of summer had cooled off, ushering us into autumn, yet the mosquitoes swarmed us both, woman and bear. I noticed an inch-long scar above Osa's right eye. It was the slightest alteration to a face that was getting older but that I now knew so well: that blond snout, the way her ears sprouted off-kilter and reminded me of a rabbit's. People had previously told me that you couldn't tell black bears apart based on appearance alone, but they were wrong. Once you spend enough time with individual bears, you can start to memorize their faces. The space between their eyes. The colour of fur around their muzzle or above their eyes. The width between their ears. The angle at which their ears are placed. The symmetry of their features. The way that bears, much like people, are inevitably scarred by age and experience. And when you recognize bears as individuals, when you look beyond the stereotypical ideas of them, only then can you learn to build a relationship.

To negotiate and share space.

To work across conflict.

To seek out solutions.

Osa's ears perked up and she gazed at something across the beaver pond, as though another bear could be close by. I saw nothing, but I trusted the bear. She hoisted herself up and headed south on the grassy road, moving with the same regal sway as her mother and the matriarchal lineage that had come before her. I filmed her walking out of sight, sensing it would be the last time I'd see Osa— a bear I'd come to call "sister"—for the season or, maybe, ever.

My brother's death had surfaced an emerging desire within for connection and intimacy of the human kind. I sensed that I was ready to migrate back into a more peopled existence; to integrate my grief into the complexity of human relationships. I longed to build a den, a sense of community, and stay open to the possibility of finding my own family.

I watched Osa disappear into the forest. She was no longer "just a black bear" to me. I was proud of the bear the same way I'd been proud of my own brother.

Osa was a sister whom I'd never forget.

As a northerly wind stripped the leaves from the trees, I set out on the road to retrieve the trail camera from the bears' rub pole. I walked slowly, trying to soak up the energy of the forest. Autumn was a season for moving slowly, ambling like a bear without hurry, who knew she was exactly where she was supposed to be. The scent of sweet decay brought me back to girlhood. It had always been my favourite season in the boreal forest.

The dogs loped ahead and flushed five or six ruffed grouse up from out of the tall grass into the trees. I'd long memorized the grouse's favourite spots by now, where they bathed their feathers in sandy bowls along the road and fed on clover in the late-day sun. Even so, I startled at the sound of the grouse's exploding feathers, and chuckled at myself, reminded of the way my brother and I used to laugh at being caught off guard by the suddenness of their flight.

I know that my brother would want me to move forward, navigating the forest without him. I'd keep the memory of him alive—honouring the wild, beautiful, and contradictory parts of who he'd been—and love and care for his children as if they were my own.

As I walked, an earthy cologne stung my nostrils. *Bear.* Her sweet musk wafted across the road. I paused and looked around. There was no one in sight, but I sensed that a bear had been here, not long before, wandering the road and grazing on the late season clover.

"I can *scent* them now," I mused to myself.

The bear smelled like honey and rotting leaves and soured raw meat. As distinct as the smell of the earth after a hard rain. A reverent scent that woke my body and mind and spirit up.

A scent that translated into: I am here even if you can't see me.